CONTENTS

Country Kitchen   C-8645, p. 16

200 Home Designs for Two-Story Living

ON THE COVER

Cover Photo: Plan AX-90307, page 25
Design: Jerold Axelrod and Associates, P.C.
Photo by: Joshua McClure

CALL TOLL-FREE TO ORDER!
1-800-547-5570

President   Jeffrey B. Heegaard
Publisher   Roger W. Heegaard
Associate Publishers   Mark Englund, Wendy Schroeder
Editor   Dianne Talmage
Associate Editors   Pamela Robertson, Eric Englund, Matthew Arthurs
Sales Operations Supervisor   Wayne Ramaker
Marketing Associates   Gene Tubbs, Mary Gehlhar, Carrie Morrison
Controller   Nancy Ness
Financial Analysts   Barbara Marquardt, Jeanne Marquardt, Tom Klauer
Information Systems Analyst   John Herber
Information Systems Associates   Kevin Gellerman, Jeffrey Tindillier
Blueprint Manager   Chuck Lantis
Staff: Amy Berdahl, Brian Boese, Daniel Brown, Shannon Christenson, Tera Girardin, Joan Jerry, Brad Johnson, April Liljedahl, Karen Liljedahl, Sarah McCadden, Monita Mohammadian, Michelle Olofson, Cindy Pai, Kellie Pierce, Michael Romain, Shelley Safratowich, Keri Schwab, Karen Zambory, Peggy Zambory

Southern Styling   E-1709, p. 55

Pure Warmth and Comfort   S-8389, p. 113

Contemporary Lines   P-7689, p. 195

Fantastic Floor Plan!   B-88015, p. 200

Home Designs for Two-Story Living, a publication of the HomeStyles Group, is published by HomeStyles Publishing and Marketing, Inc., Roger F. Heegaard, Chairman; Jeffrey B. Heegaard, President; Roger W. Heegaard, Publisher; Robert L. Pool, Executive Vice President.

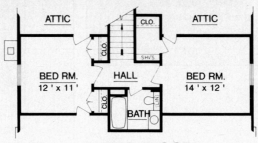

Photo courtesy of Breland & Farmer Designers, Inc.

Cost-Saving Style

- This country-style home has a classic exterior look and an open, space-saving floor plan.
- The U-shaped kitchen flows nicely into the dining room, where an angled hall stretches to the screened-in porch and the living room.
- The deluxe master bedroom is large for a home this size, and includes a separate sink and vanity area that adjoins the main bath.
- A good-sized utility room is convenient to the garage, which features a large storage area.
- The second floor offers two bedrooms, each with extra closet space, and another full bath. Both bedrooms also have access to attic storage space.

Plan E-1626

Bedrooms: 3	Baths: 2
Living Area:	
Upper floor	464 sq. ft.
Main floor	1,136 sq. ft.
Total Living Area:	**1,600 sq. ft.**
Garage	462 sq. ft.
Exterior Wall Framing:	2x6

Foundation Options:

Crawlspace
Slab
(Typical foundation & framing conversion diagram available—see order form.)

BLUEPRINT PRICE CODE: B

**NOTE:
The above photographed home may have been modified by the homeowner. Please refer to floor plan and/or drawn elevation shown for actual blueprint details.

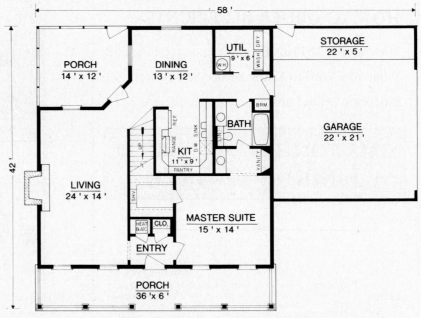

UPPER FLOOR

MAIN FLOOR

Space-Saving Floor Plan

- Easy, affordable living is the basis for this great town and country design.
- The welcoming porch and the graceful arched window give the home its curb appeal. Inside, the floor plan provides large, highly livable spaces rather than several specialized rooms.
- The foyer opens to the spacious living room. A column separates the foyer from the formal dining room, which features a bay window and an alcove that is perfect for a china hutch. The country kitchen is large enough to accommodate family and guests alike.
- A beautiful open staircase leads to the second floor, where there are three bedrooms and two baths. The master bedroom offers a tray ceiling and a luxurious bath with a sloped ceiling and a corner shower.

Plan AX-92320

Bedrooms: 3	Baths: 2½
Living Area:	
Upper floor	706 sq. ft.
Main floor	830 sq. ft.
Total Living Area:	**1,536 sq. ft.**
Standard basement	754 sq. ft.
Garage	510 sq. ft.
Exterior Wall Framing:	2x6

Foundation Options:

Standard basement

Slab

(Typical foundation & framing conversion diagram available—see order form.)

BLUEPRINT PRICE CODE:	B

**NOTE:
The above photographed home may have been modified by the homeowner. Please refer to floor plan and/or drawn elevation shown for actual blueprint details.

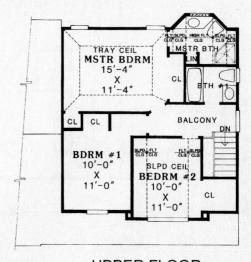

FRONT VIEW

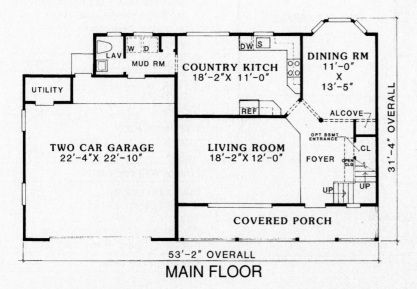

MAIN FLOOR

UPPER FLOOR

Upper Floor (plan)

SKYLITE

CER TILE LEDGE

WICL

BATH #2

BATH #1

BEDROOM #3
11'-0" x 9'-6"
CL

MASTER BEDROOM
16'-0" x 13'-2"
SPLAYED CLG

LIN
DN
CL

BEDROOM #2
13'-4" x 10'-0"
CL

CL

UPPER FLOOR

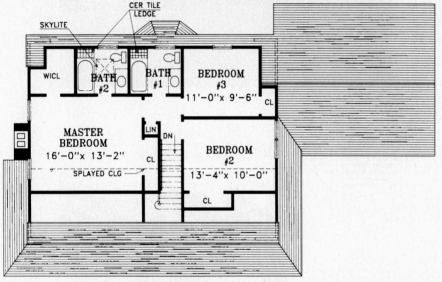

Quaint Country Design

- The renewed "country" look is evident in this simply designed two-story with wrap-around front porch.
- Functional living areas flank the entryway and stairs.
- A beautiful and spacious Great Room, with masonry fireplace and wrap-around windows, is to the left, and a nice-sized den which could serve as a library, office, guest room or fourth bedroom is to the right.
- The kitchen is a lovely space with two separate areas, an efficient work area and a distinct bay windowed dining area with center door leading to the rear yard.
- The second floor includes a master bedroom with full private bath and two large closets, plus two secondary bedrooms.

Plan AX-89311

Bedrooms: 3	Baths: 2½

Space:	
Upper floor:	736 sq. ft.
Main floor:	1,021 sq. ft.

Total living area:	**1,757 sq. ft.**
Basement:	approx. 1,021 sq. ft.
Garage:	440 sq. ft.

Exterior Wall Framing:	2x4

Foundation options:
Standard basement.
Slab.
(Foundation & framing conversion diagram available — see order form.)

Blueprint Price Code:	B

Main Floor (plan)

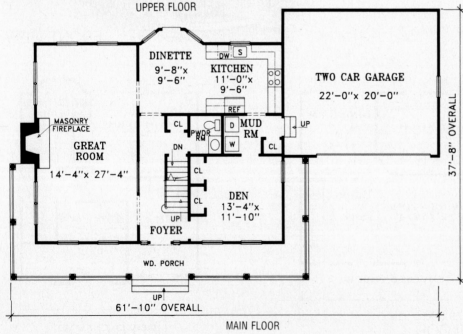

MASONRY FIREPLACE

GREAT ROOM
14'-4" x 27'-4"

DINETTE
9'-8" x 9'-6"

KITCHEN
11'-0" 9'-6"

DW S

REF

TWO CAR GARAGE
22'-0" x 20'-0"

CL

PWDR RM

D MUD RM

W

UP

CL

DN

CL

CL

DEN
13'-4" x 11'-10"

UP

FOYER

WD. PORCH

37'-8" OVERALL

UP

61'-10" OVERALL

MAIN FLOOR

Country Styling for Up-to-Date Living

- Nearly surrounded by a covered wood porch, this traditional 1,860 square-foot farm-styled home is modernized for today's active, up-to-date family.
- Inside, the efficient floor plan promotes easy mobility with a minimum of cross-traffic.
- The spacious living and dining area is warmed by a fireplace with a stone hearth; the U-shaped country kitchen is centrally located between these areas and the nook and family room with wood stove on the other side.
- Sliding glass doors lead out to both the rear patio and the deck that adjoins the dining and living rooms.
- The large master bedroom with corner window, dressing area and private bath and two other bedrooms with a second shared bath are found on the upper level.

Plans P-7677-2A & -2D	
Bedrooms: 3	Baths: 2 ½
Space:	
Upper floor	825 sq. ft.
Main floor	1,035 sq. ft.
Total Living Area	**1,860 sq. ft.**
Basement	1,014 sq. ft.
Garage	466 sq. ft.
Exterior Wall Framing	2x6
Foundation options:	Plan #
Daylight Basement	P-7677-2D
Crawlspace	P-7677-2A
(Foundation & framing conversion diagram available—see order form.)	
Blueprint Price Code	B

PLAN P-7677-2D
WITH DAYLIGHT BASEMENT

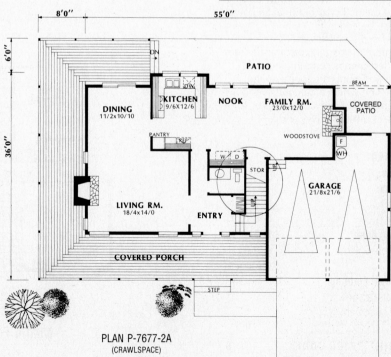

PLAN P-7677-2A
(CRAWLSPACE)

Nicely Sized and Styled

- Eye-catching entry columns and varying rooflines accent this versatile two-story.
- The vaulted entry and living room are open to the upper level. Decorative columns, a lovely corner window and a front window seat are found in the living room, which is open to the hall and the stairway.
- The roomy kitchen and breakfast area at the rear of the home offers a pantry and a bayed window that overlooks a rear patio. The kitchen also has easy access to the formal dining room and a handy pass-through to the casual family room.
- Sliding glass doors in the family room open to the patio; an optional fireplace may also be added.
- A nice-sized laundry room is convenient to the garage entrance, and a powder room is centrally located.
- All four bedrooms are found on the upper level, where a balcony overlooks the living room below. The master suite includes built-in shelves and a luxurious private bath.

Plan AG-1801

Bedrooms: 4	Baths: 2½
Living Area:	
Upper floor	890 sq. ft.
Main floor	980 sq. ft.
Total Living Area:	**1,870 sq. ft.**
Standard basement	980 sq. ft.
Garage	480 sq. ft.
Exterior Wall Framing:	2x6
Foundation Options:	

Standard basement

(All plans can be built with your choice of foundation and framing. A generic conversion diagram is available. See order form.)

BLUEPRINT PRICE CODE: B

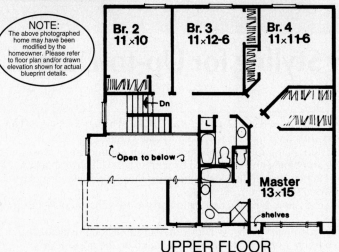

NOTE:
The above photographed home may have been modified by the homeowner. Please refer to floor plan and/or drawn elevation shown for actual blueprint details.

Br. 2
11×10

Br. 3
11×12-6

Br. 4
11×11-6

Dn

Open to below

Master
13×15

shelves

UPPER FLOOR

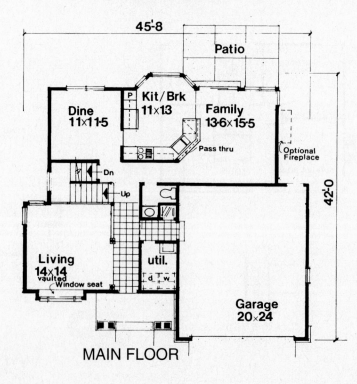

45'-8

Patio

P

Kit/Brk
11×13

Dine
11×11-5

Family
13-6×15-5

Pass thru

Optional Fireplace

42'-0

Dn

Up

Living
14×14
vaulted

Window seat

util.

d w

Garage
20×24

MAIN FLOOR

Plan AG-1801

PRICES AND DETAILS
ON PAGES 12-15

Photo by Mark Englund/HomeStyles

Master Suite Is Hard to Resist

- A covered front entry, topped by a dormer with a half-round window, gives this three-bedroom home an updated traditional look.
- Inside, volume spaces are created by high ceilings and lots of windows.
- The formal dining room is distinguished by a tray ceiling and a large picture window overlooking the front porch.
- The vaulted Great Room features floor-to-ceiling windows facing the backyard and a fireplace that can be enjoyed from the adjoining kitchen and breakfast area. The kitchen, which has a flat ceiling, includes a corner sink, an island cooktop and a large pantry. The vaulted breakfast nook is filled with glass and features a built-in desk.
- The master suite is hard to resist, with its inviting window seat and vaulted ceiling. The luxurious bath is also vaulted and boasts a garden tub in addition to a shower. A walk-in closet is opposite a clever vanity with a sit-down makeup area between the two sinks.
- The two bedrooms upstairs share another full bath.

NOTE: The above photographed home may have been modified by the homeowner. Please refer to floor plan and/or drawn elevation shown for actual blueprint details.

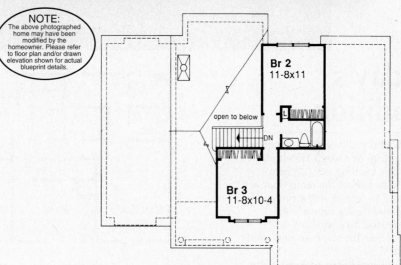

UPPER FLOOR

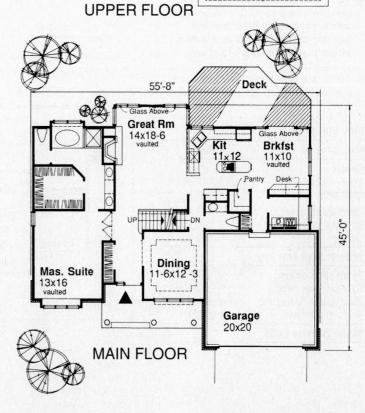

MAIN FLOOR

Plan B-89061

Bedrooms: 3	Baths: 2½
Living Area:	
Upper floor	436 sq. ft.
Main floor	1,490 sq. ft.
Total Living Area:	**1,926 sq. ft.**
Standard basement	1,490 sq. ft.
Garage	400 sq. ft.
Exterior Wall Framing:	2x4

Foundation Options:

Standard basement
(All plans can be built with your choice of foundation and framing. A generic conversion diagram is available. See order form.)

BLUEPRINT PRICE CODE:	B

Today's Tradition

- The traditional two-story design is brought up to today's standards with this exciting new design.
- The front half of the main floor is devoted to formal entertaining. The living and dining rooms offer symmetrical bay windows overlooking the wrap-around front porch.
- The informal living zone faces the rear deck and yard. It includes a family room with fireplace and beamed ceiling as well as a modern kitchen with cooktop island and snack bar.
- There are four large bedrooms and two full baths on the upper sleeping level.

Plan AGH-2143

Bedrooms: 4	Baths: 2½
Space:	
Upper floor:	1,047 sq. ft.
Main floor:	1,096 sq. ft.
Total living area:	**2,143 sq. ft.**
Daylight basement:	1,096 sq. ft.
Garage:	852 sq. ft.

Exterior Wall Framing: 2x6

Foundation options:
Daylight basement.
(Foundation & framing conversion diagram available — see order form.)

Blueprint Price Code: C

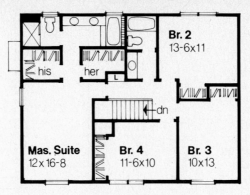

UPPER FLOOR

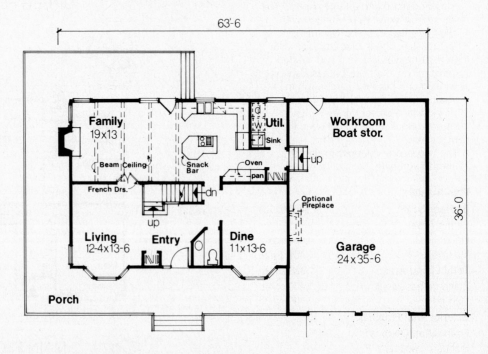

MAIN FLOOR

Plan AGH-2143

Two-Story Traditional

Plan GL-1950

Bedrooms: 3	**Baths:** 2½

Space:

Upper floor:	912 sq. ft.
Main floor:	1,038 sq. ft.
Total living area:	1,950 sq. ft.
Garage:	484 sq. ft.
Exterior Wall Framing:	2x6

Foundation options:
Standard basement.
(Foundation & framing conversion diagram available — see order form.)

Blueprint Price Code:	B

UPPER FLOOR

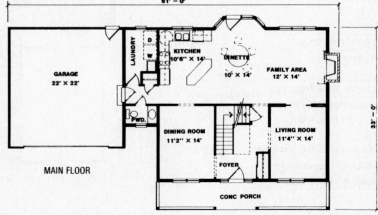

MAIN FLOOR

*TO ORDER THIS BLUEPRINT,
CALL TOLL-FREE 1-800-547-5570*

Plan GL-1950

*PRICES AND DETAILS
ON PAGES 12-15*

Colonial with a Contemporary Touch

- Open, flowing rooms highlighted by a two-story round-top window combine to give this colonial design a contemporary, today touch.
- To the left of the elegant, two-story foyer lies the living room, which flows into the rear-facing family room with fireplace.
- The centrally located kitchen serves both the formal dining room and the dinette, with a view of the family room beyond.
- All four bedrooms are located upstairs. The master suite includes a walk-in closet and private bath with double vanities, separate shower and whirlpool tub under skylights.

Plan AHP-9020

Bedrooms: 4	Baths: 2 ½
Space:	
Upper floor	1,021 sq. ft.
Main floor	1,125 sq. ft.
Total Living Area	**2,146 sq. ft.**
Basement	1,032 sq. ft.
Garage	480 sq. ft.
Exterior Wall Framing	2x6

Foundation options:

Standard Basement

Slab

(Foundation & framing conversion diagram available—see order form.)

Blueprint Price Code	C

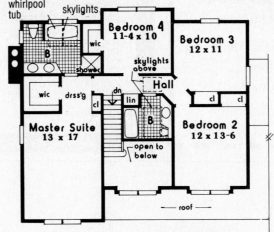

UPPER FLOOR

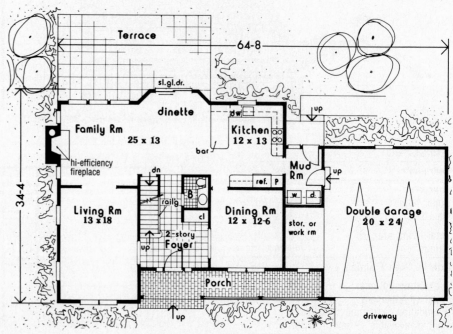

MAIN FLOOR

TO ORDER THIS BLUEPRINT, CALL TOLL-FREE 1-800-547-5570

Plan AHP-9020

PRICES AND DETAILS ON PAGES 12-15

THE "SOURCE 1"

"SOURCE 1" construction blueprints are detailed, clear and concise. All blueprints are designed by licensed architects or members of the A.I.B.D. (American Institute of Building Design), and each plan is designed to meet nationally recognized building codes (either the Uniform Building Code, Standard Building Code or Basic Building Code) at the time and place they were drawn.

The blueprints for most home designs include the following elements, but the presentation of these elements may vary depending on the size and complexity of the home and the style of the individual designer:

1. *Exterior Elevations* show the front, rear and sides of the house, including exterior materials, details and measurements.

2. *Foundation Plans* include drawings for a full, daylight or partial basement, crawlspace, slab, or pole foundation. All necessary notations and dimensions are included. (Foundation options will vary for each plan. If the home you want does not have the type of foundation you desire, a foundation conversion diagram is available from "SOURCE 1".)

3. *Detailed Floor Plans* show the placement of interior walls and the dimensions for rooms, doors, windows, stairways, etc., of each level of the house.

4. *Cross Sections* show details of the house as though it were cut in slices from the roof to the foundation. The cross sections specify the home's construction, insulation, flooring and roofing details.

5. *Interior Elevations* show the specific details of cabinets (kitchen, bathroom, and utility room), fireplaces, built-in units, and other special interior features, depending on the nature and complexity of the item. ***Note:*** *For cost savings and to accommodate your own style and taste, we suggest contacting local cabinet and fireplace distributors for sizes and styles.*

6. *Roof Details* show slope, pitch and location of dormers, gables and other roof elements, including clerestory windows and skylights. These details may be shown on the elevation sheet or on a separate diagram. ***Note:*** *If trusses are used, we suggest using a local truss manufacturer to design your trusses to comply with your local codes and regulations.*

7. *Schematic Electrical Layouts* show the suggested locations for switches, fixtures and outlets. These details may be shown on the floor plan or on a separate diagram.

8. *General Specifications* provide general instructions and information regarding structure, excavating and grading, masonry and concrete work, carpentry and wood, thermal and moisture protection, and specifications about drywall, tile, flooring, glazing, caulking and sealants.

PLANS PACKAGE

OTHER HELPFUL BUILDING AIDS

Every set of plans that you order will contain the details your builder needs. However, "Source 1" provides additional guides and information that you may order, as follows:

1. *Reproducible Blueprint Set* is useful if you will be making changes to the stock home plan you've chosen. This set consists of original line drawings produced on erasable, reproducible paper for the purpose of modification. When alterations are complete, working copies can be made.

2. *Mirror Reversed Plans* are used when building the home in reverse of the illustrated floor plan. Reversed plans are available for an additional one-time surcharge. Since the lettering and dimensions will read backwards, we recommend that you order only one or two reversed sets in addition to the regular-reading sets.

3. *Itemized List of Materials* details the quantity, type and size of materials needed to build your home. (This list is helpful in acquiring an accurate construction estimate.)

4. *Description of Materials* describes the type and quality of materials suggested for the home. This form may be required for obtaining FHA or VA financing.

5. *Typical "How-To" Diagrams — Plumbing, Wiring, Solar Heating, and Framing and Foundation Conversion Diagrams.* Each of these diagrams details the basic tools and techniques needed to plumb, wire and install a solar heating system, convert plans with 2 x 4 exterior walls to 2 x 6 (or vice versa), or adapt a plan for a basement, crawlspace or slab foundation. ***Note: These diagrams are general and not specific to any one plan.**

NOTE: Due to regional variations, local availability of materials, local codes, methods of installation, and individual preferences, it is impossible to include much detail on heating, plumbing, and electrical work on your plans. The duct work, venting, and other details will vary depending on the type of heating and cooling system (forced air, hot water, electric, solar) and the type of energy (gas, oil, electricity, solar) that you use. These details and specifications are easily obtained from your builder, contractor, and/or local suppliers.

PLEASE READ BEFORE YOU ORDER

WHO WE ARE

"Source 1" is a consortium of 45 of America's leading residential designers. All the plans presented in this book are designed by licensed architects or members of the A.I.B.D. (American Institute of Building Designers), and each plan is designed to meet nationally recognized building codes (either the Uniform Building Code, Standard Building Code or Basic Building Code) in effect at the time and place that they were drawn.

BLUEPRINT PRICES

Our sales volume allows us to offer quality blueprints at a fraction of the cost it takes to develop them. Custom designs cost thousands of dollars, usually 5 to 15% of the cost of construction. Design costs for a $100,000 home, for example, can range from $5,000 to $15,000.

Our pricing schedule is based on "Total heated living space." Garages, porches, decks and unfinished basements are <u>not</u> included.

Number of Sets	Price Code Based on Square Feet						
	A under 1,500	B 1,500- 1,999	C 2,000- 2,499	D 2,500- 2,999	E 3,000- 3,499	F 3,500- 3,999	G 4,000 & up
1	$265	$300	$335	$370	$405	$440	$475
4	$310	$345	$380	$415	$450	$485	$520
7	$340	$375	$410	$445	$480	$515	$550
Reproducible Set	$440	$475	$510	$545	$580	$615	$650

ARCHITECTURAL AND ENGINEERING SEALS

The increased concern over energy costs and safety has prompted many cities and states to require an architect or engineer to review and "seal" a blueprint prior to construction. There may be a fee for this service. Please contact your local lumber yard, municipal building department, Builders Association, or local chapter of the AIBD or AIA (American Institute of Architecture).

Note: (Plans for homes to be built in Nevada may have to be re-drawn and sealed by a Nevada-licensed design professional.)

RETURNS AND EXCHANGES

HomeStyles blueprints are satisfaction-guaranteed. If, for some reason, the blueprints you ordered cannot be used, we will be pleased to exchange them within 30 days of the purchase date. Please note that a handling fee will be assessed for all exchanges. For more information, call us toll-free. **Note: Reproducible Sets cannot be exchanged or returned.**

ESTIMATING BUILDING COSTS

Building costs vary widely depending on style, size, type of finishing materials you select, and the local rates for labor and building materials. A local average cost per square foot of construction can give you a rough estimate. To get the average cost per square foot in your area, you can call a local contractor, your state or local Builders Association, the National Association of Home Builders (NAHB), or the AIBD. A more accurate estimate will require a professional review of the working blueprints and the types of materials you will be using.

FOUNDATION OPTIONS AND EXTERIOR CONSTRUCTION

Depending on your location and climate, your home will be built with either a slab, crawlspace or basement foundation; the exterior walls will either be 2x4 or 2x6. Most professional contractors and builders can easily adapt a home to meet the foundation and exterior wall requirements that you desire.

If the home that you select does not offer the foundation or exterior wall requirements that you prefer, HomeStyles offers a typical foundation and framing conversion diagram. (See order form.)

HOW MANY BLUEPRINTS SHOULD I ORDER?

A single set of blueprints is sufficient to study and review a home in greater detail. However, if you are planning to get cost estimates or are planning to build, you will need a minimum of 4 sets. If you will be modifying your home plan, we recommend ordering a Reproducible Blueprint Set.

To help determine the exact number of sets you will need, please refer to the Blueprint Checklist below:

BLUEPRINT CHECKLIST

____**Owner (1 Set)**

____**Lending Institution (usually 1 set for conventional mortgage; 3 sets for FHA or VA loans)**

____**Builder (usually requires at least 3 sets)**

____**Building Permit Department (at least 1 set)**

REVISIONS, MODIFICATIONS AND CUSTOMIZING

The tremendous variety of designs available from "SOURCE 1" allows you to choose the home that best suits your lifestyle, budget and building site. Through your choice of siding, roof, trim, decorating, color, etc., your home can be customized easily.

Minor changes and material substitutions can be made by any professional builder without the need for expensive blueprint revisions. However, if you will be making major changes, we strongly recommend that you order a Reproducible Blueprint Set and seek the services of an architect or professional designer.

**Every state, county and municipality has its own codes, zoning requirements, ordinances, and building regulations. Modifications may be necessary to comply with your specific requirements -- snow loads, energy codes, seismic zones, etc.

COMPLIANCE WITH CODES

Depending on where you live, you may need to modify your plans to comply with local building requirements -- snow loads, energy codes, seismic zones, etc. All "SOURCE 1" plans are designed to meet the specifications of seismic zones I or II. "SOURCE 1" authorizes the use of our blueprints expressly conditioned upon your obligation and agreement to strictly comply with all local building codes, ordinances, regulations, and requirements -- including permits and inspections at the time of construction.

LICENSE AGREEMENT, COPY RESTRICTIONS, COPYRIGHT

When you purchase a "SOURCE 1" blueprint, we, as Licensor, grant you, as Licensee, the right to use these documents to construct a single unit. All of the plans in this publication are protected under the Federal Copyright Act, Title XVII of the United States Code and Chapter 37 of the Code of Federal Regulations. Each "Source 1" designer retains title and ownership of the original documents. The blueprints licensed to you cannot be resold or used by any other person, copied or reproduced by any means. **This does not apply to Reproducible Blueprints.** When you purchase a Reproducible Blueprint Set, you reserve the right to modify and reproduce the plan.

BLUEPRINT ORDER FORM

Ordering your dream home plans is as easy as 1-2-3!

Complete this order form in just 3 easy steps. Then mail in your order, or call 1-800-547-5570 for faster service!

Thank you for your order and good luck with your new home!

1. BLUEPRINTS & ACCESSORIES

SAVE $60!   **SAVE $135!**

BLUEPRINT CHART

Price Code	1 Set	4 Sets	7 Sets	Reproducible Set*
A	$265	$310	$340	$440
B	$300	$345	$375	$475
C	$335	$380	$410	$510
D	$370	$415	$445	$545
E	$405	$450	$480	$580
F	$440	$485	$515	$615
G	$475	$520	$550	$650

Prices subject to change.

*A Reproducible Set is produced on erasable paper for the purpose of modification. Available for plans with prefix: AG, AGH, AH, AHP, APS, AX, B, BOD, C, CPS, DD, DW, E, EOF, FB, GL, GML, GSA, H, HDS, HFL, J, K, KLF, LMB, LRD, M, NW, OH, PH, PI, PM, S, SDG, THD, UDG, V.

ADDITIONAL SETS: Additional sets of the plan ordered are $35 each. Save $60 to $135 when you order the 4-set or 7-set package shown above!

MIRROR REVERSED SETS: $40 Surcharge. From the total number of sets you ordered above, choose the number of these that you want to be reversed. Pay only $40. *Note: All writing on mirror reversed plans is backwards. We recommend ordering only one or two reversed sets in addition to the regular-reading sets.*

ITEMIZED LIST OF MATERIALS: Available for $40; each additional set is $10. Details the quantity, type and size of materials needed to build your home.

DESCRIPTION OF MATERIALS: Sold only in a set of two for $40. (For use in obtaining FHA or VA financing.)

TYPICAL HOW-TO DIAGRAMS: One set $12.50. Two sets $23. Three sets $30. All four sets only $35. General guides on plumbing, wiring, and solar heating, plus information on how to convert from one foundation or exterior framing to another. *Note: These diagrams are not specific to any one plan.*

2. SHIPPING AND HANDLING

Add shipping and handling costs according to chart below:

	1-3 Sets	4-6 Sets	7 Sets or more	Reproducible Set
U.S. Regular (4-6 working days)	$12.50	$15.00	$17.50	$15.00
U.S. Express (2 working days)	$25.00	$27.50	$30.00	$27.50
Canada Regular (2-3 weeks)	$12.50	$15.00	$17.50	$15.00
Canada Express (4-6 working days)	$25.00	$30.00	$35.00	$30.00
Overseas/Airmail (7-10 working days)	$50.00	$60.00	$70.00	$60.00

3. PAYMENT INFORMATION

Choose the method of payment you prefer. Send check, money order or credit card information, along with name and address to:

1. COMPLETE THIS FORM

Plan Number_____ Price Code_____

Foundation_____
(Carefully review the foundation option(s) available for your plan -- basement, crawlspace, pole, pier, or slab. If several options are offered, choose only one.)

No. of Sets:
☐ One Set
☐ Four Sets
☐ Seven Sets
☐ One Reproducible Set

$_____ (See Blueprint Chart at left)

ADDITIONAL SETS_____ (Quantity) $_____ ($35 each)

MIRROR REVERSED SETS_____ (Quantity) $_____ ($40 Surcharge)

ITEMIZED LIST OF MATERIALS_____ (Quantity) $_____ ($40; $10 for each additional)
(Available on plans with prefix: AH, AHP, APS*, AX, B*, C, CAR, CDG*, CPS, DD*, DW, E, FB, GSA, H, HFL, I, J, K, LMB*, LRD, N, NW*, P, PH, R, S, THD, U, UDG, VL.)
*Not available on all plans. Please call before ordering.

DESCRIPTION OF MATERIALS $_____ ($40 for two sets)
(Available on plans with prefix: AHP, C, DW, H, HFL, J, K, LMB, N, P, PH, VL.)

TYPICAL HOW-TO DIAGRAMS $_____ (All four only $35)
(One set $12.50. Two sets $23. Three sets $30.)
☐ Plumbing ☐ Wiring ☐ Solar Heating ☐ Framing & Foundation Conversion

SUBTOTAL $_____

SALES TAX* $_____ (*MN residents add 6.5% sales tax)

SHIPPING & HANDLING $_____ (See chart at left)

2.

GRAND TOTAL $_____

3.

☐ Check/Money Order enclosed (in U.S. funds)
☐ VISA ☐ MASTERCARD ☐ DISCOVER ☐ AMEX

Credit Card#_____ Exp. Date_____

Name_____

Address_____

City_____ State_____ Country_____

Zip_____ Daytime Phone(____)_____

Check if you are a builder: ☐   Home Phone(____)_____

Mail coupon to: HomeStyles Plan Service P.O. Box 50670 Minneapolis, MN 55405   Or Fax to: (612)338-1626

FOR FASTER SERVICE CALL 1-800-547-5570

FOR FASTER SERVICE CALL 1-800-547-5570

CP42

Country Kitchen and Deluxe Master Bath

- Front porch, dormers and shutters give this home a decidedly country look on the outside, which is complemented by an informal modern interior.
- The roomy country kitchen connects with a sunny breakfast nook and utility area on one hand and a formal dining room on the other.
- The central portion of the home consists of a large family room with

a fireplace and easy access to a rear deck.
- The downstairs master suite is particularly impressive for a home of this size, a features a majestic master bath with two walk-in closets and double vanities.
- Upstairs, you will find two more ample-sized bedrooms, a double bath and a large storage area.

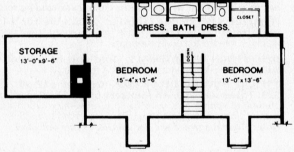

UPPER FLOOR

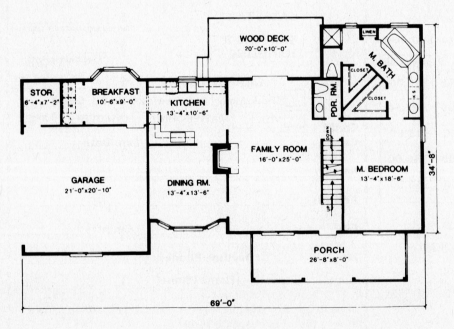

MAIN FLOOR

Plan C-8645	
Bedrooms: 3	**Baths:** 2½
Living Area:	
Upper floor	704 sq. ft.
Main floor	1,477 sq. ft.
Total Living Area:	**2,181 sq. ft.**
Daylight basement	Approx. 1,400 sq. ft.
Garage	438 sq. ft.
Storage	123 sq. ft.
Exterior Wall Framing:	2x4

Foundation Options:
Daylight basement
Crawlspace
Slab
(Typical foundation & framing conversion diagram available—see order form.)

BLUEPRINT PRICE CODE:	C

Plan C-8645

Front Porch
Invites Visitors

- This neat and well-proportioned design exudes warmth and charm.
- The roomy foyer connects the formal dining room and living room for special occasions, and the living and family rooms join together to create abundant space for large gatherings.
- The large kitchen, dinette and family room flow from one to the other for great casual family living.
- Upstairs, the roomy master suite is complemented by a master bath available in two configurations. The unique library is brightened by a beautiful arched window.

Plan GL-2161

Bedrooms: 3	Baths: 2½
Living Area:	
Upper floor	991 sq. ft.
Main floor	1,170 sq. ft.
Total Living Area	**2,161 sq. ft.**
Standard basement	1,170 sq. ft.
Garage	462 sq. ft.
Exterior Wall Framing	**2x6**
Foundation Options:	

Standard basement
(All plans can be built with your choice of foundation and framing. A generic conversion diagram is available. See order form.)

BLUEPRINT PRICE CODE	**C**

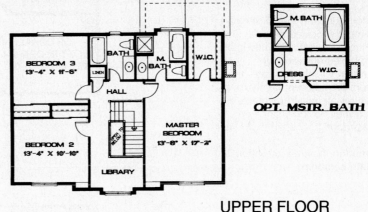

UPPER FLOOR

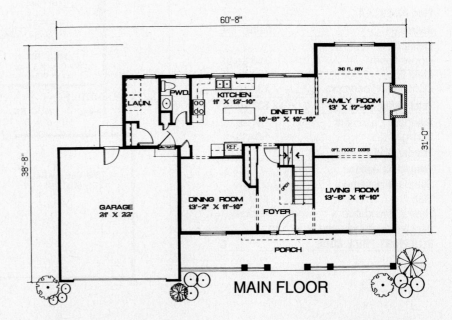

MAIN FLOOR

Affordable Country-Style

- This charming country-inspired home is economical to build and requires only a small lot.
- The powder room and the guest closet are conveniently located near the foyer and near the combination living/dining room with boxed-out window.
- A low partition visually separates the kitchen from the adjacent family room, which features an angled fireplace, a cathedral ceiling with skylight, and sliding glass doors that open to the rear yard.
- The second floor features an optional loft or fourth bedroom.

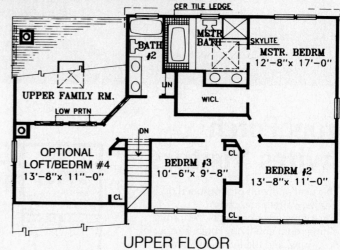

UPPER FLOOR

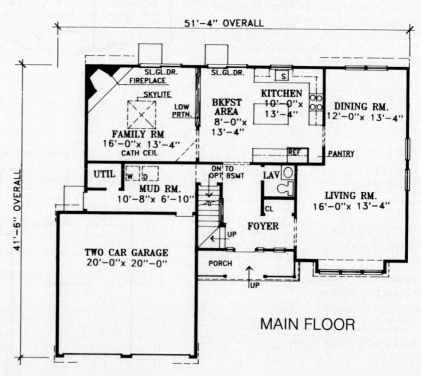

MAIN FLOOR

Plan AX-8923-A

Bedrooms: 3-4	Baths: 2½
Living Area:	
Upper floor	853 sq. ft.
Main floor	1,199 sq. ft.
Optional loft/bedroom	180 sq. ft.
Total Living Area:	**2,232 sq. ft.**
Standard basement	1,184 sq. ft.
Garage	420 sq. ft.
Exterior Wall Framing:	2x4

Foundation Options:
Standard basement
Slab
(Typical foundation & framing conversion diagram available—see order form.)

BLUEPRINT PRICE CODE: C

TO ORDER THIS BLUEPRINT, CALL TOLL-FREE 1-800-547-5570

Plan AX-8923-A

PRICES AND DETAILS ON PAGES 12-15

Skylighted Traditional

- This home features a classic traditional exterior with an exciting interior layout.
- From the vaulted foyer, guests are treated to a view through the open stairs into the vaulted Great Room, which boasts a fireplace and deck access.
- The kitchen offers an island snack bar and a pantry closet. The vaulted dinette floods the kitchen with natural light through its triple windows, sliding glass door and skylights. The formal dining room at the front of the home accommodates dinner guests.
- The master suite has a large closet and a separate dressing area. The private master bath boasts a skylighted whirlpool bath and a separate shower.
- The upstairs bedrooms are connected by a unique bridge, which offers views of the Great Room and foyer.

Plan GL-2291

Bedrooms: 3	Baths: 2½
Living Area:	
Upper floor	673 sq. ft.
Main floor	1,618 sq. ft.
Total Living Area:	**2,291 sq. ft.**
Standard basement	1,618 sq. ft.
Garage	491 sq. ft.
Exterior Wall Framing:	2x6

Foundation Options:

Standard basement
(Typical foundation & framing conversion diagram available—see order form.)

BLUEPRINT PRICE CODE:	C

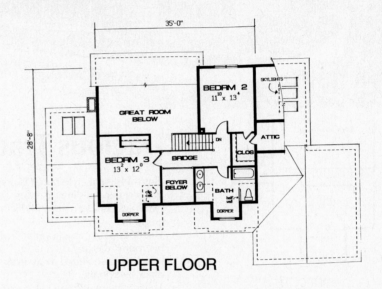

UPPER FLOOR

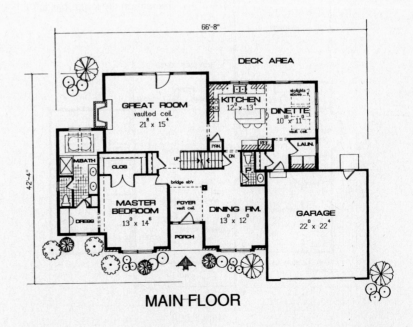

MAIN FLOOR

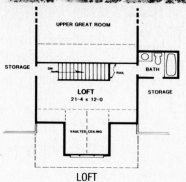

LOFT

Gracious Traditional

- This traditional-style ranch is perfect for a corner building lot. Long windows and dormers add distinctive elegance.
- The floor plan has a popular "split-bedroom" design. The master bedroom is secluded away from the other bedrooms.
- The large Great Room has a vaulted ceiling and stairs leading up to a loft.
- The upstairs loft is perfect for a recreation area, and has a full bath.

- The master bedroom bath has a large corner tub and his and hers vanities. A large walk-in closet provides plenty of storage space.
- The two other bedrooms have large walk-in closets, desks, and a shared bath.
- The kitchen and private breakfast nook are located conveniently near the utility/garage area.

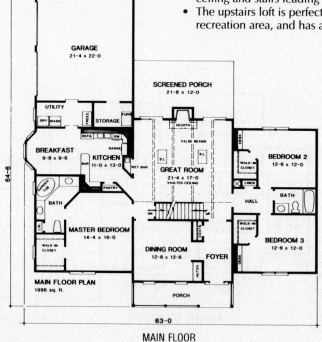

MAIN FLOOR

Plan C-8920	
Bedrooms: 3	**Baths:** 3
Living Area:	
Upper floor	305 sq. ft.
Main floor	1,996 sq. ft.
Total Living Area:	**2,301 sq. ft.**
Daylight basement	1,996 sq. ft.
Garage	469 sq. ft.
Exterior Wall Framing:	2x4

Foundation Options:
Daylight basement
Crawlspace
(Typical foundation & framing conversion diagram available—see order form.)

BLUEPRINT PRICE CODE:	C

TO ORDER THIS BLUEPRINT, CALL TOLL-FREE 1-800-547-5570

Plan C-8920

PRICES AND DETAILS ON PAGES 12-15

Vertical Sophistication

- This sophisticated two-story demands a second look. The vertical theme of the elegant exterior is also evident in the home's interior.
- Off the two-story-high foyer is a vaulted living room with a view of the expansive patio and a dynamic two-sided fireplace that is shared with the adjoining dining room. Elegant columns

visually separate the formal living room from the formal dining room.
- A skylighted sun porch to the rear of the dining room is surrounded in glass.
- A spacious island kitchen and breakfast area combine at the front of the home. A laundry room connects the kitchen to the garage.
- The elegant master suite is privately positioned to the rear. A skylighted sitting area and a private bath with dual sinks are featured.
- Two more bedrooms and another full bath share the upper floor.

Plan B-92019

Bedrooms: 3	Baths: 2½
Living Area:	
Upper floor	767 sq. ft.
Main floor	1,554 sq. ft.
Total Living Area:	**2,321 sq. ft.**
Standard basement	1,554 sq. ft.
Garage	547 sq. ft.
Exterior Wall Framing:	2x4

Foundation Options:

Standard basement
(All plans can be built with your choice of foundation and framing. A generic conversion diagram is available. See order form.)

BLUEPRINT PRICE CODE:	C

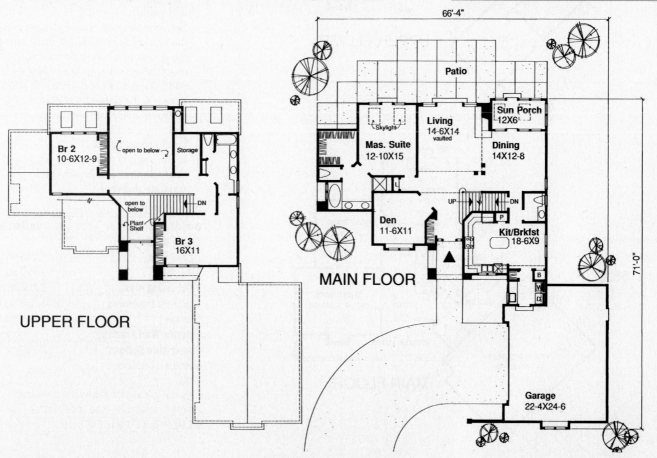

UPPER FLOOR

MAIN FLOOR

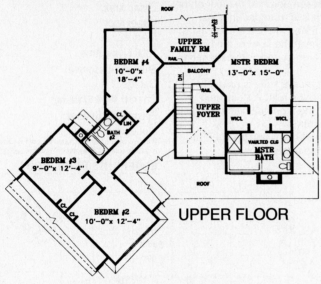

UPPER FLOOR

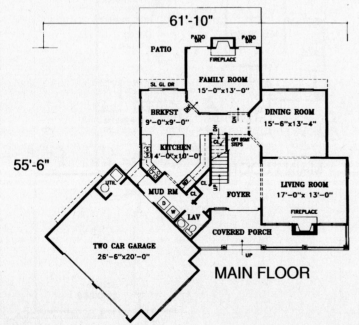

MAIN FLOOR

Angled Four-Bedroom

- A covered front porch, half-round windows and an angled garage with an attractive window treatment give this two-story an inviting look.
- Inside, the spacious foyers offers a view of the formal living room with a fireplace and a view of the front porch and yard.
- Between the formal dining room and the island kitchen and breakfast area is the generous-sized sunken family room; a second fireplace is flanked by patio doors that overlook a rear patio.
- Between the upper-level master bedroom and three secondary bedrooms is a balcony open to the family room below.
- In the vaulted master bath you'll find dual vanities, a large tub and a separate shower.

Plan AX-90309

Bedrooms: 4	Baths: 2½
Living Area:	
Upper floor	1,148 sq. ft.
Main floor	1,190 sq. ft.
Total Living Area:	**2,238 sq. ft.**
Standard basement	1,082 sq. ft.
Garage	545 sq. ft.
Exterior Wall Framing:	2x4

Foundation Options:
Standard basement
Slab
(Typical foundation & framing conversion diagram available—see order form.)

BLUEPRINT PRICE CODE: C

You Asked for It!

- Our most popular plan in recent years, E-3000, has now been downsized for affordability, without sacrificing character or excitement.
- Exterior appeal is created with a covered front porch with decorative columns, triple dormers and rail-topped bay windows.
- The floor plan has combined the separate living and family rooms available in E-3000 into one spacious family room with corner fireplace, which flows into the dining room through a columned gallery.
- The kitchen serves the breakfast room over an angled snack bar, and features a huge pantry.
- The stunning main-floor master suite offers a private sitting area, a walk-in closet and a dramatic, angled bath.
- There are two large bedrooms upstairs accessible via a curved staircase with bridge balcony.

Plan E-2307

Bedrooms: 3	Baths: 2½
Living Area:	
Upper floor	595 sq. ft.
Main floor	1,765 sq. ft.
Total Living Area:	**2,360 sq. ft.**
Standard basement	1,765 sq. ft.
Garage	484 sq. ft.
Storage	44 sq. ft.
Exterior Wall Framing:	2x6

Foundation Options:

Standard basement
Crawlspace
Slab

(All plans can be built with your choice of foundation and framing. A generic conversion diagram is available. See order form.)

BLUEPRINT PRICE CODE:	**C**

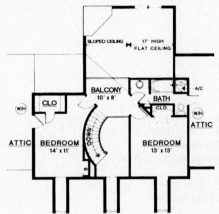

UPPER FLOOR

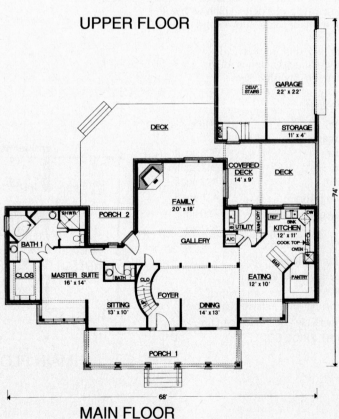

MAIN FLOOR

Old-Fashioned Charm

- A trio of dormers add old-fashioned charm to this modern design.
- Both the living room and the dining room offer vaulted ceilings, and the two rooms flow together to create a sense of even more spaciousness.
- The open kitchen, nook and family room combination features a sunny alcove, a walk-in pantry and an inviting wood stove.
- A first-floor den and a walk-through utility room are other big bonuses.
- Upstairs, the master suite includes a walk-in closet and a deluxe bath with a spa tub and a separate shower and water closet.
- Two more bedrooms, each with a window seat, and a bonus room complete this stylish design.

Plan CDG-2004

Bedrooms: 4	Baths: 2½
Living Area:	
Upper floor	928 sq. ft.
Main floor	1,317 sq. ft.
Bonus room	192 sq. ft.
Total Living Area:	**2,437 sq. ft.**
Partial daylight basement	780 sq. ft.
Garage	537 sq. ft.
Exterior Wall Framing:	2x6

Foundation Options:

Partial daylight basement

Crawlspace

(Typical foundation & framing conversion diagram available—see order form.)

BLUEPRINT PRICE CODE: C

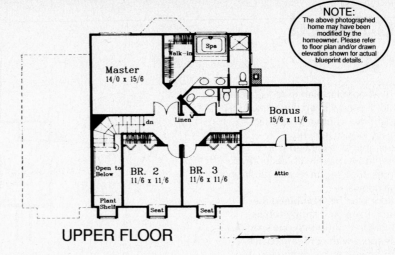

UPPER FLOOR

NOTE:
The above photographed home may have been modified by the homeowner. Please refer to floor plan and/or drawn elevation shown for actual blueprint details.

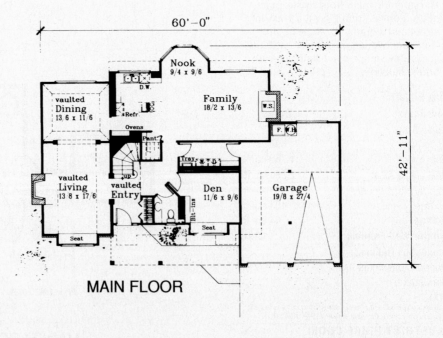

MAIN FLOOR

Plan CDG-2004

PRICES AND DETAILS
ON PAGES 12-15

Panoramic Porch

- A gracious, ornate rounded front porch and a two-story turreted bay lend a Victorian charm to this home.
- A two-story foyer with round-top transom windows and plant ledge above greets guests at the entry.
- The living room enjoys a panoramic view overlooking the front porch and yard.
- The formal dining room and den each feature a bay window for added style.
- The kitchen/breakfast room incorporates an angled island cooktop, from which the sunken family room with corner fireplace can be enjoyed.
- The three bedrooms and two full baths upstairs are highlighted by a stunning master suite. The master bath offers a quaint octagonal sitting area within the turret bay.

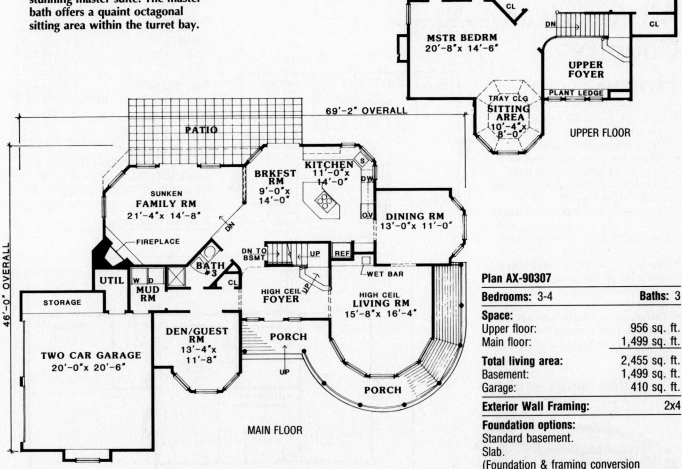

Plan AX-90307

Bedrooms: 3-4	Baths: 3

Space:

Upper floor:	956 sq. ft.
Main floor:	1,499 sq. ft.

Total living area:	2,455 sq. ft.
Basement:	1,499 sq. ft.
Garage:	410 sq. ft.

Exterior Wall Framing:	2x4

Foundation options:
Standard basement.
Slab.
(Foundation & framing conversion diagram available — see order form.)

Blueprint Price Code:	C

All-American Country Home

- Romantic, old-fashioned and spacious living areas combine to create this modern home.
- Off the entryway is the generous living room with fireplace and French doors which open onto the traditional rear porch.
- Country kitchen features an island table for informal occasions, while the adjoining family room is ideal for family gatherings.
- Practically placed, a laundry/mud room lies off the garage for immediate disposal of soiled garments.
- This plan is available with garage (H-3711-1) or without garage (H-3711-2) and with or without basement.

PLANS H-3711-2 & H-3711-2A
(WITHOUT GARAGE)

**NOTE: The above photographed home may have been modified by the homeowner. Please refer to floor plan and/or drawn elevation shown for actual blueprint details.

PLANS H-3711-1 & H-3711-1A
(WITH GARAGE)

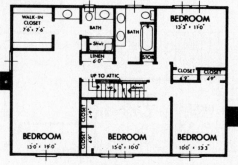

UPPER FLOOR

Plans H-3711-1/1A & -2/2A	
Bedrooms: 4	**Baths:** 2½

Space:

Upper floor:	1,176 sq. ft.
Main floor:	1,288 sq. ft.
Total living area:	2,464 sq. ft.
Basement:	approx. 1,288 sq. ft.
Garage:	505 sq. ft.

Exterior Wall Framing:	2x6

Foundation options:
Standard basement (Plans H-3711-1 & -2).
Crawlspace (Plans H-3711-1A & -2A).
(Foundation & framing conversion diagram available — see order form.)

Blueprint Price Code:	C

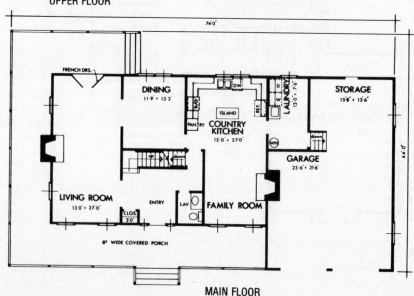

MAIN FLOOR

Plans H-3711-1/1A & -2/2A

PRICES AND DETAILS ON PAGES 12-15

Photo by Mark Englund/HomeStyles

Home Piques Interest

- A peaked roofline and dramatic arches create a striking facade that will stand out in any neighborhood.
- The high, columned entrance introduces a covered porch that wraps around the study to the master bath.
- A handsome fireplace and a tall, arched window adorn the spacious living room off the entry. The living room flows into a bright, formal dining room.
- The open island kitchen has abundant counter space, a unique corner range and a snack counter that extends into the family room.
- A bay window brings light into the adjoining morning room, which overlooks the backyard.
- The main-floor master suite is positioned for privacy. The bedroom features an oversized bay. Two walk-in closets, separate vanities and an oval tub under glass highlight the large bath.
- Two more bedrooms, a skylighted bath and a play area occupy the upper floor.

Plan DD-2524-B

Bedrooms: 3+	Baths: 2½
Living Area:	
Upper floor	584 sq. ft.
Main floor	1,956 sq. ft.
Total Living Area:	**2,540 sq. ft.**
Garage	483 sq. ft.
Exterior Wall Framing:	2x4

Foundation Options:

Slab

(All plans can be built with your choice of foundation and framing. A generic conversion diagram is available. See order form.)

BLUEPRINT PRICE CODE:	**D**

NOTE:
The above photographed home may have been modified by the homeowner. Please refer to floor plan and/or drawn elevation shown for actual blueprint details.

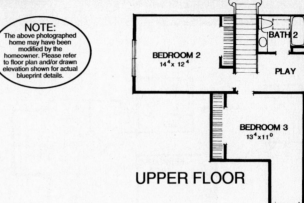

BEDROOM 2
14⁴ x 12⁴

BATH 2

PLAY

BEDROOM 3
13⁴ x 11⁰

UPPER FLOOR

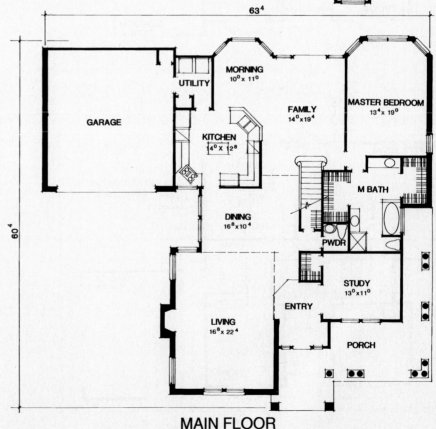

63⁴

60⁴

GARAGE

UTILITY

MORNING
10⁰ x 11⁰

KITCHEN
14⁰ x 12⁸

FAMILY
14⁰ x 19⁴

MASTER BEDROOM
13⁴ x 19⁰

M BATH

DINING
16⁸ x 10⁴

PWDR

STUDY
13⁰ x 11⁰

ENTRY

LIVING
16⁸ x 22⁴

PORCH

MAIN FLOOR

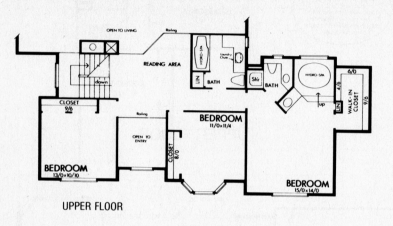

UPPER FLOOR

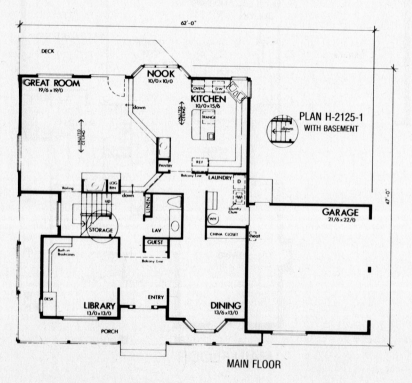

MAIN FLOOR

PLAN H-2125-1 WITH BASEMENT

Delightful Blend of Old and New

- A contemporary floor plan is hidden in a traditional farmhouse exterior.
- Vaulted entrance is open to the upper level; adjacent open stairwell is lit by a semi-circular window.
- French doors open into a library with built-in bookcase and deck.
- Sunken Great Room features a fireplace, vaulted ceiling open to the upstairs balcony, and French doors leading to a backyard deck.
- Roomy kitchen has center cooking island, eating bar, and attached nook with corner fireplace.
- Upper level has reading area and exciting master suite with hydro-spa.

Plans H-2125-1 & -1A

Bedrooms: 3	Baths: 2½
Space:	
Upper floor:	1,105 sq. ft.
Main floor:	1,554 sq. ft.
Total living area:	2,659 sq. ft.
Basement:	approx. 1,554 sq. ft.
Garage:	475 sq. ft.
Exterior Wall Framing:	2x6

Foundation options:
Standard basement (Plan H-2125-1).
Crawlspace (Plan H-2125-1A).
(Foundation & framing conversion diagram available — see order form.)

Blueprint Price Code:	D

Photo courtesy of Breland and Farmer Designers, Inc.

Verandas Add Extra Charm

- Porches, columns and dormers give this home a charming facade.
- The interior is equally appealing, with its beautiful two-story foyer and practical room arrangement.
- The central living room has a fireplace and access to a covered porch.
- A great island kitchen is conveniently situated between the two dining areas.
- A multipurpose room and an office are perfect for hobbies and projects.
- The secluded master suite offers a private study with a sloped ceiling. The master bath is large and symmetrical.
- Three bedrooms upstairs share a compartmentalized bath.

Plan E-2900

Bedrooms: 4	Baths: 2½
Living Area:	
Upper floor	903 sq. ft.
Main floor	2,029 sq. ft.
Total Living Area:	**2,932 sq. ft.**
Standard basement	2,029 sq. ft.
Garage and storage	470 sq. ft.
Exterior Wall Framing:	2x6

Foundation Options:
Standard basement
Crawlspace
Slab
(Typical foundation & framing conversion diagram available—see order form.)

BLUEPRINT PRICE CODE: D

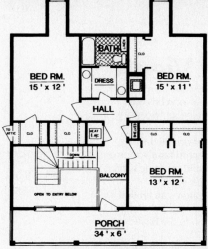

NOTE:
The above photographed home may have been modified by the homeowner. Please refer to floor plan and/or drawn elevation shown for actual blueprint details.

UPPER FLOOR

MAIN FLOOR

Dramatic Backyard Views

- Columned front and rear porches offer country styling to this elegant two-story.
- A dramatic array of windows stretches along the informal, rear-oriented living areas, including the central family room, the adjoining kitchen and morning room and the secluded master suite.
- The modern kitchen features an angled snack counter, a walk-in pantry, and a work island, in addition to the bayed morning room.
- The formal dining room and living room flank the two-story-high foyer.
- The exciting master suite has a sunny bayed sitting area with its own fireplace, large walk-in closets and a luxurious private bath with dual vanities, spa tub and separate shower.
- The centrally located stairway leads to three extra bedrooms and two full baths on the upper level.

Plan DD-2912

Bedrooms: 4	**Baths:** 3½

Space:

Upper floor	916 sq. ft.
Main floor	2,046 sq. ft.
Total Living Area	**2,962 sq. ft.**
Basement	1,811 sq. ft.
Garage	513 sq. ft.
Exterior Wall Framing	2x4

Foundation options:

Standard Basement

Crawlspace

Slab

(All plans can be built with your choice of foundation and framing. A generic conversion diagram is available. See order form.))

BLUEPRINT PRICE CODE	**D**

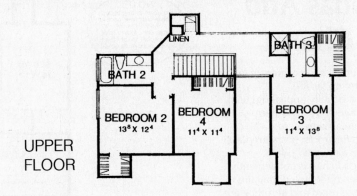

UPPER FLOOR

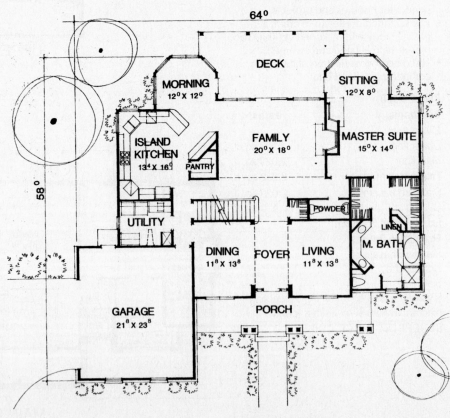

MAIN FLOOR

Photo by Gil Ford

Spacious and Stately

- Covered porches front and rear.
- Downstairs master suite with spectacular bath.
- Family/living/dining areas combine for entertaining large groups.
- Classic Creole/plantation exterior.

Plan E-3000

Bedrooms: 4		**Baths:** 3½

Space:

Upper floor:	1,027 sq. ft.
Main floor:	2,008 sq. ft.
Total living area:	**3,035 sq. ft.**
Porches:	429 sq. ft.
Basement:	2,008 sq. ft.
Garage:	484 sq. ft.
Storage:	96 sq. ft.

Exterior Wall Framing:	2x6

Typical Ceiling Heights:

Upper floor:	8'
Main floor:	9'

Foundation options:
Standard basement.
Crawlspace.
Slab.
(Foundation & framing conversion diagram available — see order form.)

Blueprint Price Code:	E

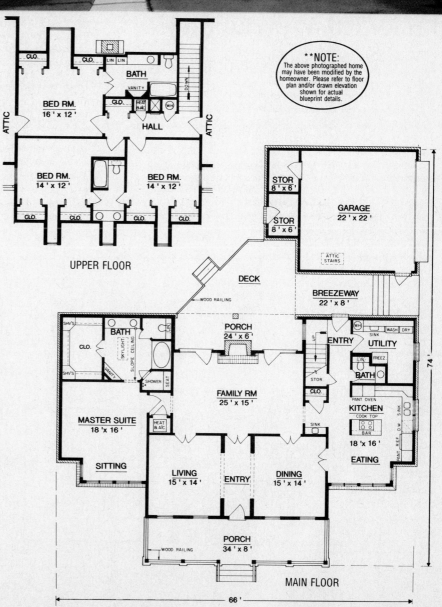

NOTE:
The above photographed home may have been modified by the homeowner. Please refer to floor plan and/or drawn elevation shown for actual blueprint details.

UPPER FLOOR

MAIN FLOOR

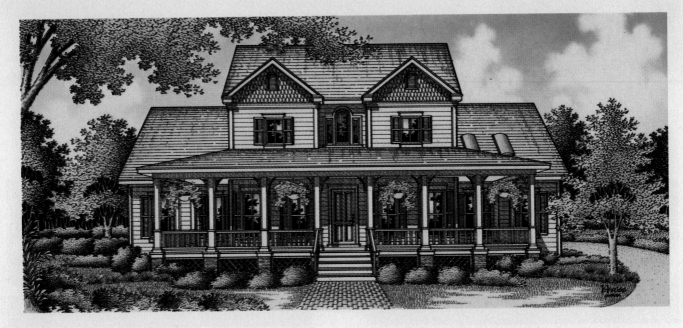

Wrap-around Porch Accents Victorian Farmhouse

- Fish-scale shingles and horizontal siding team with the detailed front porch to create this look of yesterday. The sides and rear are brick.
- The main level features a center section of informal family room and formal living and dining rooms. They can all be connected via French doors.
- A separate workshop is located on the main level and connected to the main house by a covered breezeway.
- The master bath ceiling is sloped and has built-in skylights. The kitchen and eating area have high sloped ceilings also. Typical ceiling heights are 8' on the basement and upper level and 10' on the main level.
- This home is energy efficient.
- This home is designed on a full daylight basement. The two-car garage is located under the workshop.

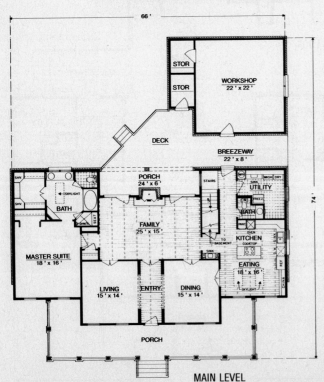

MAIN LEVEL

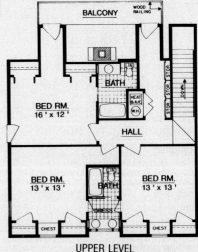

UPPER LEVEL
PLAN E-3103
WITH DAYLIGHT BASEMENT

Exterior walls are 2x6 construction.

Heated area:	3,153 sq. ft.
Unheated area	2,066 sq. ft.
Total area: (Not counting basement)	5,219 sq. ft.

Blueprint Price Code E

Plan E-3103

Open Design in Compact Traditional

- An instant feeling of spaciousness and openness is created in this hospitable home with a vaulted Great Room and open-railed stairway.
- Additional appeal comes from a wood-burning fireplace, visible from the adjoining kitchen and dining area.
- The spacious kitchen has a pantry and attached walk-in laundry room.
- The main-level master bedroom is well isolated from the living areas, yet easily accessible to the children's bedrooms on the upper level.

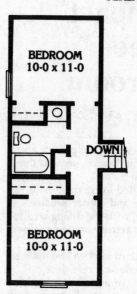

UPPER FLOOR

BEDROOM
10-0 x 11-0

DOWN

BEDROOM
10-0 x 11-0

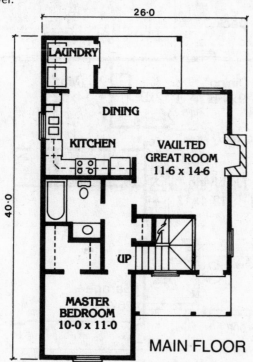

26·0

40·0

LAUNDRY

DINING

KITCHEN

VAULTED GREAT ROOM
11-6 x 14-6

UP

MASTER BEDROOM
10-0 x 11-0

MAIN FLOOR

Plan V-1098	
Bedrooms: 3	**Baths:** 2
Space:	
Upper floor	396 sq. ft.
Main floor	702 sq. ft.
Total Living Area	**1,098 sq. ft.**
Exterior Wall Framing	2x6
Foundation options:	
Crawlspace	
(Foundation & framing conversion diagram available—see order form.)	
Blueprint Price Code	**A**

Compact Three-Bedroom Home

- Both openness and privacy are possible in this economical three-bedroom home.
- The vaulted living room with fireplace and corner window combine with the dining area for an open activity and entertaining stretch.
- The modern kitchen and dining area overlook a rear deck.
- A lovely corner window brightens the private master bedroom on the main floor, two additional bedrooms and a bath share the upper loft.

Plan B-101-8501

Bedrooms: 3	Baths: 2

Space:	
Upper floor:	400 sq. ft.
Main floor:	846 sq. ft.
Total living area:	1,246 sq. ft.
Garage:	400 sq. ft.

Exterior Wall Framing:	2x4

Foundation options:
Standard basement.
(Foundation & framing conversion diagram available — see order form.)

Blueprint Price Code:	A

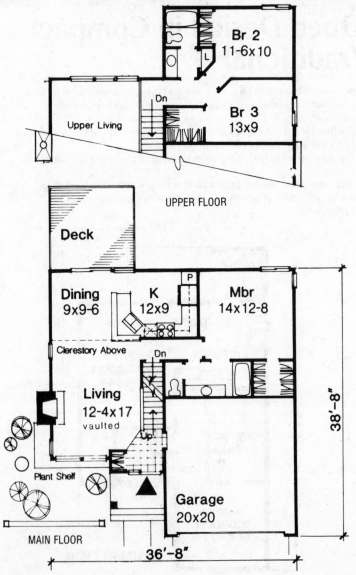

UPPER FLOOR

MAIN FLOOR

36'-8"

38'-8"

TO ORDER THIS BLUEPRINT, CALL TOLL-FREE 1-800-547-5570

Plan B-101-8501

PRICES AND DETAILS ON PAGES 12-15

Vaulted Living Room in Compact Plan

- Here's another design that proves that a compact narrow lot plan need not be plain or unattractive.
- A sheltered entry leads into a raised foyer, which introduces the vaulted living room, the stairway to the second floor, and a short hallway to the kitchen.

- A cozy breakfast nook is included in the efficient, open-design kitchen.
- Also note the convenient half-bath and storage closet between the kitchen and garage entry.
- Upstairs, the master suite includes a private bath and large walk-in closet.
- Bedroom 2 also includes a large closet.
- Bedroom 3 can be used as a loft, library, exercise room or study if not needed for sleeping.
- The upstairs hallway offers a balcony looking down into the living room below.

Plan B-224-8512

Bedrooms: 2-3	Baths: 2½
Space:	
Upper floor:	691 sq. ft.
Main floor:	668 sq. ft.
Total living area:	1,359 sq. ft.
Basement:	+/– 668 sq. ft.
Garage:	458 sq. ft.
Exterior Wall Framing:	2x4

Foundation options:
 Standard basement only.
(Foundation & framing conversion diagram available — see order form.)

Blueprint Price Code:	A

MAIN FLOOR

48'-0"

29'-10"

Deck

Brkfst
10-6x14-6

Dining
11x13-4

Kitchen

P

Garage
19-8x23-4

Living Rm
18x12-8
vaulted

DN

UP   DN

MAIN FLOOR

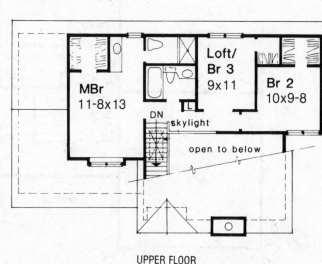

MBr
11-8x13

Loft/
Br 3
9x11

Br 2
10x9-8

DN

skylight

open to below

UPPER FLOOR

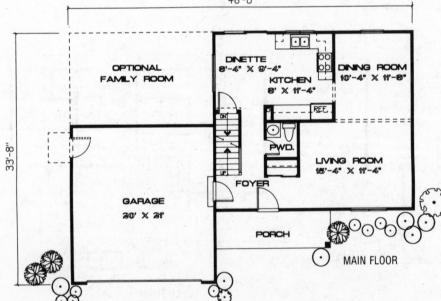

MASTER BEDROOM
13' X 11'4"

BEDROOM 3
12'8" X 10'4"

BEDROOM 2
11'8" X 12'

UPPER FLOOR

48'-0"

33'-8"

OPTIONAL
FAMILY ROOM

DINETTE
8'-4" X 9'-4"

KITCHEN
8' X 11'-4"

DINING ROOM
10'-4" X 11'-8"

REF.

PWD.

LIVING ROOM
15'-4" X 11'-4"

DN

UP

FOYER

GARAGE
20' X 21'

PORCH

MAIN FLOOR

Stylish Two-Story

- This two-story home boasts contemporary and traditional elements.
- The open main floor offers a large front living room and attached dining room.
- A sunny breakfast dinette with sliders joins a functional kitchen with plenty of counter space.
- A family room bordered by the dinette and garage may be added later. The blueprints do not show the family room.
- Three nice-sized bedrooms occupy the upper level.

Plan GL-1382

Bedrooms: 3	Baths: 2 ½
Space:	
Upper floor	710 sq. ft.
Main floor	672 sq. ft.
Total Living Area	**1,382 sq. ft.**
Basement	672 sq. ft.
Garage	420 sq. ft.
Exterior Wall Framing	2x6
Foundation options:	
Standard Basement	
(Foundation & framing conversion diagram available—see order form.)	
Blueprint Price Code	A

Plan GL-1382

PRICES AND DETAILS ON PAGES 12-15

Traditional Retreat

- This traditional vacation retreat maximizes space by offering an open, flowing floor plan.
- The spacious living room's luxurious features include a cathedral ceiling, fireplace and wet bar; its openness is extended by an exciting adjoining covered deck.
- Sweeping diagonally from the living room is the formal dining room with both front-facing and roof windows.
- The merging kitchen is separated from the living areas by a counter bar.
- The first floor bedroom features a unique triangular window seat, a dressing area and a full bath.
- The second floor is devoted entirely to a private master suite, complete with a lovely window seat, walk-in closet and attached bath.

UPPER FLOOR

CLOSET | DN | LIN. | BATH | DRESS

OPEN TO BELOW

MASTER BEDROOM
17' x 18'

Plan NW-334

Bedrooms: 2	Baths: 2
Space:	
Upper floor:	438 sq. ft.
Main floor:	1,015 sq. ft.
Total living area:	1,453 sq. ft.
Carport:	336 sq. ft.
Exterior Wall Framing:	2x6

Foundation options:
Crawlspace.
(Foundation & framing conversion diagram available — see order form.)

Blueprint Price Code: A

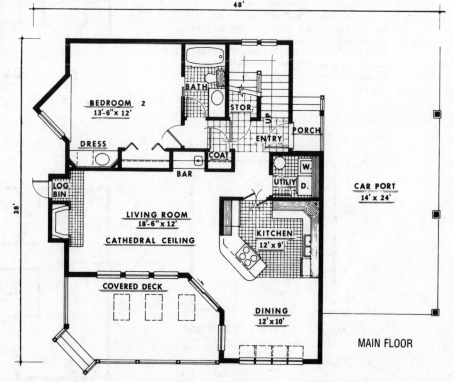

48'

38'

BEDROOM 2
13'-6" x 12'

DRESS

BATH

STOR.

UP

PORCH

ENTRY

COAT

BAR

LOG BIN

W.

UTILIY

D.

CAR PORT
14' x 24'

LIVING ROOM
18'-6" x 12'
CATHEDRAL CEILING

KITCHEN
12' x 9'

COVERED DECK

DINING
12' x 10'

MAIN FLOOR

Timeless Cape Cod

First floor:	1,008 sq. ft.
Second floor:	456 sq. ft.
Total living area: (Not counting garage)	1,464 sq. ft.

The reason for the timeless popularity of the Cape Cod concept, even during periods of revolutionary style change, is that it continues to be one of our most efficient and economical solutions to the housing problem. This home, for example, provides 1,464 sq. ft. of living area on a foundation measuring about 1,000 sq. ft.

Centralization and the over and under location of rooms guarantee lifelong savings in heating and cooling costs. Roofing and painting upkeep are far less than in equivalent one-story homes. Another important consideration is the centralization of plumbing, resulting in lower installation and operational costs. It has been estimated that nearly one-third of the water heating expense in a rambling style home is caused by water left to cool unused in extended pipe runs. In compact homes such as this, efficiency is much greater.

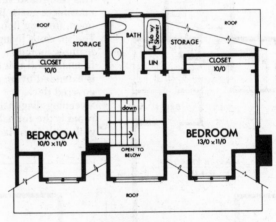

SECOND FLOOR
456 SQUARE FEET

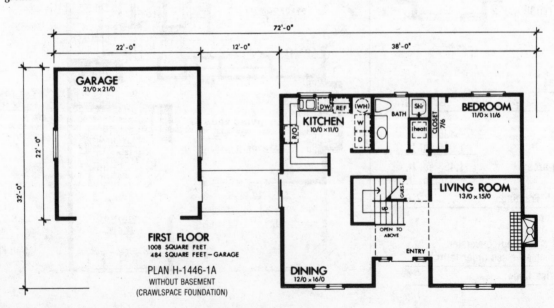

FIRST FLOOR
1008 SQUARE FEET
484 SQUARE FEET – GARAGE

PLAN H-1446-1A
WITHOUT BASEMENT
(CRAWLSPACE FOUNDATION)

Blueprint Price Code A

Plan H-1446-1A

TO ORDER THIS BLUEPRINT,
CALL TOLL-FREE 1-800-547-5570

PRICES AND DETAILS
ON PAGES 12-15

Pleasantly Peaceful

- You'll enjoy relaxing on the covered front porch of this pleasant two-story traditional home.
- Off the open foyer is an oversized family room, drenched with sunlight streaming through a French door and windows on three sides. A nice fireplace also adds warmth.
- A neatly arranged kitchen is conveniently nestled between a formal dining room and a sunny, casual breakfast room. A pantry and a powder room adjoin the breakfast room.
- The stairway to the upper floor is located in the family room. Closets and a sizable laundry room isolate the master suite from the two secondary bedrooms.
- The master bedroom features a tray ceiling, a huge walk-in closet and a private bath with a vaulted ceiling and a separate tub and shower.

Plan FB-1466

Bedrooms: 3	Baths: 2½
Living Area:	
Upper floor	703 sq. ft.
Main floor	763 sq. ft.
Total Living Area:	**1,466 sq. ft.**
Daylight basement	763 sq. ft.
Garage	426 sq. ft.
Storage	72 sq. ft.
Exterior Wall Framing:	2x4

Foundation Options:
Daylight basement
Crawlspace
(Typical foundation & framing conversion diagram available—see order form.)

BLUEPRINT PRICE CODE: A

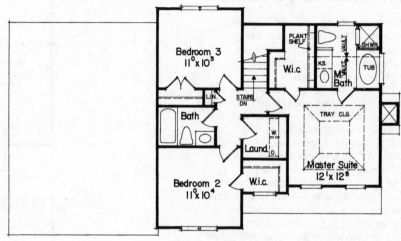

UPPER FLOOR

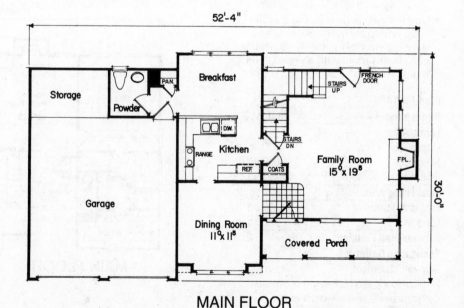

MAIN FLOOR

All the Options

- Attention-getting gables and decorative window details characterize this spacious home, which features an optional bonus room for future expansion possibilities.
- A two-story foyer leads into the main living areas. The vaulted family room is warmed by a fireplace and has French-door access to the backyard. The adjoining dining room leads to a bright breakfast area, where another French door opens to a covered porch.
- The centrally located kitchen services the entire living area, with a convenient serving bar to the breakfast area and a pass-through to the dining room.
- The elegant master suite is distinguished with a tray ceiling and a vaulted bath. The luxurious bath offers a garden tub, a separate shower and a deluxe walk-in closet adorned with a plant shelf.
- Upstairs, two bedrooms share a full bath. A balcony overlook provides a stunning view of the family room. The huge bonus room with a sloped ceiling is a nice option.

Plan FB-1469

Bedrooms: 3+	Baths: 2½
Living Area:	
Upper floor	409 sq. ft.
Main floor	1,060 sq. ft.
Optional bonus room	251 sq. ft.
Total Living Area:	**1,720 sq. ft.**
Daylight basement	1,060 sq. ft.
Garage	420 sq. ft.
Exterior Wall Framing:	2x4

Foundation Options:

Daylight basement
(Typical foundation & framing conversion diagram available—see order form.)

BLUEPRINT PRICE CODE: B

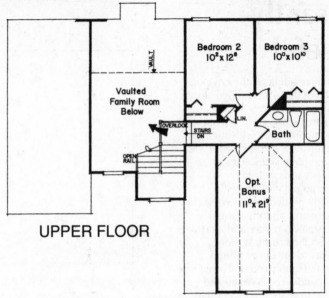

UPPER FLOOR

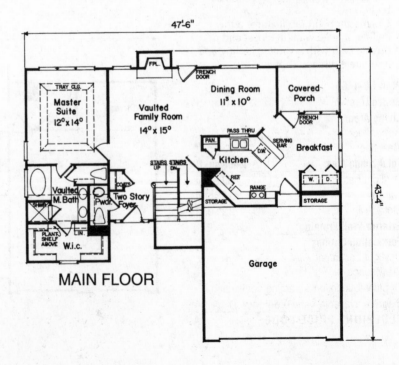

MAIN FLOOR

Compact, Cozy, Inviting

- Liberal-sized living room is centrally located and features corner fireplace and sloped ceilings.
- Separate two-car garage is included with plan.
- Two-bedroom loft overlooks living room and entryway below.
- Full-width porches, both front and rear, invite guests and family alike for leisure time rest and relaxation.

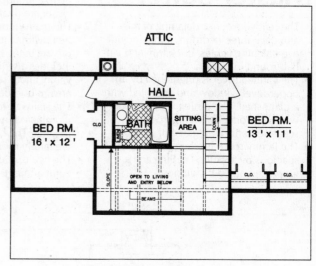

ATTIC

HALL

BED RM.
16' x 12'

BATH

SITTING AREA

DOWN

BED RM.
13' x 11'

OPEN TO LIVING AND ENTRY BELOW

SLOPE

BEAMS

CLO. CLO.

UPPER FLOOR

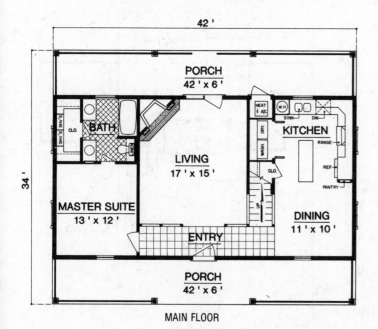

42'

PORCH
42' x 6'

BATH

HEAT & A/C

W.H

SINK   DW

KITCHEN

DRY

RANGE

LIVING
17' x 15'

WASH

CLO.

REF

34'

PANTRY

MASTER SUITE
13' x 12'

DINING
11' x 10'

ENTRY

PORCH
42' x 6'

MAIN FLOOR

Plan E-1421

Bedrooms: 3	Baths: 2
Space:	
Upper floor:	561 sq. ft.
Main floor:	924 sq. ft.
Total living area:	1,485 sq. ft.
Basement:	approx. 924 sq. ft.
Porches:	504 sq. ft.
Exterior Wall Framing:	2x6

Foundation options:
Standard basement.
Crawlspace.
Slab.
(Foundation & framing conversion diagram available — see order form.)

Blueprint Price Code: A

Main-Floor Master Suite!

- The refined exterior detailing of this attractive three-bedroom home includes eye-catching gables, brick trim and half-round louvers.
- The vaulted foyer is brightened by an upper-level window and accented with a plant shelf. The dining room merges with the wonderful family room, separated only by a graceful column.
- The family room is made even more spacious by a vaulted ceiling and a fireplace framed by windows.

- The breakfast nook combines with the kitchen to create an everyday living area that is hidden from view. A half-bath, a laundry closet and a coat closet are nearby.
- The main-floor master suite is a real treat, with its elegant tray ceiling and private bath. The luxurious bath includes a whirlpool tub, a dual-sink vanity and a separate shower and tub area, plus a deluxe walk-in closet.
- The stairway to the upper floor is illuminated by a window at the landing. The balcony hall overlooks the family room and the foyer below.
- The two upstairs bedrooms share a compartmentalized bath.

Plan FB-1529	
Bedrooms: 3	**Baths:** 2½
Living Area:	
Upper floor	431 sq. ft.
Main floor	1,098 sq. ft.
Total Living Area:	**1,529 sq. ft.**
Daylight basement	1,098 sq. ft.
Garage	432 sq. ft.
Storage	72 sq. ft.
Exterior Wall Framing:	2x4
Foundation Options:	
Daylight basement	
Crawlspace	
Slab	
(Typical foundation & framing conversion diagram available—see order form.)	
BLUEPRINT PRICE CODE:	**B**

MAIN FLOOR

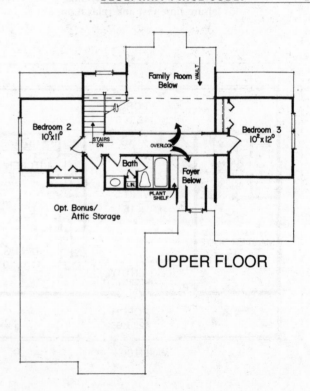

UPPER FLOOR

Open Kitchen/Family Room Combination

- This compact plan is designed to provide maximum casual living space for a small but busy family.
- A large family room/kitchen combination opens onto a large deck.
- The great room features an impressive corner fireplace and a vaulted ceiling and adjoins the

dining room to create a liberal space for entertaining.
- Upstairs, the master suite includes a private bath and large closet.
- Bedroom 2 boasts a large gable window, two closets and easy access to a second upstairs bath.
- The loft area is available for study, play, an exercise area or third bedroom.

Plan B-88006

Bedrooms: 2-3	Baths: 2½
Space:	
Upper floor:	732 sq. ft.
Main floor:	818 sq. ft.
Total living area:	**1,550 sq. ft.**
Basement:	818 sq. ft.
Garage:	374 sq. ft.

Exterior Wall Framing:	2x4

Foundation options:
Standard basement only.
(Foundation & framing conversion diagram available — see order form.)

Blueprint Price Code:	B

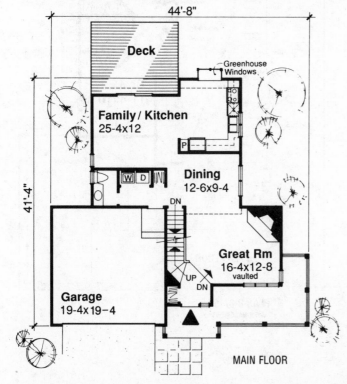

MAIN FLOOR

UPPER FLOOR

Cozy, Rustic Comfort

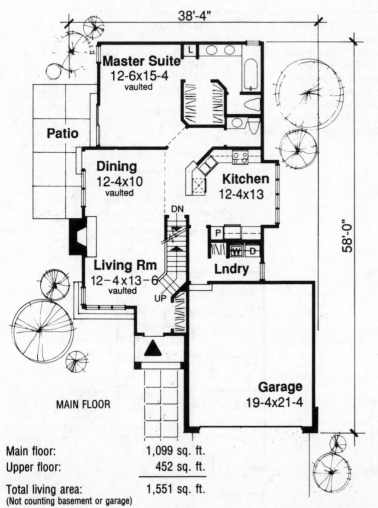

38'-4"

Master Suite
12-6x15-4
vaulted

L

Patio

Dining
12-4x10
vaulted

Kitchen
12-4x13

DN

Living Rm
12-4x13-6
vaulted

UP

P

W   D

Lndry

58'-0"

Garage
19-4x21-4

MAIN FLOOR

Main floor: 1,099 sq. ft.
Upper floor: 452 sq. ft.

Total living area: 1,551 sq. ft.
(Not counting basement or garage)

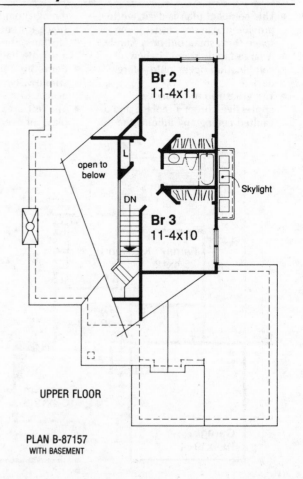

Br 2
11-4x11

open to
below

L

DN

Skylight

Br 3
11-4x10

UPPER FLOOR

PLAN B-87157
WITH BASEMENT

Blueprint Price Code B

Plan B-87157

PRICES AND DETAILS
ON PAGES 12-15

Deluxe Master Bedroom Suite in Compact Two-Story

- Plenty of luxuries are found in this compact two-story.
- A massive corner fireplace, corner window, vaulted ceiling and library alcove highlight the living room.
- A rear window wall in the dining room overlooks a rear deck that joins the bayed breakfast area and kitchen.
- The vaulted master suite offers corner window, plant shelf and a private bath.
- Up one step are two extra bedrooms and the hall loft that views the living room and entryway below.

Plan B-88002

Bedrooms: 3	Baths: 2½
Space:	
Upper floor:	833 sq. ft.
Main floor:	744 sq. ft.
Total living area:	**1,577 sq. ft.**
Garage:	528 sq. ft.
Exterior Wall Framing:	2x4

Foundation options:
Standard basement.
(Foundation & framing conversion diagram available — see order form.)

Blueprint Price Code:	B

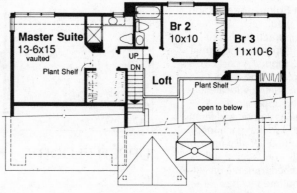

UPPER FLOOR

MAIN FLOOR

Luxury and Livability

- Big on style, this modest-sized home features a quaint Colonial exerior and an open interior plan.
- The covered front porch leads to a vaulted foyer that opens to the formal living and dining rooms. A coat closet, an attractive display niche and a powder room are centrally located, as is the stairway to the upper floor.
- The kitchen, breakfast nook and family room are designed so that each room has its own definition yet also functions as part of a whole. The angled sink separates the kitchen from the breakfast nook, which is outlined by bay windows. The large family room includes a fireplace.
- The upper floor has a hard-to-miss master suite, featuring a tray ceiling in the large sleeping area and a vaulted ceiling in the spa bath.
- Two more bedrooms and a balcony hall add to this home's luxury and livability.

Plan FB-1600

Bedrooms: 3	Baths: 2½
Living Area:	
Upper floor	772 sq. ft.
Main floor	828 sq. ft.
Total Living Area:	**1,600 sq. ft.**
Standard basement	828 sq. ft.
Garage	473 sq. ft.
Exterior Wall Framing:	2x4

Foundation Options:

Standard basement
Crawlspace
Slab

(Typical foundation & framing conversion diagram available—see order form.)

BLUEPRINT PRICE CODE:	B

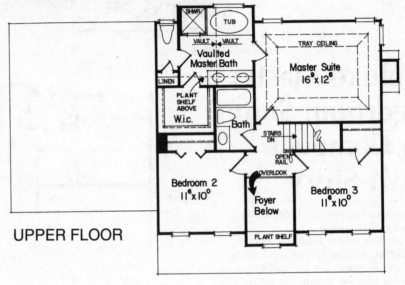

UPPER FLOOR

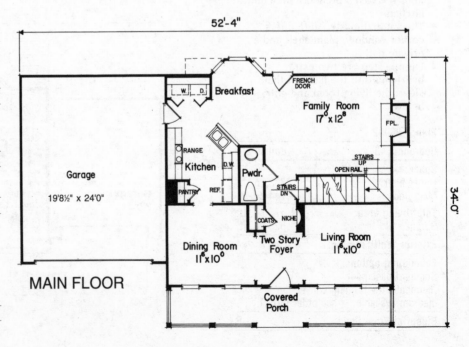

MAIN FLOOR

Classy Touches in Compact Home

- Charming window treatments, a quality front door, covered porch and detailed railings add class to this smaller home.
- The beautiful kitchen is brightened and enlarged by a sunny bay window.
- The spacious family room enjoys easy access to a patio in the back yard.
- The roomy living room features an impressive corner fireplace and a large bay window in the front.
- The master bedroom boasts a large bathroom, dressing area and closet in addition to the sleeping area.
- Both secondary bedrooms feature cozy window seats.

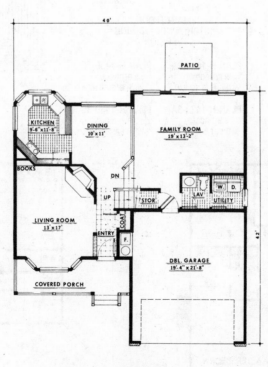

MAIN FLOOR

UPPER FLOOR

Plan NW-836

Bedrooms: 3	Baths: 2½

Space:	
Upper floor:	684 sq. ft.
Main floor:	934 sq. ft.

Total living area:	1,618 sq. ft.
Garage:	419 sq. ft.

Exterior Wall Framing:	2x6

Foundation options:
Crawlspace only.
(Foundation & framing conversion diagram available — see order form.)

Blueprint Price Code:	B

Functional, Nostalgic Home Offers Choices in Floor Plans

- Your choice of first- and second-floor room arrangements and foundation plans is required when ordering this design.
- Pick from a family room/kitchen combination with a separate living room, or an expansive living/dining room adjoining a kitchen and nook with either two or three bedrooms.
- In both cases, front entry parlor has an open stairway brightened by a round glass window.
- 8' wide front porch connects with a covered walk to a detached double-car garage.

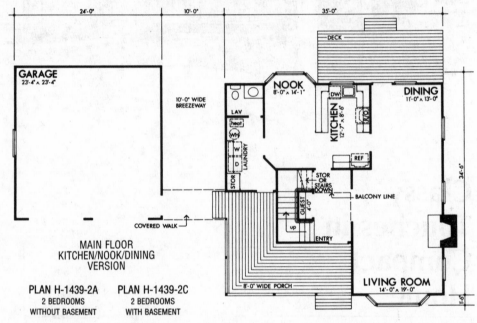

MAIN FLOOR
KITCHEN/NOOK/DINING
VERSION

PLAN H-1439-2A
2 BEDROOMS
WITHOUT BASEMENT

PLAN H-1439-2C
2 BEDROOMS
WITH BASEMENT

PLAN H-1439-3A
3 BEDROOMS
WITHOUT BASEMENT

PLAN H-1439-3C
3 BEDROOMS
WITH BASEMENT

(See facing page for alternate main floor)

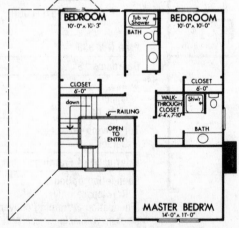

SECOND FLOOR - THREE BEDROOMS
678 SQUARE FEET

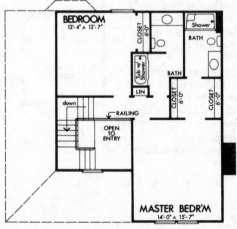

SECOND FLOOR - TWO BEDROOMS
678 SQUARE FEET

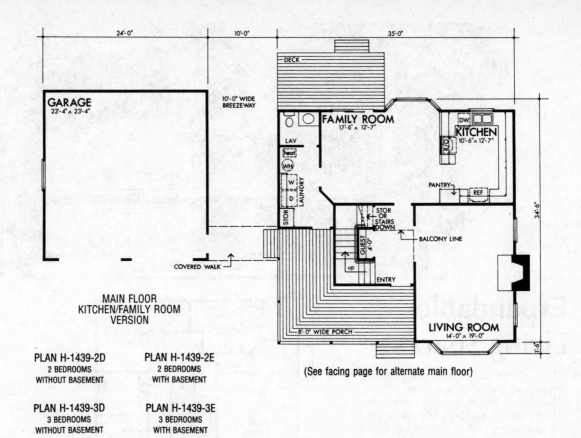

MAIN FLOOR
KITCHEN/FAMILY ROOM
VERSION

(See facing page for alternate main floor)

PLAN H-1439-2D
2 BEDROOMS
WITHOUT BASEMENT

PLAN H-1439-2E
2 BEDROOMS
WITH BASEMENT

PLAN H-1439-3D
3 BEDROOMS
WITHOUT BASEMENT

PLAN H-1439-3E
3 BEDROOMS
WITH BASEMENT

Plans H-1439-2A, -2C, -3A & -3C
Plans H-1439-2D, -2E, -3D & -3E

Bedrooms: 2-3	Baths: 2½
Space:	
Upper floor:	678 sq. ft.
Main floor:	940 sq. ft.
Total living area:	1,618 sq. ft.
Basement:	approx. 940 sq. ft.
Garage:	544 sq. ft.
Exterior Wall Framing:	2x6

Foundation options:
Standard basement (Plans H-1439-2C, -3C, -2E & -3E).
Crawlspace (Plans H-1439-2A, -3A, -2D & -3D).
(Foundation & framing conversion diagram available — see order form.)

Blueprint Price Code: B

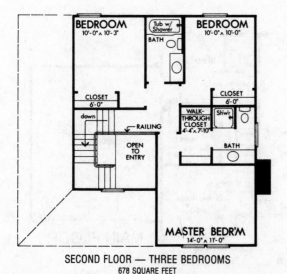

SECOND FLOOR — THREE BEDROOMS
678 SQUARE FEET

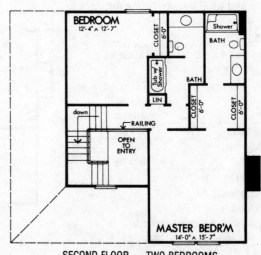

SECOND FLOOR — TWO BEDROOMS
678 SQUARE FEET

TO ORDER THIS BLUEPRINT,
CALL TOLL-FREE 1-800-547-5570 Plans H-1439-2D, -2E, -3D & -3E PRICES AND DETAILS ON PAGES 12-15   **49**

Expandable Living Spaces!

- Expandable spaces make this attractive two-story a great choice for growing families. The formal dining room or the living room could be easily converted into a library or den, while the optional bonus room above the garage provides a host of possible uses.

- The nice-sized family room offers an inviting fireplace and access to the backyard. The sunny breakfast room is just a few steps away and adjoins an efficient L-shaped kitchen.

- The upper floor features a balcony hall that overlooks the two-story-high foyer. The master suite is dignified by a tray ceiling in the sleeping area and a vaulted ceiling in the private bath with a corner spa tub. The large walk-in closet includes a handy linen closet and sports a decorative plant shelf.

- A convenient laundry closet, two bedrooms and a full bath complete the upper floor.

Plan FB-1631

Bedrooms: 3+	Baths: 2½
Living Area:	
Upper floor	787 sq. ft.
Main floor	844 sq. ft.
Bonus room	340 sq. ft.
Total Living Area:	**1,971 sq. ft.**
Daylight basement	844 sq. ft.
Garage	460 sq. ft.
Exterior Wall Framing:	2x4

Foundation Options:

Daylight basement
(Typical foundation & framing conversion diagram available—see order form.)

BLUEPRINT PRICE CODE: B

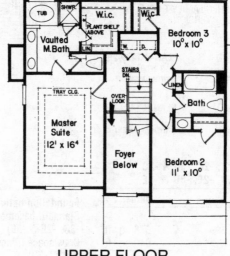

UPPER FLOOR

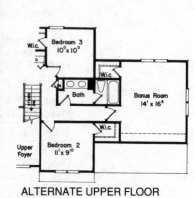

ALTERNATE UPPER FLOOR

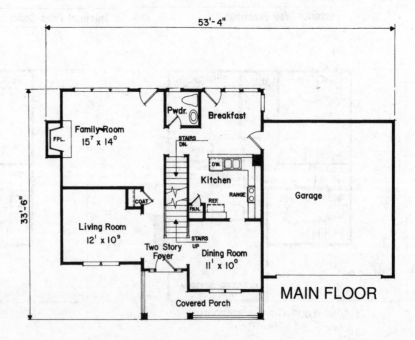

MAIN FLOOR

TO ORDER THIS BLUEPRINT,
CALL TOLL-FREE 1-800-547-5570

Plan FB-1631

PRICES AND DETAILS
ON PAGES 12-15

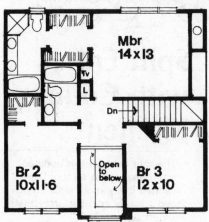

UPPER FLOOR

MAIN FLOOR

Smart Farmhouse

- This smart-looking farmhouse boasts a front wrapping porch, overlooked from the dining and living rooms.
- The two-story-high foyer reveals a decorative plant shelf and entry columns that accent and define these formal spaces.
- The informal living areas merge at the rear of the home and look out over the adjoining patio. The large family room shows off a big fireplace and shares a handy pass-through serving counter with the kitchen and the breakfast nook.
- A washer and dryer are neatly located in a laundry closet on the main floor.
- A nice-sized master bedroom with TV niche and private bath shares the upper floor with two additional bedrooms and a second bath.

Plan AG-9102

Bedrooms: 3	Baths: 2½
Living Area:	
Upper floor	769 sq. ft.
Main floor	910 sq. ft.
Total Living Area:	**1,679 sq. ft.**
Standard basement	910 sq. ft.
Garage	480 sq. ft.
Exterior Wall Framing:	2x6

Foundation Options:

Standard basement
(All plans can be built with your choice of foundation and framing. A generic conversion diagram is available. See order form.)

BLUEPRINT PRICE CODE:	B

Split Entry with Country Kitchen

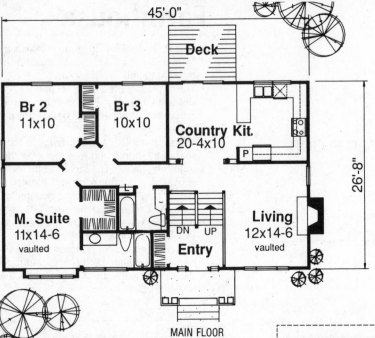

45'-0"

Deck

Br 2 11x10

Br 3 10x10

Country Kit. 20-4x10

P

26'-8"

M. Suite 11x14-6 vaulted

Entry

DN UP

Living 12x14-6 vaulted

MAIN FLOOR

- The split entry of this updated traditional opens up to a large vaulted living room with fireplace and a lovely country kitchen with sliders to a deck.
- Down the hall you'll find the vaulted master suite with large walk-in closet and private bath.
- Two additional bedrooms and a second bath are also included.
- The lower level is unfinished and left up to the owner to choose its function; room for a third bath and laundry facilities is provided.

Plan B-90012

Bedrooms: 3		Baths: 2-3
Space:		
Main/upper level:		1,203 sq. ft.
Basement:		460 sq. ft.
Total living area:		1,663 sq. ft.
Garage:		509 sq. ft.
Exterior Wall Framing:		2x4

Foundation options:
Daylight basement.
(Foundation & framing conversion diagram available — see order form.)

Blueprint Price Code: B

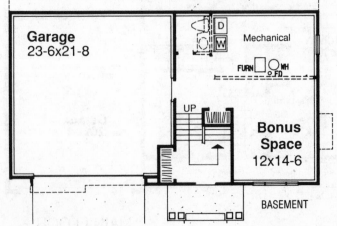

Garage 23-6x21-8

Mechanical

D
W

FURN □ ○ WH
○ FD

UP

Bonus Space 12x14-6

BASEMENT

TO ORDER THIS BLUEPRINT, CALL TOLL-FREE 1-800-547-5570

Plan B-90012

PRICES AND DETAILS ON PAGES 12-15

Plenty of Presence

- A stucco facade complemented by fieldstone, handsome keystones accenting the interesting window treatments and an imposing roofline give this home lots of presence.
- Inside, a two-story foyer an open stairway with a balcony overlook above provides an impressive welcome. Straight ahead, the huge family room is expanded by a vaulted ceiling, plus a tall window and a French door that frame the fireplace.
- The adjoining dining room flows into the kitchen and breakfast room, which feature an angled serving bar, lots of sunny windows and a French door that opens to a covered patio.
- The main-floor master suite is the pride of the floor plan, offering a tray ceiling, a vaulted spa bath and a spacious walk-in closet brightened by a window.
- The upper floor has two bedrooms, each with a walk-in closet, and a full bath. Abundant attic storage space is easily accessible.

Plan FB-1681

Bedrooms: 3	Baths: 2½
Living Area:	
Upper floor	449 sq. ft.
Main floor	1,232 sq. ft.
Total Living Area:	**1,681 sq. ft.**
Daylight basement	1,232 sq. ft.
Garage	420 sq. ft.
Storage	15 sq. ft.
Exterior Wall Framing:	2x4

Foundation Options:
Daylight basement
Slab
(Typical foundation & framing conversion diagram available—see order form.)

BLUEPRINT PRICE CODE:	B

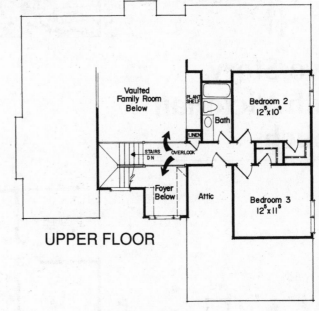

UPPER FLOOR

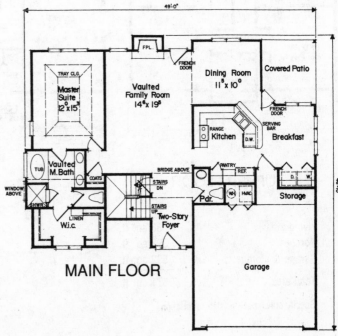

MAIN FLOOR

Two-Story
with Victorian
Touch

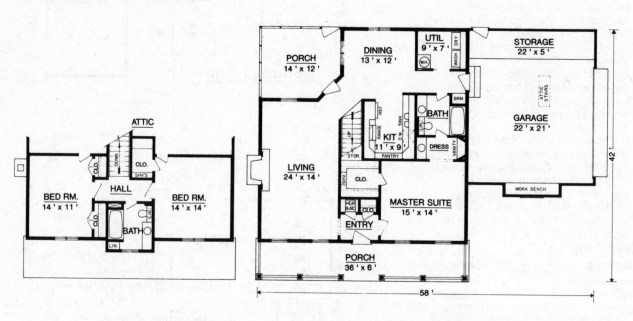

UPPER FLOOR

MAIN FLOOR

Living area:	1,686 sq. ft.
Porches:	393 sq. ft.
Garage & storage:	592 sq. ft.
Total area:	2,671 sq. ft.

Specify crawlspace or slab foundation.

Blueprint Price Code B

Plan E-1631

Southern Styling

- Classic Southern plantation styling is recreated with a full width covered front porch, triple roof dormers and stucco exterior.
- Once inside, the interior feels open, airy and bright with the living room merging into the dining room, both overlooked by the kitchen's serving and entertaining wet bar.
- The living room features a fireplace and three pairs of French doors.
- The dining room has rear access to a covered porch, connecting the two-car garage to the house.
- The main-floor master suite has two pairs of French doors leading to the front porch. The master bath includes a raised marble tub, sloped ceiling with skylight, and a walk-in closet.
- There are two bedrooms upstairs which share a second full bath and each feature a quaint dormer to let the light shine in.

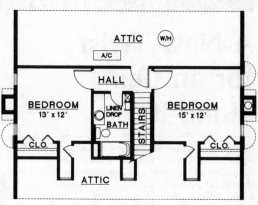

UPPER FLOOR

MAIN FLOOR

Plan E-1709

Bedrooms: 3	**Baths:** 2 ½

Space:

Upper floor	540 sq. ft.
Main floor	1,160 sq. ft.
Total Living Area	**1,700 sq. ft.**
Basement	1,160 sq. ft.
Garage	484 sq. ft.
Exterior Wall Framing	2x6

Foundation options:

Standard Basement
Crawlspace
Slab
(Foundation & framing conversion diagram available—see order form.)

Blueprint Price Code	B

A New Twist for an Old Stand-By

An exterior reminiscent of the homesteads of an earlier America conceals a floor plan as modern as the latest contemporary. An elegant central entry hall serves to channel traffic without interrupting ongoing activities in any way. Guests being entertained in the living room might be completely unaware of activities in another part of the home.

You will find no cramped dining space or tiny breakfast nook, but rather a huge kitchen/family room with plenty of dining space for even the largest family. And if all this does not provide adequate space, a large passive sun room will not only accommodate the overflow but help keep everyone warm in the bargain.

A beautiful open stairway leads upstairs. The master bedroom is larger than the living rooms of many contemporary homes. A private bath twice the size of the common "hardly-room-to-turn-around-bathroom", serves the master bedroom, together with large "his" and "hers" wardrobe closets. The other bedrooms, each with equally large wardrobes, are served by a second large bathroom.

Returning to the passive sun room, which was unheard of in original early farm homes, a thermal heat collecting storage floor and similar heat collecting masonry interior wall gather solar heat through 10 large glazed roof openings and retain it to be distributed throughout the rest of the home as the need arises. Such an arrangement can effect a surprising savings in heating costs, and also provides an unexpectedly bright and cheerful activity room.

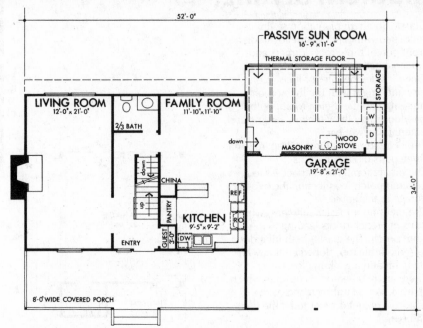

PLAN H-3727-1
WITH BASEMENT
MAIN FLOOR
704 SQUARE FEET
240 SQUARE FEET - PASSIVE SUN ROOM

PLAN H-3727-1A
WITHOUT BASEMENT - HAS CRAWLSPACE
FURNACE AND WATER HEATER IN
FURNACE PIT (ACCESS UNDER STAIR)

First floor:	704 sq. ft.
Sun Room:	240 sq. ft.
Second floor:	768 sq. ft.
Total living area:	1,712 sq. ft.

(Not counting basement or garage)

Blueprint Price Code B

SECOND FLOOR
768 SQUARE FEET

TO ORDER THIS BLUEPRINT,
CALL TOLL-FREE 1-800-547-5570

Plans H-3727-1 & -1A

PRICES AND DETAILS
ON PAGES 12-15

Compact and Efficient

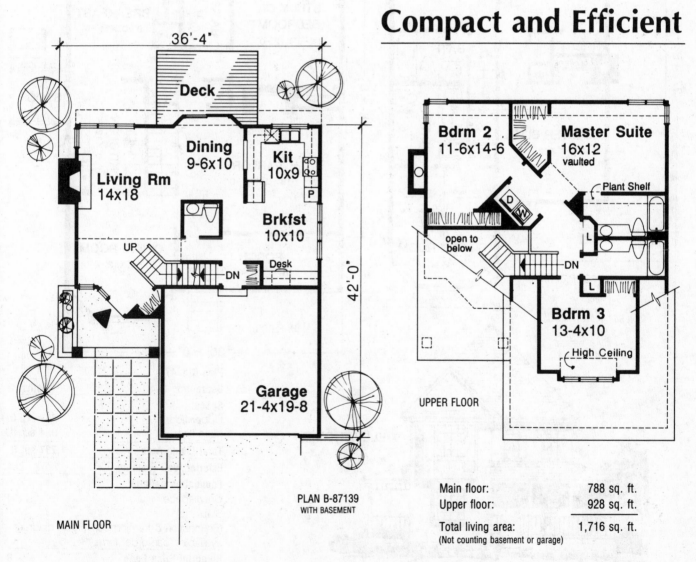

MAIN FLOOR

36'-4"

Deck

Dining
9-6x10

Kit
10x9

Living Rm
14x18

P

Brkfst
10x10

UP

Desk

DN

42'-0"

Garage
21-4x19-8

PLAN B-87139
WITH BASEMENT

UPPER FLOOR

Bdrm 2
11-6x14-6

Master Suite
16x12
vaulted

Plant Shelf

open to
below

DN

L

D
W

L

Bdrm 3
13-4x10

High Ceiling

Main floor:	788 sq. ft.
Upper floor:	928 sq. ft.
Total living area:	1,716 sq. ft.

(Not counting basement or garage)

TO ORDER THIS BLUEPRINT,
CALL TOLL-FREE 1-800-547-5570

Blueprint Price Code B
Plan B-87139

PRICES AND DETAILS
ON PAGES 12-15

57

Compact Victorian

ELEVATION A

- This compact Victorian design incorporates four bedrooms and three full baths into a home that's only 30 feet wide.
- The upstairs master suite includes a deluxe bath and a bayed sitting area.
- The roomy parlor includes a fireplace, and the formal dining room has a beautiful bay window.
- The downstairs bedroom, with its adjoining full bath, makes a great office or guest bedroom.
- Specify Elevation A or B when ordering. An attached two-car garage off the kitchen is also available upon request.

UPPER FLOOR

BEDROOM 9'-4"X9'-6"

BEDROOM 11'-2"X9'-6"

CLOSET

CLOSET LINEN

CLOSET FLUE

BATH

DOWN RAIL

WHIRLPOOL

BATH

CLOSET

MASTER SUITE 12'-0"X12'-4"

CATHEDRAL CEILING

CEILING FAN

SITTING ROOM 11'-4"X12'-4"

37' – 6"

24' – 0"

MAIN FLOOR

STUDY OR BEDROOM 11'-6"X12'-0"

BATH

WASH DRY

PANT.

BREAKFAST 9'-0"X11'-8"

CLOSET

FURN.

COATS

REF'G.

STOOP

RAIL

PARLOR 18'-0"X13'-0"

RAIL UP RANGE KITCHEN 8'-0"X12'-0" D.W. SINK

PORCH 18'-0"X6'-0"

RAIL

DINING ROOM 11'-4"X12'-8"

28' – 6"

30' – 0"

Plan C-8347

Bedrooms: 3-4	Baths: 3
Space:	
Upper floor	783 sq. ft.
Main floor	954 sq. ft.
Total Living Area	**1,737 sq. ft.**
Exterior Wall Framing	2x4

Foundation options:
Crawlspace
Slab
(Foundation & framing conversion diagram available—see order form.)

Blueprint Price Code	**B**

ELEVATION B

TO ORDER THIS BLUEPRINT, CALL TOLL-FREE 1-800-547-5570

Plan C-8347

PRICES AND DETAILS ON PAGES 12-15

Elevation B

Elevation A

Traditional Twosome

- This plan offers a choice of two elevations. Elevation A has an upper-level Palladian window, while Elevation B has a stately Georgian entry. Both versions are included in the blueprints.
- A vaulted entry foyer leads to formal living and dining rooms.
- The family room, nook and kitchen are combined to create one huge casual living area.
- The second-floor master suite is roomy and includes a beautiful, skylighted bath and a large closet.

Plan S-22189

Bedrooms: 3	Baths: 2½
Living Area:	
Upper floor	774 sq. ft.
Main floor	963 sq. ft.
Total Living Area:	**1,737 sq. ft.**
Standard basement	963 sq. ft.
Garage	462 sq. ft.
Exterior Wall Framing:	2x6

Foundation Options:
Standard basement
Crawlspace
Slab
(Typical foundation & framing conversion diagram available—see order form.)

BLUEPRINT PRICE CODE: **B**

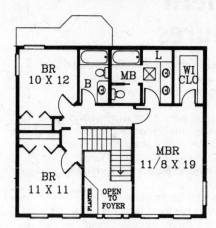

UPPER FLOOR

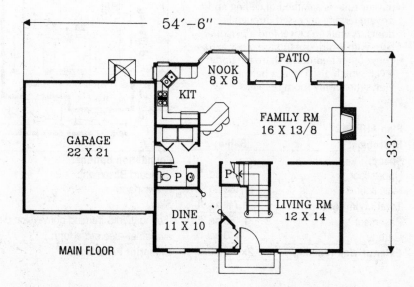

MAIN FLOOR

Colonial Has Modern Features

- This stately Colonial is as distinguished on the inside as it is on the outside.
- The dramatic entrance reveals a spacious living room with a big fireplace and a front bay window and an adjoining family room separated only by a decorative see-through wood divider. A sloped ceiling and French doors to the rear terrace are highlights in the family room.
- The high-tech kitchen has an island work area, a pantry, a handy laundry closet and a sunny, circular dinette.
- Featured in the private main-floor master suite is a cathedral ceiling and a private terrace accessed through French doors. A walk-in closet and a personal bath with whirlpool tub are other extras.
- Three other bedrooms share the upper level, which also offers a balcony that views the family room below.

Plan AHP-9121

Bedrooms: 4	Baths: 2 ½
Space:	
Upper floor	557 sq. ft.
Main floor	1,183 sq. ft.
Total Living Area	**1,740 sq. ft.**
Basement	1,183 sq. ft.
Garage	440 sq. ft.
Exterior Wall Framing	**2x4 or 2x6**

Foundation options:
Standard Basement
Crawlspace
Slab
(Foundation & framing conversion diagram available—see order form.)
Blueprint Price Code   **B**

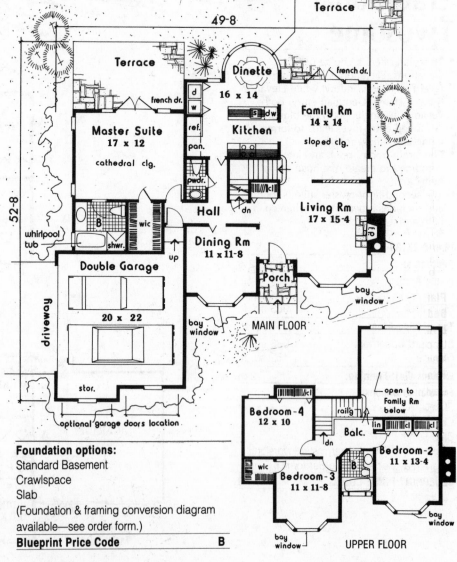

MAIN FLOOR

UPPER FLOOR

Plan AHP-9121

PRICES AND DETAILS ON PAGES 12-15

Class with Comfort

- Twin gables, great window treatments and the rich look of brick lend a sophisticated air to this design.
- Inside, the floor plan is comfortable and unpretentious. The foyer is open to the formal spaces, which flow freely into the casual living areas.
- The kitchen, breakfast nook and family room combine to create a highly livable area with no wasted space.
- The kitchen's angled serving bar accommodates those in the family room and in the nook. The bay-windowed nook has a convenient, space-saving laundry closet. The family room's fireplace warms the entire area.
- The upper floor is highlighted by an irresistible master suite featuring his-and-hers walk-in closets and a vaulted bath with a garden tub.

Plan FB-1744-L

Bedrooms: 4	**Baths:** 2½

Living Area:

Upper floor	860 sq. ft.
Main floor	884 sq. ft.
Total Living Area:	**1,744 sq. ft.**
Daylight basement	884 sq. ft.
Garage	456 sq. ft.
Exterior Wall Framing:	2x4

Foundation Options:

Daylight basement
Crawlspace
Slab
(Typical foundation & framing conversion diagram available—see order form.)

BLUEPRINT PRICE CODE:	B

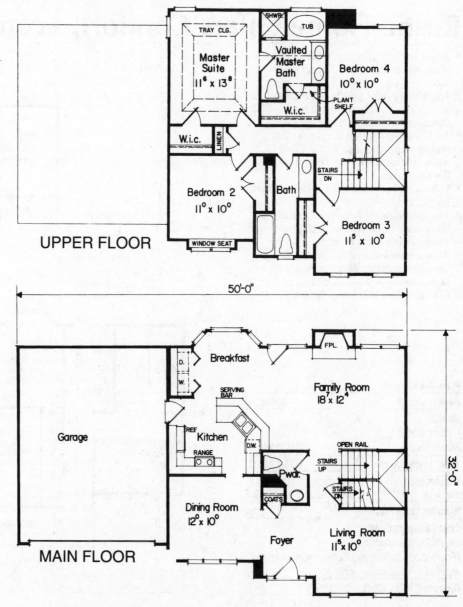

UPPER FLOOR

MAIN FLOOR

Rustic Home Offers Comfort, Economy

- Rustic and compact, this home offers economy of construction and good looks.
- The homey front porch, multi-paned windows, shutters and horizontal siding combine to create a rustic exterior.
- An L-shaped kitchen is open to the dining room and also to the living room to create a Great Room feel to the floor plan.
- The living room includes a raised-hearth fireplace.
- The main-floor master suite features a large walk-in closet and a double vanity in the master bath.
- An open two-story-high foyer leads to the second floor, which includes two bedrooms with walk-in closets and a full bath with two linen closets.

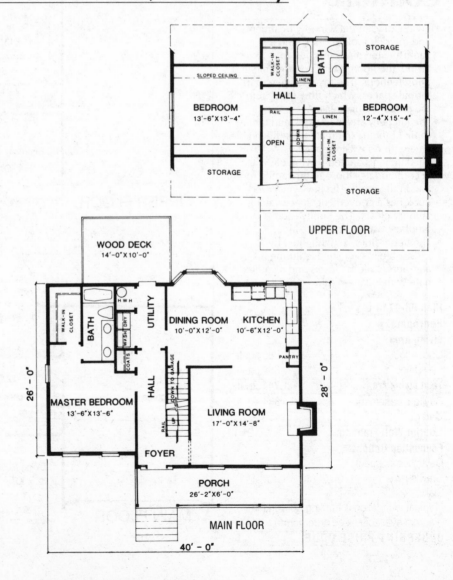

Plan C-8339	
Bedrooms: 3	**Baths:** 2
Space:	
Upper floor	660 sq. ft.
Main floor	1,100 sq. ft.
Total Living Area	**1,760 sq. ft.**
Basement	approx. 1,100 sq. ft.
Garage	Included in basement
Exterior Wall Framing	2x4
Foundation options:	
Daylight Basement	
(Foundation & framing conversion diagram available—see order form.)	
Blueprint Price Code	**B**

Plan C-8339

PRICES AND DETAILS
ON PAGES 12-15

Modern Country Cottage for Small Lot

This drive-under garage design is great for smaller lots. But even though the home is relatively compact, it's still loaded with modern features. The deluxe master bedroom has a large bath with garden tub and shower. The country kitchen/dining room combination has access to a deck out back. The large living room with fireplace is accessible from the two story foyer.

The upper floor has two large bedrooms and a full bath, and the large basement has room for two cars and expandable living areas.

This plan is available with basement foundation only.

Main floor:	1,100 sq. ft.
Second floor:	664 sq. ft.
Total living area: (Not counting basement or garage)	1,764 sq. ft.
Basement:	1,100 sq. ft.

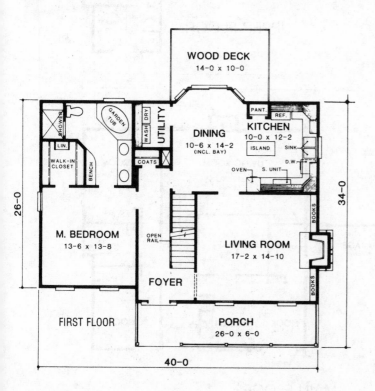

PLAN C-8870
WITH BASEMENT

**TO ORDER THIS BLUEPRINT,
CALL TOLL-FREE 1-800-547-5570**

Blueprint Price Code B
Plan C-8870

**PRICES AND DETAILS
ON PAGES 12-15**

63

Compact and Luxurious

- The best from the past and the present is bundled up in this compact design, reminiscent of a New England saltbox.
- The cozy kitchen has a center island with a breakfast counter and a built-in range and oven. The corner sink saves on counter space.
- A decorative railing separates the formal dining room from the sunken living room.
- The living room features a vaulted ceiling, built-in shelves, a central fireplace and access to a large rear deck.
- The upper-floor master suite boasts a spa bath, a separate shower and a walk-in closet.

Plan H-1453-1A

Bedrooms: 3	Baths: 2
Living Area:	
Upper floor	386 sq. ft.
Main floor	1,385 sq. ft.
Total Living Area:	**1,771 sq. ft.**
Garage	409 sq. ft.
Exterior Wall Framing:	2x6

Foundation Options:

Crawlspace

(Typical foundation & framing conversion diagram available—see order form.)

BLUEPRINT PRICE CODE: B

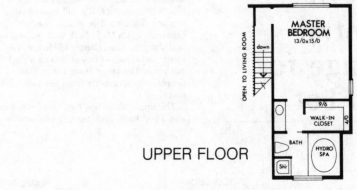

UPPER FLOOR

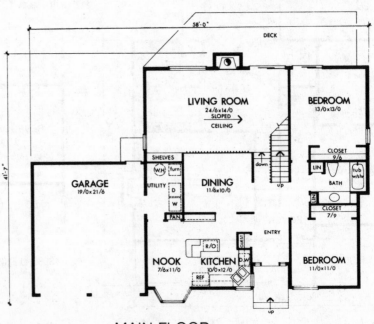

MAIN FLOOR

Plan H-1453-1A

PRICES AND DETAILS ON PAGES 12-15

Plan J-8895

Bedrooms: 3	Baths: 2½

Space:

Upper floor:	860 sq. ft.
Main floor:	919 sq. ft.

Total living area:	**1,779 sq. ft.**
Basement:	919 sq. ft.
Optional carport:	462 sq. ft.
Porch:	466 sq. ft.

Exterior Wall Framing:	2x4

Foundation options:
Standard basement.
Crawlspace.
Slab.
(Foundation & framing conversion
diagram available — see order form.)

Blueprint Price Code:	B

Expansive Porch Offers Warm Welcome

- This gracious design conjures up images of family and friends sipping iced tea on the veranda during warm summer evenings.
- Inside, a relatively compact floor plan still offers abundant space for family life and entertaining.
- The spacious living room includes a fireplace and built in cabinetry.

- The open kitchen/dining room design provides space for food preparation, eating and cleanup without the confined feeling found in many kitchens.
- The second floor consists of three good-sized bedrooms, two mirror-image baths and a hobby area.

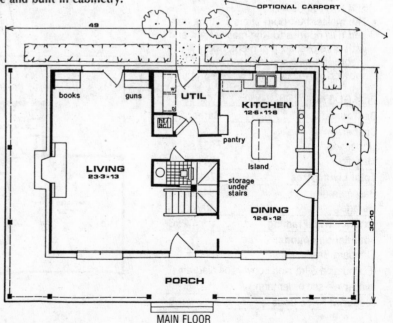

UPPER FLOOR

MAIN FLOOR

Country Serenity

- The full porch gives a nice country look and homey feel to this 1,781 square foot, two-story home.
- A spacious Great Room awaits guests to the right of the entry, highlighted by a fireplace and three walls of windows.
- The kitchen is well-placed between the formal dining room, the informal breakfast eating area, and the laundry/mud room with garage access.
- The upper floor houses three bedrooms and two full baths.
- The master bedroom offers a sitting area and two options for the master bath and walk-in closet arrangement, one incorporating a separate tub and shower.

Plan GL-1781

Bedrooms: 3	Baths: 2 ½
Space:	
Upper floor	837 sq. ft.
Main floor	944 sq. ft.
Total Living Area	**1,781 sq. ft.**
Basement	944 sq. ft.
Garage	400 sq. ft.
Exterior Wall Framing	2x6
Foundation options:	
Standard Basement	
(Foundation & framing conversion diagram available—see order form.)	
Blueprint Price Code	**B**

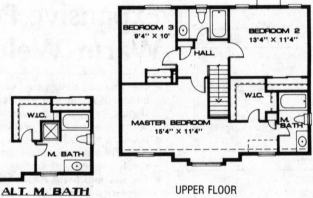

ALT. M. BATH

UPPER FLOOR

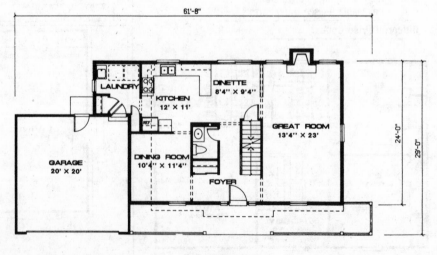

MAIN FLOOR

TO ORDER THIS BLUEPRINT, CALL TOLL-FREE 1-800-547-5570

Plan GL-1781

PRICES AND DETAILS ON PAGES 12-15

Two Story Impact

- The main, or upper level of this quaint retreat is accessed via a stairway and bordering deck.
- The upper foyer first leads to the Grand room, highlighted by a large fireplace, TV accommodations, sliding glass doors and a snack bar that separates it from the adjoining kitchen.
- The large island kitchen has walk-in pantry and attached morning room brightened by incoming light from three walls of glass.
- The magnificent master suite also has deck access; other amenities include a dressing area, walk-in closet and attached bath with sunken shower and drying area.
- The lower foyer accesses the secondary bedrooms, a second bath, laundry facilities and the two-car garage.

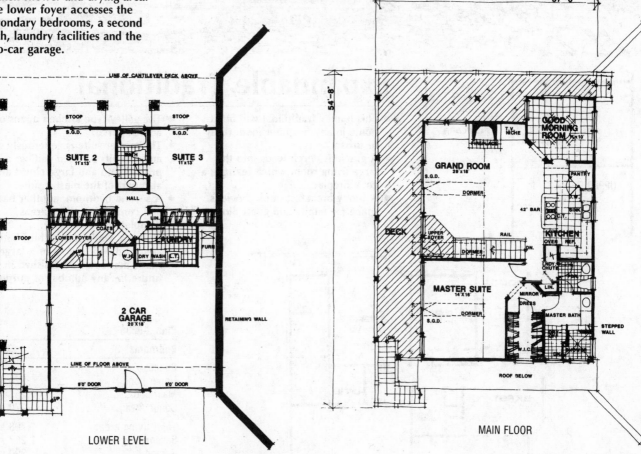

LOWER LEVEL

MAIN FLOOR

Plan EOF-15

Bedrooms: 3	**Baths:** 2

Space:
Main floor:	1,193 sq. ft.
Lower level:	593 sq. ft.

Total living area:	1,786 sq. ft.
Garage:	360 sq. ft.

Exterior Wall Framing: 2x4

Foundation options:
Daylight basement.
(Foundation & framing conversion diagram available — see order form.)

Blueprint Price Code: B

Expandable Traditional

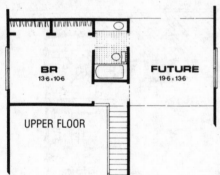

BR
13·6 x 10·6

FUTURE
19·6 x 13·6

UPPER FLOOR

- This homey traditional will be at home in any neighborhood, rural or urban.
- A gracious porch leads into the large living room which features a cozy fireplace.
- A sunny breakfast nook provides space for family and guest dining.

- The galley-type kitchen opens onto a back porch.
- The master suite is generously sized and exhibits a raised ceiling; a private bath and large closet are also part of the master suite.
- A second bedroom, another bath and convenient utility areas complete the first floor.
- Upstairs, you'll find a third bath and third bedroom, plus a large space that could be finished in the future for any number of purposes.

PORCH

BR
11·6 x 10·3

MBR
16·6 x 13
RAISED CEILING

KIT
10 x 8

BKFST
13 x 11

UTIL

LIVING
15·6 x 15

GARAGE
19·3 x 19·3

PORCH
20 x 6

MAIN FLOOR

50·4

40

Plan J-8636

Bedrooms: 3	**Baths: 3**
Space:	
Upper floor:	270 sq. ft.
Main floor:	1,253 sq. ft.
Bonus area:	270 sq. ft.
Total living area:	1,793 sq. ft.
Basement:	1,287 sq. ft.
Garage:	390 sq. ft.
Porches:	155 sq. ft.
Exterior Wall Framing:	2x4

Foundation options:
Standard basement.
Crawlspace.
Slab.
(Foundation & framing conversion diagram available — see order form.)

Blueprint Price Code:	B

Plan J-8636

*PRICES AND DETAILS
ON PAGES 12-15*

A Present From the Past

- A covered front porch with Victorian trim and an exterior with half-round windows and classic, high-pitched gables give today's homebuyers a present from the past.
- Arriving guests enjoy an open view into the Great Room with fireplace and the formal dining room with window wall.
- The kitchen incorporates a breakfast bay with rear access and adjacent laundry room.
- Up the double-stairs, lit by a round-top window, are three bedrooms and two full baths.
- All of the main-floor rooms are enhanced by 10-ft. ceilings. The upper floor has standard 8-ft. ceilings.

Plan V-1803

Bedrooms: 3	Baths: 2½
Living Area:	
Upper floor	875 sq. ft.
Main floor	928 sq. ft.
Total Living Area:	**1,803 sq. ft.**
Exterior Wall Framing:	2x6

Foundation Options:
Crawlspace
(Typical foundation & framing conversion diagram available—see order form.)

BLUEPRINT PRICE CODE:	B

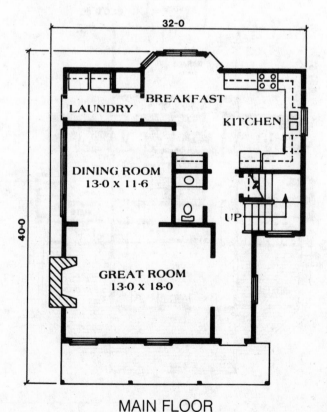

MAIN FLOOR

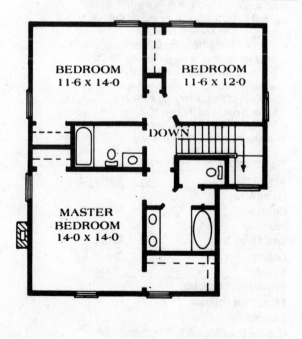

UPPER FLOOR

Unique Inside and Out

- This delightful design is as striking on the inside as it is on the outside.
- The focal point of the home is the huge Grand Room, which features a vaulted ceiling, plant shelves and lots of glass, including a clerestory window. French doors flanking the fireplace lead to the covered porch and the two adjoining sun decks.
- The centrally located kitchen offers easy access from any room in the house, and a full bath, a laundry area and the garage entrance are nearby.
- The two main-floor master suites are another unique design element of the home. Both of the suites showcase a volume ceiling, a sunny window seat, a walk-in closet, a private bath and French doors that open to a sun deck.
- Upstairs, two guest suites overlook the vaulted Grand Room below.

Plan EOF-13

Bedrooms: 4	Baths: 3
Living Area:	
Upper floor	443 sq. ft.
Main floor	1,411 sq. ft.
Total Living Area:	**1,854 sq. ft.**
Garage	264 sq. ft.
Storage	50 sq. ft.
Exterior Wall Framing:	2x6

Foundation Options:

Crawlspace

(Typical foundation & framing conversion diagram available—see order form.)

BLUEPRINT PRICE CODE: B

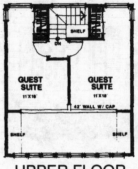

UPPER FLOOR

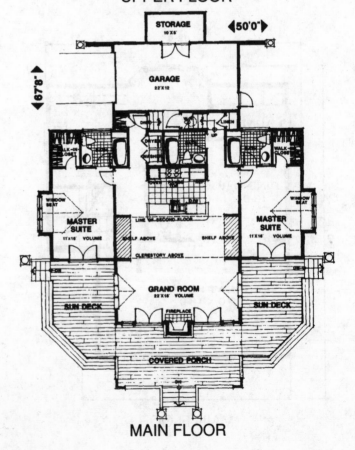

MAIN FLOOR

Plan EOF-13

FRONT VIEW

REAR VIEW

Bungalow Style for Today

- Many of the features of the once-popular bungalow are preserved and improved upon in this plan.
- A special touch is the pergola — the wooden trelliswork attached to the porch roof and supported by tapered columns.
- The spacious foyer has doors opening from both the porch and the opposing garage.
- The sunken living room is separated from the dining room by a custom-designed handrail.
- French doors close off the den or third bedroom from the living room.
- The expansive kitchen features an island work center, a pantry, a bay window with built-in desk, and access to the rear deck.
- The master suite has numerous frills.

Plans H-1459-1 & -1A

Bedrooms: 2	Baths: 2
Space:	
Upper floor	658 sq. ft.
Main floor	1,201 sq. ft.
Total Living Area	**1,859 sq. ft.**
Basement	630 sq. ft.
Garage	280 sq. ft.
Exterior Wall Framing	2x6

Foundation options:

Partial Basement
Crawlspace
(Foundation & framing conversion diagram available—see order form.)

Blueprint Price Code	**B**

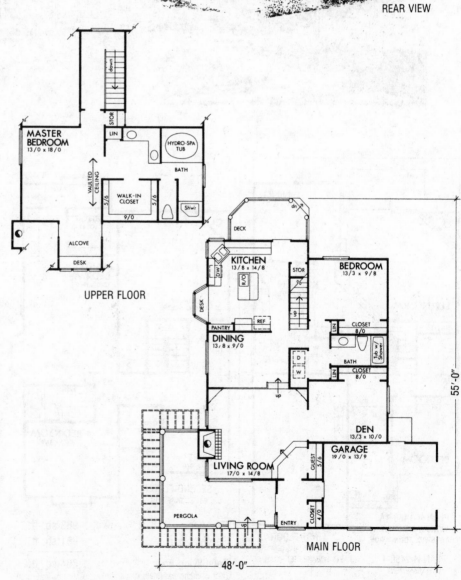

UPPER FLOOR

MAIN FLOOR

FRONT VIEW

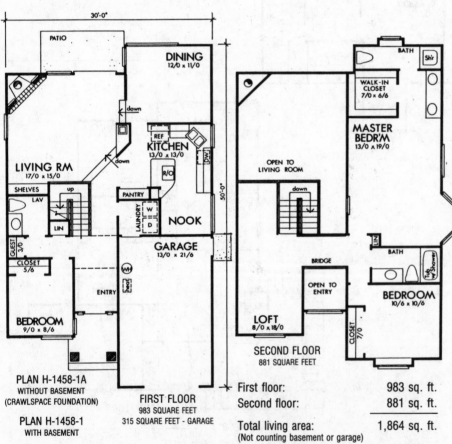

30'-0"

PATIO

DINING
12/0 x 11/0

down

REF
KITCHEN
13/0 x 13/0

R/O

LIVING RM
17/0 x 15/0

down

SHELVES

LAV

up

PANTRY

LIN

LAUNDRY

W

D

NOOK

GUEST
3/0

GARAGE
13/0 x 21/6

CLOSET
5/6

ENTRY

BEDROOM
9/0 x 8/6

50'-0"

PLAN H-1458-1A
WITHOUT BASEMENT
(CRAWLSPACE FOUNDATION)

PLAN H-1458-1
WITH BASEMENT

FIRST FLOOR
983 SQUARE FEET
315 SQUARE FEET - GARAGE

BATH

Sh'r

WALK-IN
CLOSET
7/0 x 6/6

MASTER
BEDR'M
13/0 x 19/0

OPEN TO
LIVING ROOM

down

LIN

BATH

BRIDGE

tub
w/shower

OPEN TO
ENTRY

BEDROOM
10/6 x 10/6

LOFT
8/0 x 18/0

CLOSET
7/0

SECOND FLOOR
881 SQUARE FEET

First floor: 983 sq. ft.

Second floor: 881 sq. ft.

Total living area: 1,864 sq. ft.
(Not counting basement or garage)

Queen Anne with Contemporary Interior

This gracious home offers numerous features for convenience and charm:
- 1,864 sq. ft. of living area.
- 2 bedrooms, plus den.
- Traditional exterior style.
- 30' wide at first floor, 32' wide at second floor.
- Versatile kitchen with range/oven/eating bar combination.
- Practical spice cabinet, pantry and nook.
- Sunken living room with vaulted ceiling, fireplace, French doors, wet bar and built-in shelves.
- Dramatic open staircase.
- Interesting entry open to bridge above.
- 2½ baths.
- Cozy loft open to living area.
- Spacious and elegant master bedroom with bay window, walk-in closet, separate shower, double-sink vanity and window overlooking living/loft area.
- Energy-efficient specifications throughout, including 2x6 wall framing.

Blueprint Price Code B

Plans H-1458-1 & 1A

TO ORDER THIS BLUEPRINT,
CALL TOLL-FREE 1-800-547-5570

PRICES AND DETAILS
ON PAGES 12-15

Octagonal Dining Bay

- Classic traditional styling is recreated with a covered front porch and triple dormers with half-round windows.
- Once inside, the interior feels open, airy and bright.
- The living room with fireplace leads into the formal dining room with octagonal bay windows.
- The island kitchen overlooks the breakfast bay and family room with second fireplace and sliders to the rear deck.
- A skylit hallway connects the four upstairs bedrooms and two full baths.

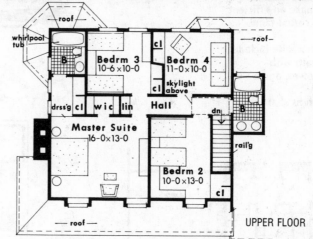

Plan K-680-R

Bedrooms: 4	Baths: 2½
Space:	
Upper floor	853 sq. ft.
Main floor	1,015 sq. ft.
Total Living Area	**1,868 sq. ft.**
Basement	1,015 sq. ft.
Garage & Mud Room	504 sq. ft.
Exterior Wall Framing	**2x4**

Foundation options:

Standard Basement

Slab

(Foundation & framing conversion diagram available—see order form.)

Blueprint Price Code	**B**

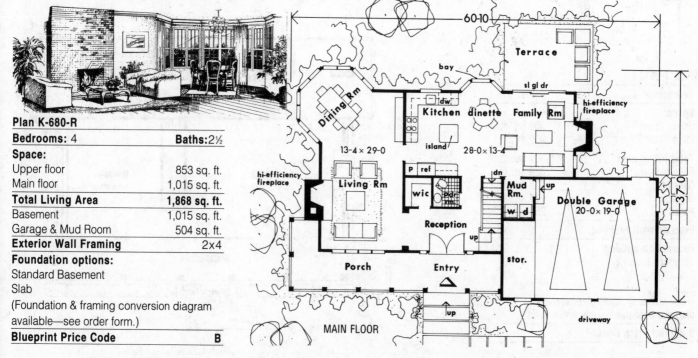

UPPER FLOOR

MAIN FLOOR

Cost-Efficient Cottage with Luxury Features

- This country cottage is easy to build, economical and attractive.
- The basic rectangular shape simplifies construction, and the steeply pitched roof accommodates upstairs bedrooms in space that would often otherwise be simply attic overhead.
- A huge living room with fireplace dominates the main floor.
- The dining room, kitchen, utility area and half bath make an efficient and livable area for casual family life.
- The main-floor master suite includes a spacious private bath with separate tub and shower, and a large closet.
- Upstairs, two bedrooms share another full bath.

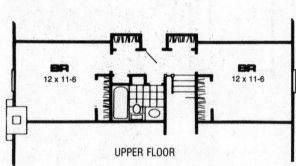

UPPER FLOOR

Plan J-86131

Bedrooms: 3	Baths: 2½
Space:	
Upper floor:	500 sq. ft.
Main floor:	1,369 sq. ft.
Total living area:	**1,869 sq. ft.**
Basement:	1,369 sq. ft.
Carport:	416 sq. ft.
Storage:	124 sq. ft.
Porch:	258 sq. ft.
Exterior Wall Framing:	2x4

Foundation options:
Standard basement.
Crawlspace.
Slab.
(Foundation & framing conversion diagram available — see order form.)

Blueprint Price Code:	B

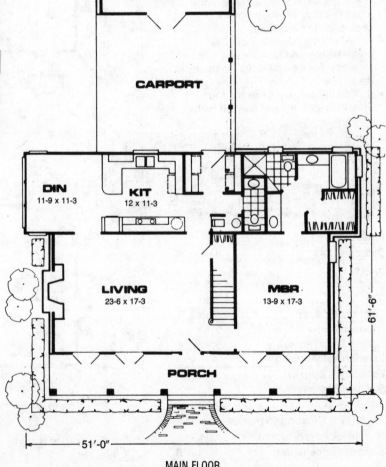

MAIN FLOOR

TO ORDER THIS BLUEPRINT, CALL TOLL-FREE 1-800-547-5570

Plan J-86131

PRICES AND DETAILS ON PAGES 12-15

Customize Your Floor Plan!

- An optional bonus room and a choice between a loft or a bedroom allow you to customize the floor plan of this striking two-story traditional.

- The vaulted foyer leads guests past a handy powder room and directly into the vaulted family room straight ahead or into the formal dining room on the right. A beautiful open-railed staircase pleasantly breaks up the spaces while giving more privacy to the kitchen and the breakfast room.

- The sunny breakfast room is open to the island kitchen. A pantry closet, loads of counter space and direct access to the laundry room and the garage add to the kitchen's efficiency.

- The main-floor master suite is a treasure, with its tray ceiling and vaulted, amenity-filled master bath.

- Upstairs, two bedrooms, a full bath and an optional loft as well as a bonus room provide plenty of opportunity for expansion and customization.

Plan FB-1874

Bedrooms: 3+	Baths: 2½
Living Area:	
Upper floor	554 sq. ft.
Main floor	1,320 sq. ft.
Bonus room	155 sq. ft.
Total Living Area:	**2,029 sq. ft.**
Daylight basement	1,320 sq. ft.
Garage	240 sq. ft.
Storage	38 sq. ft.
Exterior Wall Framing:	2x4

Foundation Options:

Daylight basement
(Typical foundation & framing conversion diagram available—see order form.)

BLUEPRINT PRICE CODE:	C

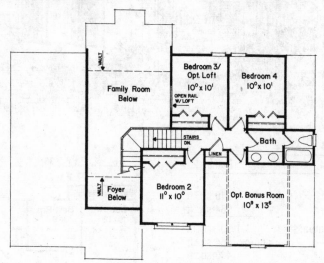

UPPER FLOOR

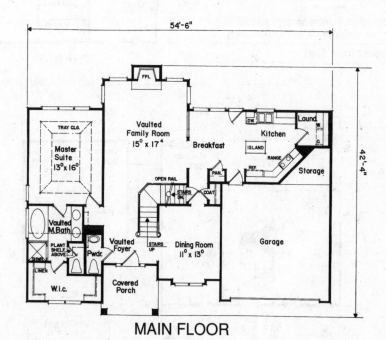

MAIN FLOOR

Plan M-2214

Bedrooms: 4	Baths: 2½

Space:

Upper floor:	940 sq. ft.
Main floor:	964 sq. ft.
Total living area:	**1,904 sq. ft.**
Basement:	approx. 964 sq. ft.
Garage:	440 sq. ft.

Exterior Wall Framing:	2x4

Foundation options:
Standard basement only.
(Foundation & framing conversion
diagram available — see order form.)

Blueprint Price Code:	B

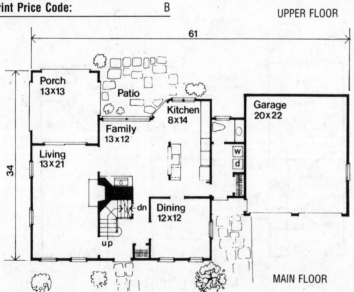

UPPER FLOOR

MAIN FLOOR

Traditional Saltbox Roofline

- This classic saltbox exterior offers an open, flexible interior, with well-planned space for the large, busy family.
- The spacious living room includes an impressive fireplace and sliding doors to a screened porch at the rear of the home.
- The large, open-design kitchen blends in with the family room to create a delightful space for food preparation and family life.
- A formal dining room is found at the right as you enter the foyer.
- Upstairs, a deluxe master suite includes a private bath and large closet.
- Three secondary bedrooms share a second upstairs bath.
- Note the convenient washer/dryer area and half-bath off the kitchen.

Plan M-2214

PRICES AND DETAILS
ON PAGES 12-15

A Blend of Extras

- A sophisticated blend of country and contemporary design flows through this exceptional home.
- Specially designed for a side sloping lot, the home has a tuck-under garage and an open, economical interior.
- Attractive features include vaulted ceilings, a front wrapping deck, a rear deck off the family room, skylights, interior plant shelves in the kitchen and master bath, and an optional fourth bedroom, guest room or study.
- The vaulted family room is uniquely set below the main level, separated from the nook by a handrail.
- Three bedrooms and two full baths are found on the upper floor.

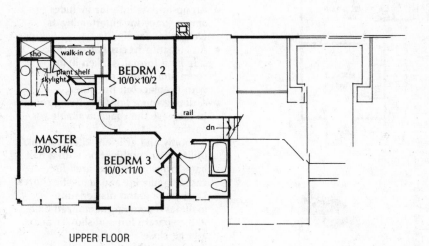

UPPER FLOOR

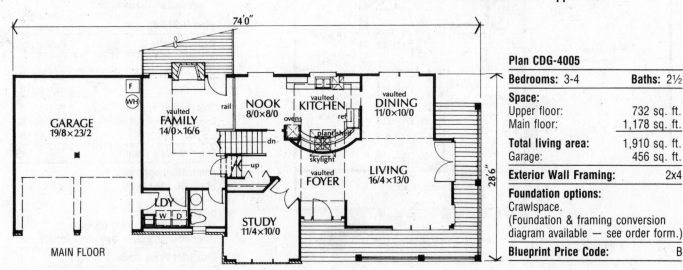

MAIN FLOOR

Plan CDG-4005

Bedrooms: 3-4	Baths: 2½

Space:

Upper floor:	732 sq. ft.
Main floor:	1,178 sq. ft.

Total living area:	1,910 sq. ft.
Garage:	456 sq. ft.

Exterior Wall Framing:	2x4

Foundation options:
Crawlspace.
(Foundation & framing conversion diagram available — see order form.)

Blueprint Price Code:	B

Farmhouse for Today

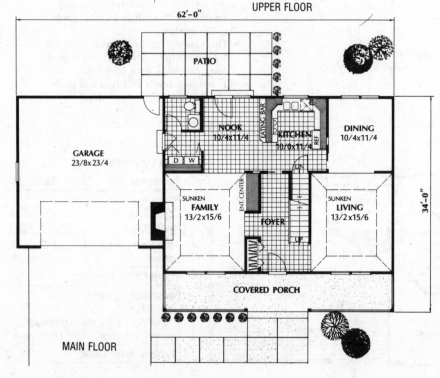

DECK

SHWR · TUB

DRESSING

BDRM. 2
12/2 x 11/6

MASTER
13/2 x 14/2

TUB

RAILING   DN

BDRM. 3
10/8 x 11/6

DESK

FOYER BELOW

UPPER FLOOR

62'-0"

PATIO

GARAGE
23/8 x 23/4

NOOK
10/4 x 11/4

EATING BAR

KITCHEN
10/0 x 11/4

REF

DINING
10/4 x 11/4

D   W

ENT. CENTER

SUNKEN
FAMILY
13/2 x 15/6

FOYER

UP

SUNKEN
LIVING
13/2 x 15/6

34'-0"

UP

COVERED PORCH

MAIN FLOOR

- An inviting veranda and charming dormer windows lend traditional warmth to this attractive design.
- An up-to-date interior includes ample space for entertaining as well as for family life.
- An elegant foyer is flanked on one side by a formal, sunken living room and a sunken family room with fireplace on the other.
- A dining room joins the living room to increase the space available for parties.
- A roomy and efficient kitchen/nook/ utility area combination with a half bath forms a spacious area for casual family life and domestic chores.
- Upstairs, a grand master suite includes a compartmentalized bath with separate tub and shower and a large closet.
- A second full bath serves the two secondary bedrooms.

Plan U-87-203

Bedrooms: 3	Baths: 2½
Space:	
Upper floor:	857 sq. ft.
Main floor:	1,064 sq. ft.
Total living area:	**1,921 sq. ft.**
Basement:	1,064 sq. ft.
Garage:	552 sq. ft.
Exterior Wall Framing:	2x4 & 2x6

Foundation options:
Standard basement.
Crawlspace.
Slab.
(Foundation & framing conversion diagram available — see order form.)

Blueprint Price Code:	B

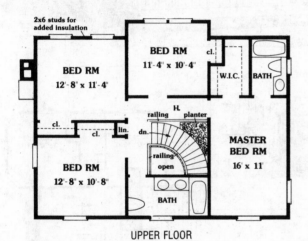

UPPER FLOOR

2x6 studs for added insulation

BED RM
12'-8" x 11'-4"

BED RM
11'-4" x 10'-4"

cl.

W.I.C.

BATH

cl.

cl.

lin.

BED RM
12'-8" x 10'-8"

H.

railing

planter

dn.

railing

open

BATH

MASTER
BED RM
16' x 11'

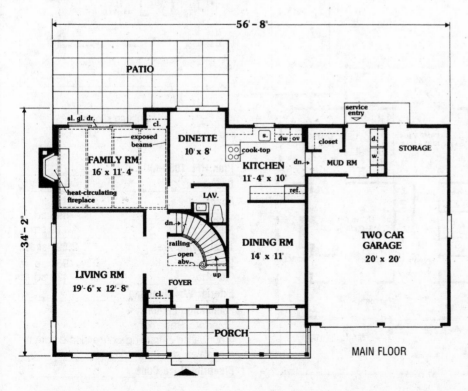

MAIN FLOOR

56' - 8"

34' - 2"

PATIO

sl. gl. dr.

cl.

exposed beams

FAMILY RM
16' x 11'-4"

heat-circulating fireplace

DINETTE
10' x 8'

s.

cook-top

dw ov

closet

MUD RM

d.

w.

STORAGE

KITCHEN
11'-4" x 10'

dn.

ref.

service entry

LAV.

LIVING RM
19'-6" x 12'-8"

dn.

railing

open abv.

up

FOYER

cl.

DINING RM
14' x 11'

TWO CAR
GARAGE
20' x 20'

PORCH

Distinctive Colonial Farmhouse

- Although a casual living theme flows throughout this farmhouse, elegance is not forgotten.
- A beautiful circular stair ascends from the central foyer to the bedrooms on the upper level.
- Formal living and dining rooms flank the foyer.
- The informal family room at the rear captures an Early American style with exposed beams, wood paneling and a brick fireplace wall. Sliding glass doors provide access to the adjoining patio.
- A sunny dinette opens to an efficiently arranged kitchen with a handy laundry room near the garage entrance.
- A decorative railing and a planter adorn the second-floor balcony that overlooks the foyer below. Four generous-sized bedrooms and two baths share this level.

Plan HFL-1010-CR

Bedrooms: 4	**Baths:** 2 ½

Space:

Upper floor	932 sq. ft.
Main floor	1,099 sq. ft.
Total Living Area	**2,031 sq. ft.**
Basement	998 sq. ft.
Garage and storage	476 sq. ft.
Exterior Wall Framing	2x4

Foundation options:

Standard Basement

Slab

(Foundation & framing conversion diagram available—see order form.)

Blueprint Price Code	**C**

Romantic Victorian

- This plan proves the romance of Victorian styling can be achieved without sacrificing modern lifestyles.
- The exterior is classic, while the interior admirably meets the needs of today's families.
- While the home totals just over 2,000 sq. ft., it includes many features found in larger homes — such as a bright, airy formal dining room, a roomy foyer and a large family room.
- The living room is especially large for a home of this total size and features a massive fireplace.
- Upstairs, a majestic master suite includes tower windows and access to a private deck. Two other bedrooms share a double-vanity bath.

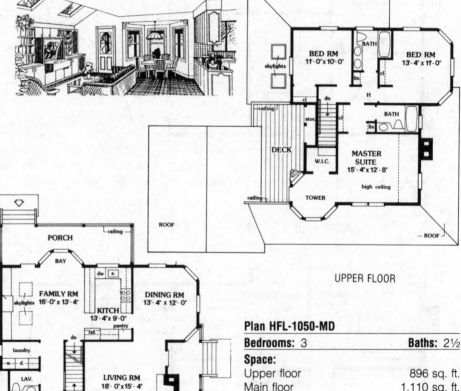

UPPER FLOOR

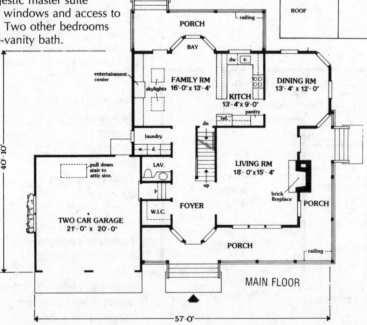

MAIN FLOOR

40'-0"

57'-0"

Plan HFL-1050-MD

Bedrooms: 3	Baths: 2½
Space:	
Upper floor	896 sq. ft.
Main floor	1,110 sq. ft.
Total Living Area	**2,006 sq. ft.**
Basement	967 sq. ft.
Garage	420 sq. ft.
Exterior Wall Framing	2x6

Foundation options:

Standard Basement
(Foundation & framing conversion diagram available—see order form.)

Blueprint Price Code	C

TO ORDER THIS BLUEPRINT, CALL TOLL-FREE 1-800-547-5570

Plan HFL-1050-MD

PRICES AND DETAILS ON PAGES 12-15

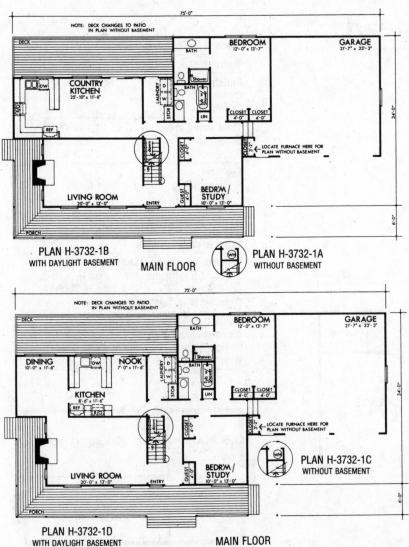

Old Homestead

Almost everyone has a soft place in his heart for a certain home in his childhood. A home like this one, with understated farmhouse styling and wrap-around porch, may be the image of "Home" that your children remember.

Two versions of the first floor plan provide a choice between a country kitchen and a more formal dining room.

All versions feature 2x6 exterior wall framing.

Upper floor:	626 sq. ft.
Main floor:	1,359 sq. ft.
Total living area:	1,985 sq. ft.

(Not counting basement or garage)
(Non-basement versions designed with crawlspace)

Garage:	528 sq. ft.

PLAN H-3732-1B
WITH DAYLIGHT BASEMENT

MAIN FLOOR

PLAN H-3732-1A
WITHOUT BASEMENT

PLAN H-3732-1D
WITH DAYLIGHT BASEMENT

MAIN FLOOR

PLAN H-3732-1C
WITHOUT BASEMENT

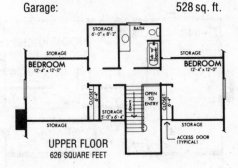

UPPER FLOOR
626 SQUARE FEET

Blueprint Price Code B

TO ORDER THIS BLUEPRINT, CALL TOLL-FREE 1-800-547-5570
Plans H-3732-1A, -1B, -1C & -1D
PRICES AND DETAILS ON PAGES 12-15

81

Classic Homestead

SECOND FLOOR

- WALK-IN CLOSET
- LAV
- W.C.
- sh'w'r
- BEDROOM 11'-0" x 11'-5"
- CLOSET
- CLOSET
- BEDROOM 10'-0" x 11'-5"
- LINEN
- BEDROOM 13'-0" x 15'-0"
- down
- BEDROOM 10'-0" x 11'-5"
- BATH
- LAV
- W.C.
- CLOSET

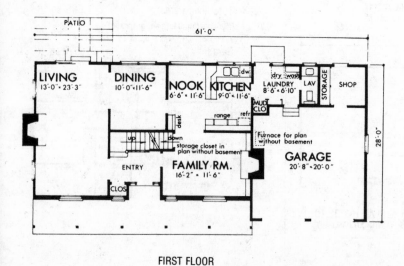

FIRST FLOOR

- PATIO
- 61'-0"
- LIVING 13'-0" x 23'-3"
- DINING 10'-0" x 11'-6"
- NOOK 6'-6" x 11'-6"
- KITCHEN 9'-0" x 11'-6"
- dw
- dry wash
- LAUNDRY 8'-6" x 6'-10"
- LAV
- STORAGE
- SHOP
- MUD CLO
- desk
- range
- refr
- Furnace for plan without basement
- up
- down
- storage closet in plan without basement
- ENTRY
- FAMILY RM. 16'-2" x 11'-6"
- GARAGE 20'-8" x 20'-0"
- CLOS
- 28'-0"

Plans H-3678-3 & H-3678-3A

Bedrooms: 4	Baths: 2½

Finished space:
Upper floor:	960 sq. ft.
Main floor:	1,036 sq. ft.

Total living area:	1,996 sq. ft.
Basement:	900 sq. ft.
Garage:	413 sq. ft.

Features:
Spacious living room and large family room.
Convenient nook/kitchen/laundry arrangement.
Inviting porch and roomy entry area.

Exterior Wall Framing:	2x4

Foundation options: (Specify)
Standard Basement: Plan H-3678-3
Crawlspace: Plan H-3678-3A
(Foundation & framing conversion diagram available — see order form.)

Blueprint Price Code:
Without finished basement design:	B
With finished basement design:	D

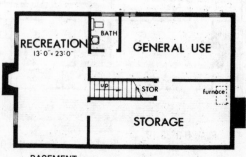

BASEMENT

- RECREATION 13'-0" x 23'-0"
- BATH
- GENERAL USE
- up
- STOR
- furnace
- STORAGE

Classic Economy

- The basic rectangular shape of this two-story makes it economical to build. All four bedrooms are located on the upper level.
- The main-floor central hallway is decorated by an open stairway; it is flanked by a dining room and a formal living room with an attractive fireplace that can be seen from the foyer. Sliding glass doors at the rear overlook the back porch.
- A brilliant family room, bayed dinette and kitchen combine at the rear for an open, yet intimate, atmosphere. A wood-beam ceiling adds a homey touch.
- Main-floor laundry facilities, a half-bath and a handy service porch are located near the garage access.

VIEW OF KITCHEN AND DINETTE FROM FAMILY ROOM.

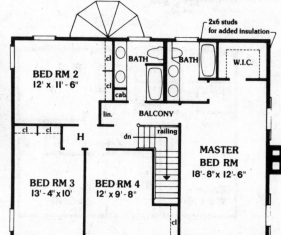

UPPER FLOOR

Plan HFL-1070-RQ

Bedrooms: 4	**Baths:** 2 ½

Space:	
Upper floor	1,013 sq. ft.
Main floor	983 sq. ft.
Total Living Area	**1,996 sq. ft.**
Basement	889 sq. ft.
Garage	403 sq. ft.
Exterior Wall Framing	2x6

Foundation options:
Standard Basement
Slab
(Foundation & framing conversion diagram available—see order form.)

Blueprint Price Code	**B**

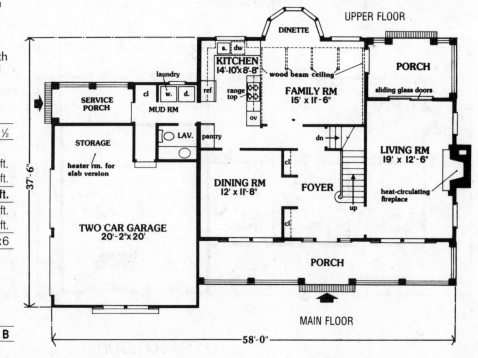

MAIN FLOOR

Relax on the Front Porch

- Summer evenings will be a breeze on the quaint front porch of this affordable two story home.
- A very efficient floor plan keeps hallways at a minimum and living spaces at a maximum.
- The front entry opens into a dramatic two story space with stairway, plant shelf and transom windows. To the left and right of the entry are the formal living and dining rooms.
- The informal family room with fireplace is only a half-wall away from the island kitchen and breakfast eating area.
- The upper floor feels spacious with the open stairwell. It houses three bedrooms, two full baths and a handy laundry room.

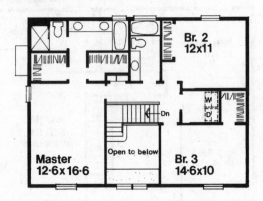

Br. 2
12x11

Master
12·6 x 16·6

Open to below   Dn

Br. 3
14·6x10

UPPER FLOOR

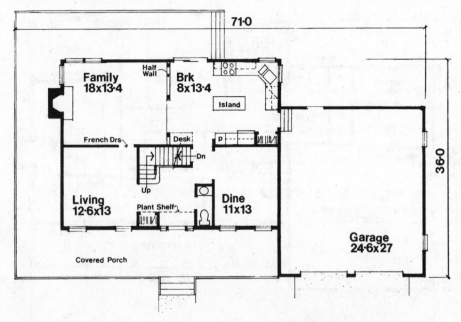

71·0

Family
18x13·4

Half Wall

Brk
8x13·4

Island

French Drs

Desk

p

Dn

36·0

Living
12·6x13

Plant Shelf

Up

Dine
11x13

Garage
24·6x27

Covered Porch

MAIN FLOOR

Plan AGH-1997	
Bedrooms: 3	**Baths:** 2 ½
Space:	
Upper floor	933 sq. ft.
Main floor	1,064 sq. ft.
Total Living Area	**1,997 sq. ft.**
Basement	1,064 sq. ft.
Garage	662 sq. ft.
Exterior Wall Framing	2x4

Foundation options:

Standard Basement

(Foundation & framing conversion diagram available—see order form.)

Blueprint Price Code	B

Plan AGH-1997

Classic Colonial

- This classic Colonial is distinguished by a curved, columned portico that leads into a breathtaking two-story gallery, highlighted by a curved staircase.
- The adjacent living room offers bright windows and an efficient fireplace.
- The sunny dining room features sliding glass doors to a rear terrace and easy access to the kitchen, which has ample counter space and an eating bar.
- The family room has its own high-efficiency fireplace, while the nearby dinette offers a circular snack bar and sliding glass doors to another terrace.
- Upstairs, the open-railed gallery leads to the spacious master suite, boasting a walk-in closet and a private bath with a whirlpool tub.
- Two additional large bedrooms share a second full bath. A fourth bedroom with built-in shelves makes an ideal den or guest room.

Plan K-655-U

Bedrooms: 4	Baths: 2½
Living Area:	
Upper floor	944 sq. ft.
Main floor	1,054 sq. ft.
Total Living Area:	**1,998 sq. ft.**
Standard basement	994 sq. ft.
Garage and storage	450 sq. ft.
Exterior Wall Framing:	2x4 or 2x6
Foundation Options:	
Standard basement	
Slab	
BLUEPRINT PRICE CODE:	**B**

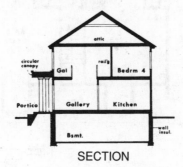

SECTION

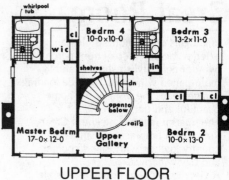

UPPER FLOOR

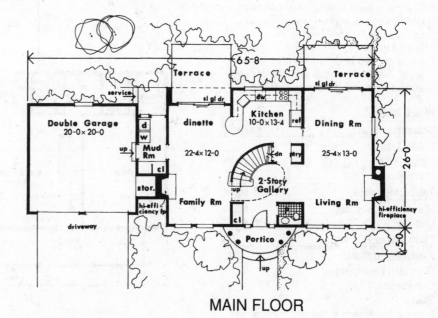

MAIN FLOOR

Country Kitchen and Great Room

- Highlights of this home's pleasant exterior include a cozy front porch, two dormers, stylish shutters and multi-paned windows. The side-loading garage keeps the front of the home beautiful and uncluttered.
- The interior features a central Great Room with fireplace and an eat-in country kitchen with island counter and bay windows.
- A view to the wood deck is possible from the Great Room and the adjoining dining room.
- The main-floor master suite boasts a walk-in closet and private access to a compartmentalized bath with oversized linen closet.
- Upstairs, two bedrooms with window seats share a full bath. A large storage area is found above the garage.

Plan C-8040

Bedrooms: 3	Baths: 2
Living Area:	
Upper floor:	718 sq. ft.
Main floor	1,318 sq. ft.
Total Living Area:	**2,036 sq. ft.**
Standard basement	1,221 sq. ft.
Garage	436 sq. ft.
Exterior Wall Framing:	2x4

Foundation Options:

Standard basement
Crawlspace
Slab
(Typical foundation & framing conversion diagram available—see order form.)

BLUEPRINT PRICE CODE:	C

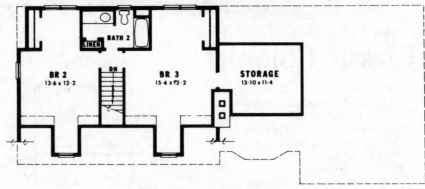

UPPER FLOOR

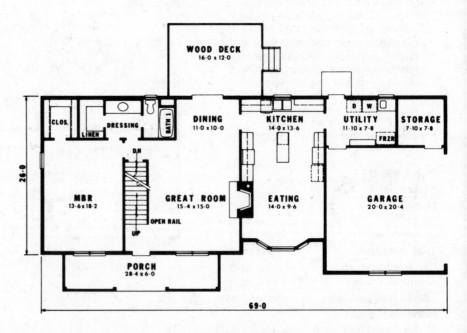

MAIN FLOOR

TO ORDER THIS BLUEPRINT, CALL TOLL-FREE 1-800-547-5570

Plan C-8040

PRICES AND DETAILS ON PAGES 12-15

Farmhouse with Modern Touch

- This classic center-hall design features an All-American Farmhouse exterior wrapped around a super-modern interior.
- A large family room features a built-in entertainment center and adjoins a convenient dinette for quick family meals.
- The spacious living and dining rooms adjoin to provide abundant space for large gatherings.

- An inviting porch leads into a roomy foyer which highlights a curved staircase.
- The second floor features a deluxe master suite and three secondary bedrooms.

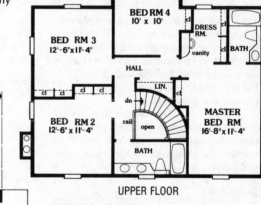

VIEW INTO LIVING ROOM FROM FOYER.

UPPER FLOOR

BED RM 4
10' x 10'

BED RM 3
12'-6"x11'-4"

DRESS RM.
vanity
BATH

HALL

BED RM 2
12'-6" x 11'-4"

LIN.
dn
rail   open

MASTER BED RM
16'-8" x 11'-4"

BATH

Plan HFL-1040-MB

Bedrooms: 4	Baths: 2½
Space:	
Upper floor	936 sq. ft.
Main floor	1,094 sq. ft.
Total Living Area	**2,030 sq. ft.**
Basement	1,022 sq. ft.
Garage	420 sq. ft.
Exterior Wall Framing	2x6

Foundation options:
Standard Basement
Slab
(Foundation & framing conversion diagram available—see order form.)

Blueprint Price Code C

60'-0"

TERRACE

sliding glass doors

s. dw

range

sliding glass doors

service entry

MUD RM   cl

KITCHEN
10'-8" x 10'

DINETTE
8'-8" x 8'-8"

LAUNDRY
d. w.

ref.

LAV.

DINING RM
12'-6" x 11'-6"

35'-6"

heat-circulating fireplace

dn

railing   open

FAMILY RM
16' x 12'-2' (avg.)

entertainment center

TWO CAR GARAGE
21'-4" x 19'-8"

LIVING RM
19'-8" x 12'-6"

FOYER

up

cl

high ceiling

PORCH

MAIN FLOOR

Volume with Charm

- This charming two-story has an interesting variety of exterior elements and an open, airy interior.
- The two-story foyer has direct access to the main living areas. The formal spaces are oriented to the front of the home and include a dining room that overlooks a covered porch.
- A long view into the family room reveals a dramatic fireplace flanked by windows. The vaulted family room can also be viewed from the balcony above.
- A large kitchen and a vaulted breakfast room adjoin the family room. The breakfast room features a built-in work desk and a bayed sitting area. The kitchen offers a pantry closet and two convenient serving bars.
- A spectacular vaulted master suite is the perfect adult retreat. The bedroom opens to a private vaulted bath with a corner tub, a separate shower, dual sinks and a walk-in closet.

Plan FB-2081

Bedrooms: 4	Baths: 2½
Living Area:	
Upper floor	492 sq. ft.
Main floor	1,589 sq. ft.
Bonus room	226 sq. ft.
Total Living Area:	**2,307 sq. ft.**
Daylight basement	1,589 sq. ft.
Garage	400 sq. ft.
Storage	24 sq. ft.
Exterior Wall Framing:	2x4

Foundation Options:

Daylight basement

(Typical foundation & framing conversion diagram available—see order form.)

BLUEPRINT PRICE CODE:	C

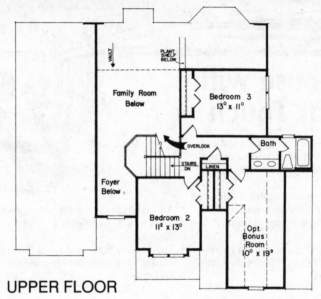

UPPER FLOOR

MAIN FLOOR

Quality Four-Bedroom Design

- Here's another fine example of a traditional plan that has faithfully stood the test of time.
- While not huge, the interior provides plenty of space for a busy family.
- The large family room includes a fireplace and adjoins the casual dinette area.
- A big kitchen includes a handy work island and is open to the dinette area.
- The living and dining rooms flow together when big space is needed for formal entertaining or large family gatherings.
- Upstairs, you'll find four roomy bedrooms and two full baths, one of which is private to the master bedroom.
- Also note the balcony overlooking the foyer below.

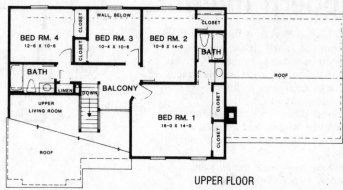

UPPER FLOOR

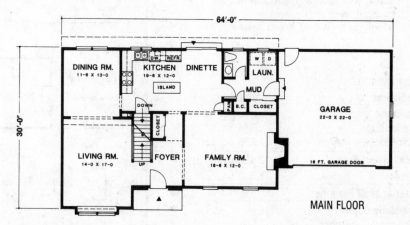

MAIN FLOOR

Plan A-2109-DS

Bedrooms: 4	**Baths:** 2½

Space:
Upper floor: 942 sq. ft.
Main floor: 1,148 sq. ft.

Total living area: 2,090 sq. ft.
Basement: 1,148 sq. ft.
Garage: 484 sq. ft.

Exterior Wall Framing: 2x4

Foundation options:
Standard basement only.
(Foundation & framing conversion diagram available — see order form.)

Blueprint Price Code: C

Victorian Exterior, Modern Interior

- This classic exterior is built around an interior that offers all the amenities wanted by today's families.
- A Great Room provides ample space for large gatherings and multiple family activities.
- A formal dining room is available for special occasions, and a casual breakfast nook serves everyday dining needs.
- A deluxe main-floor master suite features a cathedral ceiling.
- Upstairs, two secondary bedrooms share a full bath and a balcony overlooking the Great Room below.

Plan DW-2112	
Bedrooms: 3	**Baths:** 2½
Space:	
Upper floor	514 sq. ft.
Main floor	1,598 sq. ft.
Total Living Area	**2,112 sq. ft.**
Basement	1,598 sq. ft.
Exterior Wall Framing	2x4

Foundation options:
Standard Basement
Crawlspace
Slab
(Foundation & framing conversion diagram available—see order form.)

Blueprint Price Code   C

UPPER FLOOR

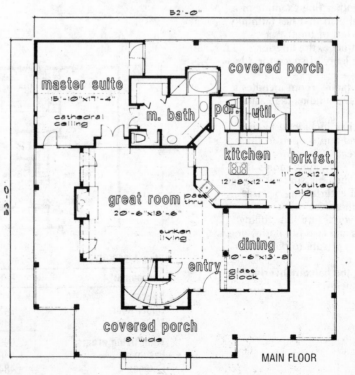

MAIN FLOOR

TO ORDER THIS BLUEPRINT, CALL TOLL-FREE 1-800-547-5570   Plan DW-2112   **PRICES AND DETAILS ON PAGES 12-15**

A Colonial for Today

- Designed for a growing family, this handsome traditional home offers four bedrooms plus a den and three complete baths. The Colonial exterior is updated by a covered front entry porch topped off with a fanlight window above.

- The dramatic tiled foyer is two stories high and provides direct access to all the home's living areas. The spacious living room has an inviting brick fireplace and sliding pocket doors to the adjoining dining room.

- Overlooking the backyard, the huge combination kitchen/family room is the home's hidden charm. The family room has a window wall with sliding glass doors that open to an enticing terrace. The kitchen features a peninsula breakfast bar with seating for six. A built-in entertainment center and bookshelves line one wall of the family room.

- The adjacent mudroom is just off the garage entrance and includes a pantry closet. A full bath and a large den complete the first floor.

- The second floor is highlighted by a beautiful balcony that is open to the foyer below. The luxurious master suite is brightened by a skylight and boasts two closets, including an oversized walk-in closet. The master bath has a whirlpool tub and dual-sink vanity.

- The three remaining bedrooms are generously sized and have plenty of storage space. Another full bath serves these bedrooms.

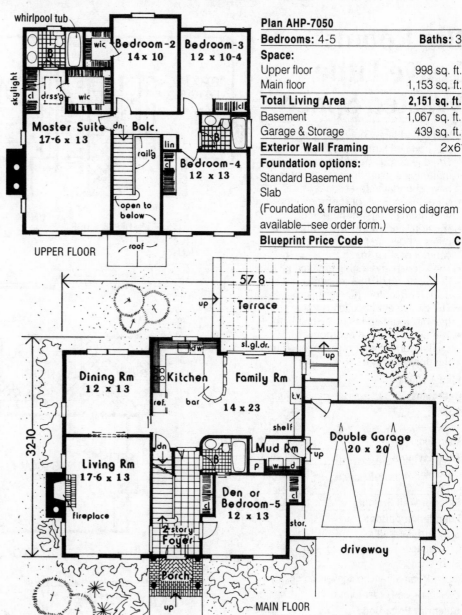

Plan AHP-7050	
Bedrooms: 4-5	**Baths:** 3
Space:	
Upper floor	998 sq. ft.
Main floor	1,153 sq. ft.
Total Living Area	**2,151 sq. ft.**
Basement	1,067 sq. ft.
Garage & Storage	439 sq. ft.
Exterior Wall Framing	2x6
Foundation options:	
Standard Basement	
Slab	
(Foundation & framing conversion diagram available—see order form.)	
Blueprint Price Code	**C**

Big Rooms Leave Little Wasted Space

- You'll find large, open living areas in this updated farmhouse design.
- Three generous-sized bedrooms, including a main-floor master suite, have abundant closet space.
- All of the main-floor rooms overlook the welcoming wraparound porch.
- Spacious and sunny, the living room offers a huge fireplace and flanking cabinet or shelf space.
- The kitchen and dining area merge to the rear, and feature a counter bar and deck for overflow dining space.
- The garage entrance leads to the laundry room and hallway half-bath.
- The two additional bedrooms with quaint dormer windows are found on the upper level.

Plan J-90013

Bedrooms: 3	Baths: 2 ½
Space:	
Upper floor	823 sq. ft.
Main floor	1,339 sq. ft.
Total Living Area	**2,162 sq. ft.**
Basement	1,339 sq. ft.
Garage	413 sq. ft.
Exterior Wall Framing	2x4

Foundation options:

Standard Basement
Crawlspace
Slab

(Foundation & framing conversion diagram available—see order form.)

Blueprint Price Code	C

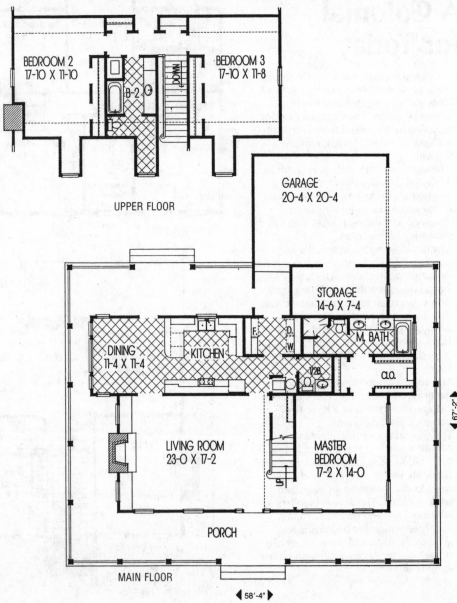

BEDROOM 2
17-10 X 11-10

BEDROOM 3
17-10 X 11-8

UPPER FLOOR

GARAGE
20-4 X 20-4

STORAGE
14-6 X 7-4

M. BATH

DINING
11-4 X 11-4

KITCHEN

LIVING ROOM
23-0 X 17-2

MASTER BEDROOM
17-2 X 14-0

PORCH

MAIN FLOOR

67'-2"

58'-4"

Plan J-90013

PRICES AND DETAILS ON PAGES 12-15

Energy-Efficient Colonial Home

- This home combines classic Colonial styling with passive-solar energy efficiency. Insulated thermal flooring collects heat during the day to warm the home at night.
- An air-lock vestibule, which minimizes heat loss, leads into a spacious, elegant reception area.
- The bayed living room features optional folding doors to the family room, which offers a high-efficiency fireplace and two sets of sliding glass doors to a bright rear terrace.
- The expansive formal dining room leads into an efficient U-shaped kitchen, which boasts a pantry and a dinette with sliding glass doors to a glass-roofed sun room.
- The upper floor features an electrically operated skylight above the stairs.
- The master suite offers a walk-in closet and a private bath with a whirlpool tub.
- Three additional bedrooms share a second full bath.

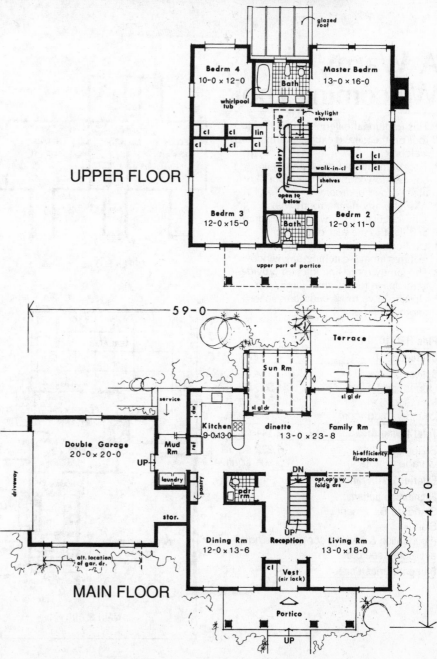

Plan K-508-B

Bedrooms: 4	Baths: 2½
Living Area:	
Upper floor	1,003 sq. ft.
Main floor	1,072 sq. ft.
Sun room	101 sq. ft.
Total Living Area:	**2,176 sq. ft.**
Partial basement	633 sq. ft.
Garage and storage	458 sq. ft.
Exterior Wall Framing:	2x4 or 2x6

Foundation Options:

Partial basement
Slab
(Typical foundation & framing conversion diagram available–see order form.)

BLUEPRINT PRICE CODE: C

A Warm, Welcoming Look

- This traditional exterior with the saltbox roof on the garage exudes warmth and welcome.
- The roomy main floor includes a bay-windowed master bedroom plus a nice second bedroom.
- A bright, airy dining room with a semi-circular window wall adds drama and light to the rear of the home.
- Up front, the spacious living room also features an eye-catching bay window.
- The family room and kitchen provide great space for informal family life.
- Upstairs, two more bedrooms share another full bath.

Plan HFL-1030-DL

Bedrooms: 4	Baths: 3

Space:

Upper floor	530 sq. ft.
Main floor	1,515 sq. ft.
Laundry, mud room	99 sq. ft.
Total Living Area	**2,144 sq. ft.**
Basement	1,222 sq. ft.
Garage & storage	501 sq. ft.
Exterior Wall Framing	**2x6**

Foundation options:

Standard Basement
Slab
(Foundation & framing conversion diagram available—see order form.)

Blueprint Price Code	**C**

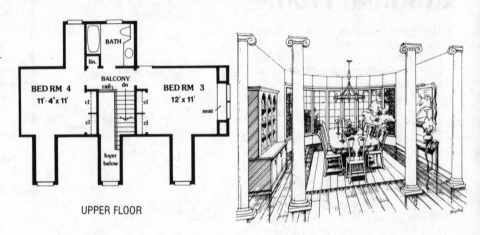

UPPER FLOOR

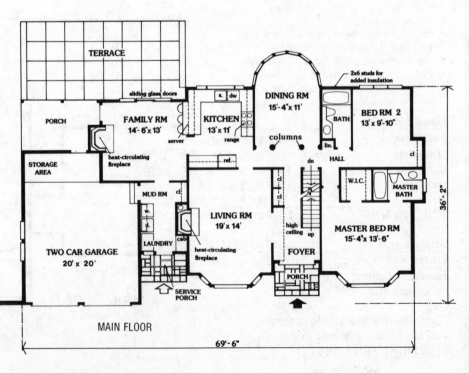

MAIN FLOOR

Distinct Formal Spaces

- This attractive traditional home boasts room for up to four bedrooms plus formal living spaces that can be closed off from the informal areas.
- The two-story foyer features two handy coat closets and a decorative upper-level plant shelf.
- A large gourmet kitchen with a work island and an adjoining breakfast room each overlook an oversized rear deck. The breakfast room opens to the family room, which features a cozy fireplace.
- The laundry closet is conveniently located on the upper level, close to the bedrooms.
- The master bedroom has a tray ceiling and a private bath. The bath boasts his-and-hers walk-in closets, separate vanities and a toilet compartment.
- The bonus room can serve as a fourth bedroom, hobby room or playroom.

Plan APS-1905

Bedrooms: 3-4	Baths: 2½
Living Area:	
Upper floor	915 sq. ft.
Main floor	1,084 sq. ft.
Bonus room/ 4th Bedroom	224 sq. ft.
Total Living Area:	**2,223 sq. ft.**
Standard basement	1,064 sq. ft.
Garage	440 sq. ft.
Exterior Wall Framing:	2x4
Foundation Options:	
Standard basement	
(Typical foundation & framing conversion diagram available—see order form.)	
BLUEPRINT PRICE CODE:	C

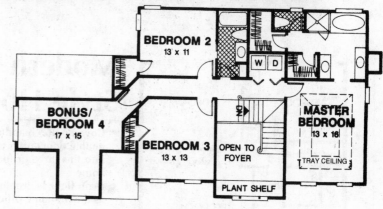

UPPER FLOOR

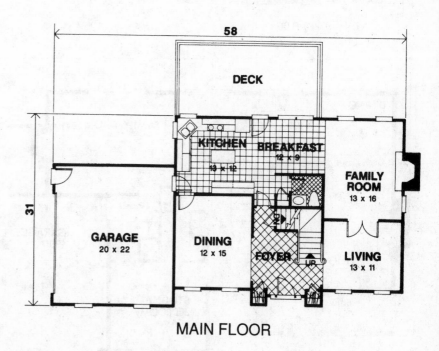

MAIN FLOOR

Modern Traditional-Style Home

UPPER FLOOR

- Covered porch and decorative double doors offer an invitation into this three or four bedroom home.
- Main floor bedroom may be used as a den, home office, or guest room, with convenient bath facilities.
- Adjoining dining room makes living room seem even more spacious; breakfast nook enlarges the look of the attached kitchen.
- Brick-size concrete block veneer and masonry tile roof give the exterior a look of durability.

PLAN H-1351-M1A
WITHOUT BASEMENT
(CRAWLSPACE FOUNDATION)

Plans H-1351-M1 & -M1A	
Bedrooms: 3-4	**Baths: 3**
Space:	
Upper floor:	862 sq. ft.
Main floor:	1,383 sq. ft.
Total living area:	**2,245 sq. ft.**
Basement:	1,383 sq. ft.
Garage:	413 sq. ft.
Exterior Wall Framing:	**2x6**

Foundation options:
Standard basement (Plan H-1351-M1).
Crawlspace (Plan H-1351-M1A).
(Foundation & framing conversion diagram available — see order form.)

Blueprint Price Code:	C

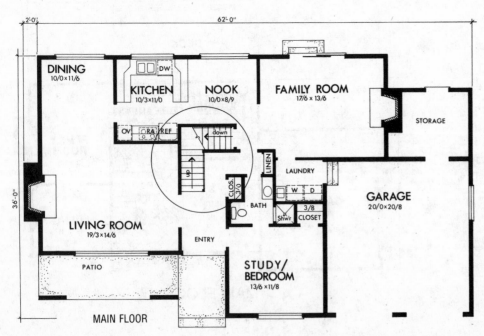

MAIN FLOOR

Plans H-1351-M1 & -M1A

PRICES AND DETAILS
ON PAGES 12-15

Narrow-Lot Luxury

- At only 40 ft. wide, this 1½-story home is ideal for a narrow lot.
- Vaulted ceilings in the entry, living room, family room and master suite contribute to the overall spaciousness of the home's open design.
- Special touches – like a plant shelf above the vaulted entry, decorative columns between the dining room and the living room and a loft with two

overlooks – make an exciting interior statement.
- The main-floor master suite opens to a private deck and features his-and-hers closets. The personal bath boasts a vaulted ceiling, double sinks, an oval tub and a separate shower.
- The family gathering area includes an open kitchen, a sunny breakfast room and a vaulted family room with a fireplace and an adjoining deck.
- A second bedroom and another bath share the upper floor, along with a loft area that could serve as an extra bedroom, a TV room or a home office.

Plan B-90002	
Bedrooms: 2+	**Baths:** 2½
Living Area:	
Upper floor	527 sq. ft.
Main floor	1,730 sq. ft.
Total Living Area:	**2,257 sq. ft.**
Standard basement	1,730 sq. ft.
Garage	406 sq. ft.
Exterior Wall Framing:	2x6
Foundation Options:	
Standard basement	
(Typical foundation & framing conversion diagram available—see order form.)	
BLUEPRINT PRICE CODE:	C

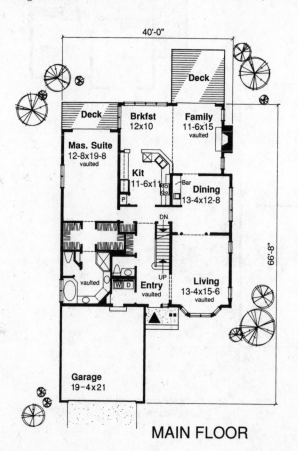

MAIN FLOOR

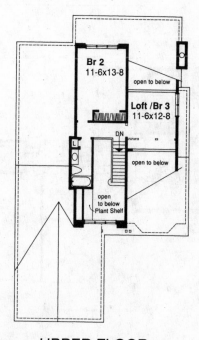

UPPER FLOOR

Two-Story Features
Deluxe Master Bedroom

First floor:	1,442 sq. ft.
Second floor:	823 sq. ft.
Total living area:	2,265 sq. ft.
Basement (Optional):	688 sq. ft.

SECOND FLOOR

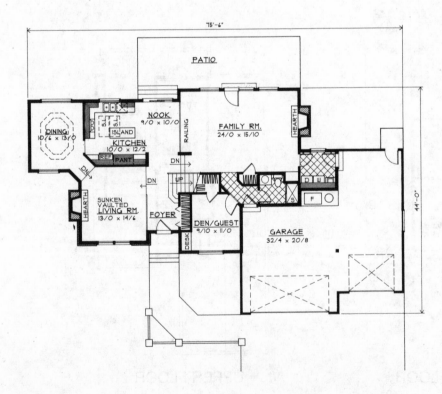

Specify basement, crawlspace
or slab foundation.

Blueprint Price Code C

Plan U-88-201

Decorative and Distinctive

- A decorative covered front entry and shuttered windows create a distinctive facade for this traditional two-story.
- The two-story foyer is flanked by two large formal spaces. The dining room features a lovely bay window and easy access to the kitchen.
- A coat closet and a powder room are located off the hall that leads to the family room. This spacious family activity area is warmed by a nice fireplace and has a beautiful French door that provides outdoor access.
- The adjoining kitchen has a serving bar that extends to the family room as well as to the sunny breakfast area. A pantry and a laundry room are discreetly placed near the entrance to the garage.
- The upper floor houses four bedrooms, three with walk-in closets. The master bedroom has a private, vaulted bath.

Plan FB-2279

Bedrooms: 4	Baths: 2½
Living Area:	
Upper floor	1,190 sq. ft.
Main floor	1,089 sq. ft.
Total Living Area:	**2,279 sq. ft.**
Daylight basement	1,089 sq. ft.
Garage	410 sq. ft.
Storage	66 sq. ft.
Exterior Wall Framing:	2x4

Foundation Options:
Daylight basement
Crawlspace
Slab
(Typical foundation & framing conversion diagram available—see order form.)

BLUEPRINT PRICE CODE:	C

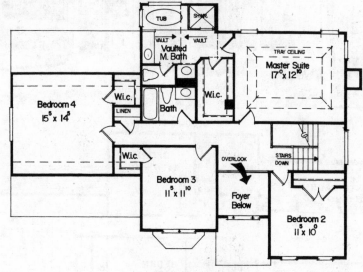

UPPER FLOOR

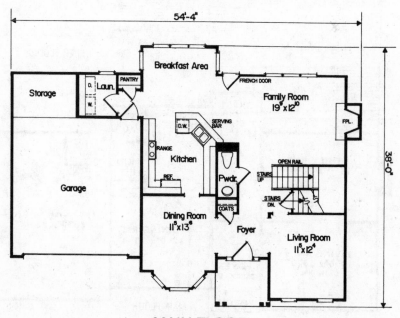

MAIN FLOOR

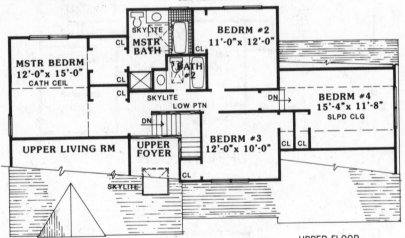

CER TILE LEDGE

SKYLITE
MSTR BATH
BATH #2

MSTR BEDRM
12'-0" x 15'-0"
CATH CEIL

CL
CL

BEDRM #2
11'-0" x 12'-0"

CL

SKYLITE
LOW PTN
DN

BEDRM #4
15'-4" x 11'-8"
SLPD CLG

DN

UPPER LIVING RM

UPPER FOYER

BEDRM #3
12'-0" x 10'-0"

CL CL

SKYLITE

CL

UPPER FLOOR

Distinctive Two-Story

- A playful and distinctive exterior invites you into a functional, contemporary interior.
- The sunken living room features a soaring cathedral ceiling open to the second floor balcony.
- The adjoining step-down family room is connected to allow for overflow and easy circulation of traffic.
- A luxurious master suite and room for three additional bedrooms are found on the second floor, with a dramatic balcony and a view of the foyer and the living room.

Plan AX-8922-A

Bedrooms: 3-4	Baths: 2½
Living Area:	
Upper floor	840 sq. ft.
Main floor	1,213 sq. ft.
Optional fourth bedroom	240 sq. ft.
Total Living Area:	**2,293 sq. ft.**
Standard basement	1,138 sq. ft.
Garage	470 sq. ft.
Exterior Wall Framing:	2x4

Foundation Options:
Standard basement
Slab
(Typical foundation & framing conversion diagram available—see order form.)

BLUEPRINT PRICE CODE: C

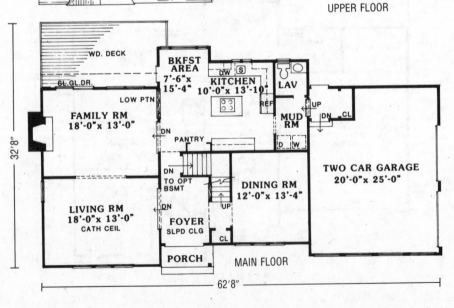

WD. DECK

BKFST AREA
7'-6" x 15'-4"

DW S

KITCHEN
10'-0" x 13'-10"

LAV

GL. GL. DR.

LOW PTN

FAMILY RM
18'-0" x 13'-0"

REF

MUD RM

UP

DN CL

32'-8"

DN

PANTRY

DN UP

DN TO OPT BSMT

DINING RM
12'-0" x 13'-4"

TWO CAR GARAGE
20'-0" x 25'-0"

D W

LIVING RM
18'-0" x 13'-0"
CATH CEIL

DN

FOYER
SLPD CLG

CL

PORCH

MAIN FLOOR

62'-8"

TO ORDER THIS BLUEPRINT, CALL TOLL-FREE 1-800-547-5570

Plan AX-8922-A

PRICES AND DETAILS ON PAGES 12-15

Doors Isolate Formal Areas

- This elegant European stucco design has plenty of living space, including room for four bedrooms.
- The dramatic two-story foyer offers two coat closets and a decorative upper-level plant shelf.
- Bay windows accent both front-facing formal living areas.
- Double doors close off the family room from the living room. The kitchen and breakfast room can be isolated from the foyer and from the formal dining room as well. A center work island is useful in the gourmet kitchen, and the breakfast room offers access to the attached deck, ideal for entertaining or for outdoor dining.
- Convenient laundry facilities accommodate the bedrooms on the upper level.

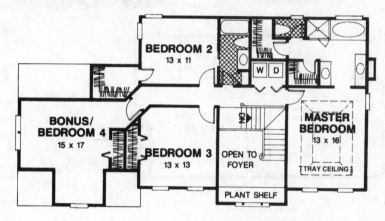

UPPER FLOOR

Plan APS-2015

Bedrooms: 3-4	**Baths:** 2½
Living Area:	
Upper floor	934 sq. ft.
Main floor	1,112 sq. ft.
Bonus room/4th bedroom	254 sq. ft.
Total Living Area:	**2,300 sq. ft.**
Standard basement	1,112 sq. ft.
Garage	440 sq. ft.
Exterior Wall Framing:	2x4

Foundation Options:

Standard basement

(Typical foundation & framing conversion diagram available—see order form.)

BLUEPRINT PRICE CODE:	C

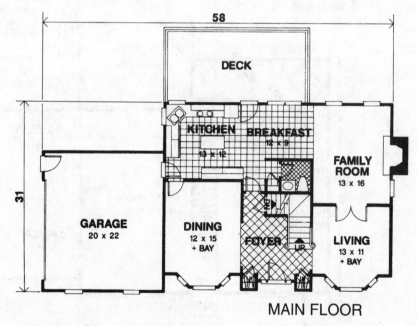

MAIN FLOOR

TO ORDER THIS BLUEPRINT,
CALL TOLL-FREE 1-800-547-5570

Plan APS-2015

PRICES AND DETAILS
ON PAGES 12-15

101

Traditional Touches Dress Up a Country Cottage

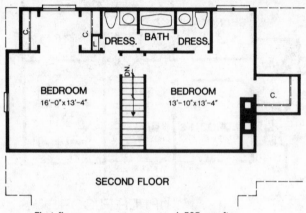

SECOND FLOOR

Bedroom 16'-0" x 13'-4"
Bedroom 13'-10" x 13'-4"
DRESS. BATH DRESS.

First floor:	1,535 sq. ft.
Second floor:	765 sq. ft.
Total living area:	2,300 sq. ft.

(Not counting basement or garage)

PLAN C-8535
WITH BASEMENT

Multipaned windows, shutters and a covered porch embellish the traditional exterior of this country cottage. The floor plan incorporates a central Great Room. A raised-hearth stone fireplace forms part of a wall separating the Great Room from the kitchen.

The large country kitchen features an island and abundant counter space. The breakfast room includes a bay window. A large dining room faces the front.

First-level master bedroom has its own super bath with separate shower, garden tub, twin vanities and walk-in closets. Two large bedrooms, separate dressing areas and compartment tub occupy the second level.

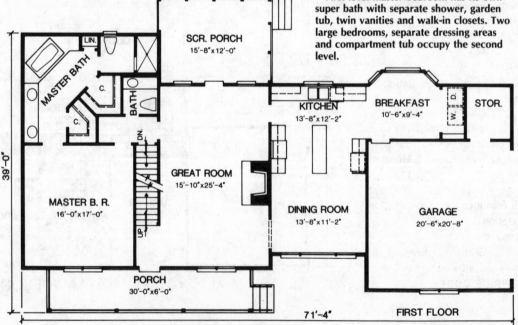

MASTER BATH
SCR. PORCH 15'-8" x 12'-0"
KITCHEN 13'-8" x 12'-2"
BREAKFAST 10'-6" x 9'-4"
STOR.
BATH
GREAT ROOM 15'-10" x 25'-4"
MASTER B. R. 16'-0" x 17'-0"
DINING ROOM 13'-8" x 11'-2"
GARAGE 20'-6" x 20'-8"
39'-0"
PORCH 30'-0" x 6'-0"
71'-4"
FIRST FLOOR

Blueprint Price Code C
Plan C-8535

PRICES AND DETAILS ON PAGES 12-15

Formal Yet Friendly

- The formal yet friendly atmosphere of this elegant two-story home draws immediate attention.
- The two-story entry extends a warm welcome, with its columned court, gabled roof and exciting windows. Inside, the raised, vaulted entry focuses on the family room fireplace, which is surrounded by two-story-high windows.
- The eat-in kitchen is open to the family room and has a bay window viewing out to the deck.
- The upstairs is highlighted by a bridge that is flooded with light and overlooks the vaulted family room and entry.

Plan B-91011

Bedrooms: 3-5	Baths: 3
Living Area:	
Upper floor	961 sq. ft.
Main floor	1,346 sq. ft.
Total Living Area:	**2,307 sq. ft.**
Standard basement	1,346 sq. ft.
Garage	480 sq. ft.
Exterior Wall Framing:	2x4

Foundation Options:

Standard basement

(Typical foundation & framing conversion diagram available—see order form.)

BLUEPRINT PRICE CODE: C

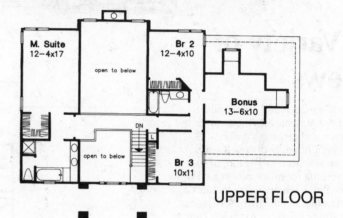

UPPER FLOOR

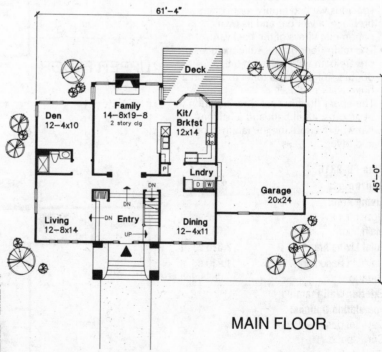

MAIN FLOOR

REAR VIEW

A Variety of Views

- The stone-accented entry of this traditional home sets the tone for its unique and elegant interior.
- The light-filled, two-story foyer is flanked by front-facing formal spaces. The dining room is easily served by the adjoining kitchen, which features a pantry and a convenient serving bar.
- The sunny breakfast room has French-door access to the outdoors. The spacious vaulted family room offers a fireplace, a wet bar and its own panoramic views of the backyard.
- The main-floor master suite includes a private bath with a garden tub, a double-sink vanity, a toilet room and a huge walk-in closet.
- The upper floor houses three additional bedrooms, a full bath and a balcony hallway overlooking the family room and foyer.

Plan FB-2316	
Bedrooms: 4	**Baths:** 2½
Living Area:	
Upper floor	786 sq. ft.
Main floor	1,530 sq. ft.
Total Living Area:	**2,316 sq. ft.**
Daylight basement	1,530 sq. ft.
Garage	488 sq. ft.
Exterior Wall Framing:	2x4
Foundation Options:	
Daylight basement	
Crawlspace	
(Typical foundation & framing conversion diagram available—see order form.)	
BLUEPRINT PRICE CODE:	**C**

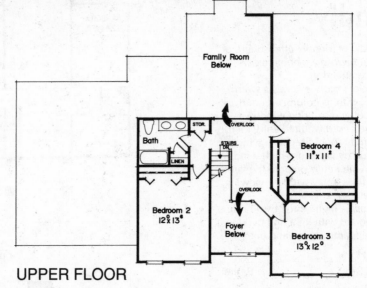

UPPER FLOOR

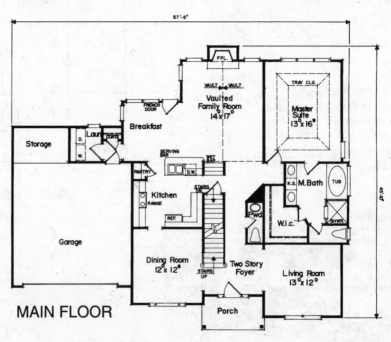

MAIN FLOOR

Plan FB-2316

PRICES AND DETAILS ON PAGES 12-15

Great Family Living Areas

- The covered front porch and multi-windowed facade give this home its countrypolitan appeal and comfort.
- Inside, a wonderful kitchen, breakfast nook and family room combination steals the show. The step-saving kitchen includes a large pantry closet, an oversized worktop island/snack bar and a built-in desk. The bay-windowed breakfast nook steps down to the vaulted family room with fireplace.
- The formal living room includes an optional fireplace, while the dining room has an optional bay window.
- A half-bath is just off the foyer, as is a study. The laundry room is convenient to both the kitchen and the garage.
- The upper floor features a spectacular master suite, offering a vaulted ceiling in the sleeping area, a dressing area with a walk-in closet and a skylighted bath with a corner platform tub.
- The blueprints for this plan include details for finishing the exterior with brick or with wood siding.

Plan CH-240-A

Bedrooms: 4-5	Baths: 2½
Living Area:	
Upper floor	1,019 sq. ft.
Main floor	1,300 sq. ft.
Total Living Area:	**2,319 sq. ft.**
Basement	1,300 sq. ft.
Garage	384 sq. ft.
Exterior Wall Framing:	2x4

Foundation Options:
Daylight basement
Standard basement
Crawlspace
(Typical foundation & framing conversion diagram available—see order form.)

BLUEPRINT PRICE CODE: C

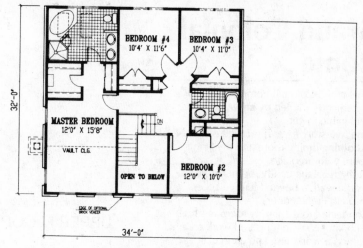

UPPER FLOOR

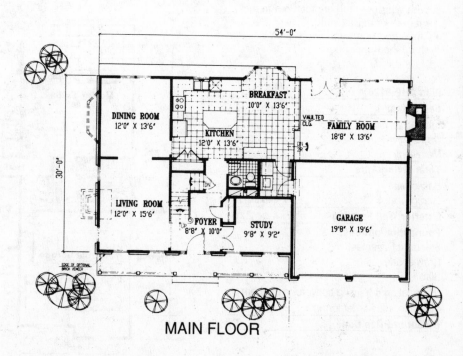

MAIN FLOOR

**TO ORDER THIS BLUEPRINT,
CALL TOLL-FREE 1-800-547-5570**

Plan CH-240-A

**PRICES AND DETAILS
ON PAGES 12-15**

105

Grand Colonial Home

- This grand Colonial home boasts a porch entry framed by bay windows and gable towers.
- The two-story foyer directs guests to the adjoining dining room and the living room with fireplace.
- At the rear, the family room features a media wall, a bar and terrace access through French doors.
- Connected to the family room is a high-tech kitchen with an island work area, a pantry, a work desk and a circular dinette.
- A private terrace, a romantic fireplace, a huge walk-in closet and a lavish bath with whirlpool tub are featured in the main-floor master suite.
- Three bedrooms and two full baths share the upper floor.

Plan AHP-9120

Bedrooms: 4	Baths: 3½
Space:	
Upper floor	776 sq. ft.
Main floor	1,551 sq. ft.
Total Living Area	**2,327 sq. ft.**
Basement	1,580 sq. ft.
Garage	440 sq. ft.
Exterior Wall Framing	2x4 or 2x6

Foundation options:

Standard Basement
Crawlspace
Slab

(Foundation & framing conversion diagram available—see order form.)

Blueprint Price Code	C

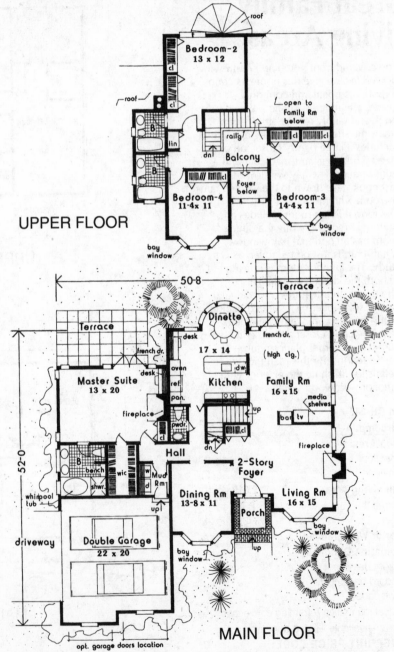

UPPER FLOOR

MAIN FLOOR

Plan AHP-9120

UPPER FLOOR

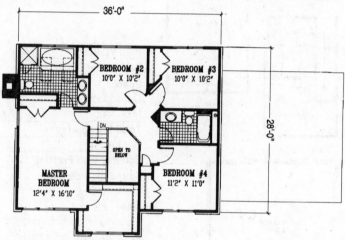

36'-0"

28'-0"

BEDROOM #2
10'0" X 10'2"

BEDROOM #3
10'0" X 10'2"

MASTER
BEDROOM
12'4" X 16'10"

OPEN TO
BELOW

DN

BEDROOM #4
11'2" X 11'0"

Style and Function

- This spacious home offers both style and function for the large, established, or growing family.
- The formal living room at the front of the home has a private study with boxed window; the dining room, opposite, has bay window.
- Elegant double doors enter the family room which offers a large fireplace and rear bay area with skylights and access to a possible patio.
- The upper level boasts four bedrooms, including a roomy master suite with private luxury bath and generous walk-in closet.

Plan CH-107-A

Bedrooms: 4	**Baths:** 2 ½
Space:	
Upper floor	1,007 sq. ft.
Main floor	1,326 sq. ft.
Total Living Area	**2,333 sq. ft.**
Basement	1,200 sq. ft.
Garage	462 sq. ft.
Exterior Wall Framing	2x4

Foundation options:
Daylight Basement
Standard Basement
Crawlspace
(Foundation & framing conversion diagram available—see order form.)

Blueprint Price Code	C

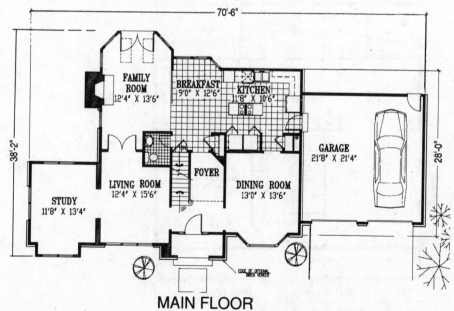

70'-6"

38'-2"

28'-0"

FAMILY
ROOM
12'4" X 13'6"

BREAKFAST
9'0" X 12'6"

KITCHEN
11'8" X 10'6"

GARAGE
21'8" X 21'4"

STUDY
11'8" X 13'4"

LIVING ROOM
12'4" X 15'6"

FOYER

DINING ROOM
13'0" X 13'6"

UP

EDGE OF OPTIONAL
BRICK VENEER

MAIN FLOOR

TO ORDER THIS BLUEPRINT,
CALL TOLL-FREE 1-800-547-5570

Plan CH-107-A

PRICES AND DETAILS
ON PAGES 12-15

107

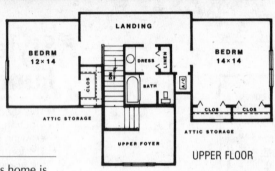

LANDING

BEDRM
12×14

DRESS   LINEN

CLOS   DR

BATH   A/C

BEDRM
14×14

ATTIC STORAGE

CLOS   CLOS

UPPER FOYER

ATTIC STORAGE

UPPER FLOOR

Simply Beautiful

- The beautiful symmetry of this home is marked by the double-door entry with overhead dormer windows and the full-width porch with columns and railings. The clean-cut lines of the design belie the home's 2,360 sq. ft. of luxurious living space.

- Guests are greeted by a two-story-high foyer that is flooded with light from the elegant, half-round dormer window above. Abundant closet space and a half-bath are just ahead.

- The home's spaciousness is enhanced by 9-ft. ceilings throughout the first floor. The large living room features a centrally located fireplace that can also be enjoyed from the adjoining dining room.

- Storage space is again well accounted for in the kitchen. An island cooktop counter is convenient to the full-glass nook. A French door in the nook opens to a covered porch for outdoor entertaining.

- An oversized utility room has plenty of space for a freezer, plus a clothes-folding table with extra storage below.

- The first-floor master suite is an appreciated feature, with an enticing master bath that includes a whirlpool tub, shower, dual vanities and a walk-in closet.

- The two spacious bedrooms upstairs share a compartmentalized bath.

Plan VL-2360	
Bedrooms: 3	**Baths:** 2 ½
Space:	
Upper floor	683 sq. ft.
Main floor	1,677 sq. ft.
Total Living Area	**2,360 sq. ft.**
Garage	458 sq. ft.
Exterior Wall Framing	2x4
Foundation options:	
Crawlspace	
Slab	
(Foundation & framing conversion diagram available—see order form.)	
Blueprint Price Code	C

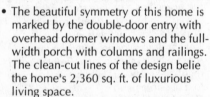

GARAGE
20×22

67'

DINING
12×14

UTIL

W DRY WASH

DIVIDER

NOOK
9×9

PORCH

STO

FRZR

RNG

D/W

BATH

CLOSET

KIT'N
12×12
OVENS

PAN   REF

1/2 BATH

LIN WH

LIVING RM
16×20

CLOSET

STO

A/C

MASTER SUITE
16×20

F/P

FOYER

PORCH

9'-0" CEILINGS 1ST. FLOOR

46'

MAIN FLOOR

 TO ORDER THIS BLUEPRINT, CALL TOLL-FREE 1-800-547-5570   Plan VL-2360   **PRICES AND DETAILS ON PAGES 12-15**

Appealing Arches

- Elegant arches add drama to the covered front porch of this two-story.
- Interior arches offer an attractive entrance to the formal dining room and the living room, which flank the foyer.
- The decorative niche off the foyer attractively displays your favorite conversation pieces.
- A dramatic fireplace and an array of windows frame the spacious two-story family room. An arched opening leads into the adjoining kitchen, which offers a convenient serving bar. A pantry closet and open shelving are featured in the sunny attached breakfast area.
- The upper floor includes a large master suite, three secondary bedrooms, and a compartmentalized bath. Bedroom 2 has a window seat, while Bedroom 4 has a private dressing area.
- The master bedroom flaunts a tray ceiling, a beautiful window showpiece and a private vaulted bath with a garden tub. The bedroom may be extended to include a sitting area.

Plan FB-2368

Bedrooms: 4	Baths: 2½
Living Area:	
Upper floor	1,168 sq. ft.
Main floor	1,200 sq. ft.
Total Living Area:	**2,368 sq. ft.**
Daylight basement	1,200 sq. ft.
Garage	504 sq. ft.
Exterior Wall Framing:	2x4

Foundation Options:
Daylight basement
Slab
(Typical foundation & framing conversion diagram available—see order form.)

BLUEPRINT PRICE CODE:	C

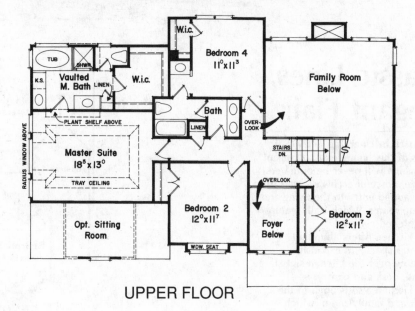

UPPER FLOOR

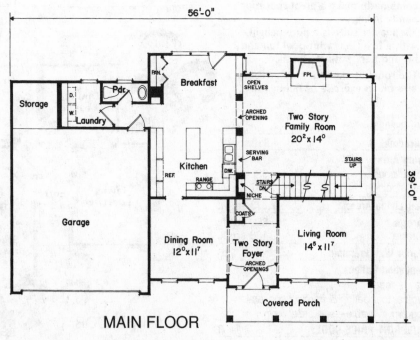

MAIN FLOOR

Classic Lines, Elegant Flair

- The rich brick arches and classic lines of this home lend an elegant air which will never be outdated.
- Inside, graceful archways lead from the vaulted entry to the living and dining rooms, which both feature heightened ceilings.
- The kitchen offers abundant counter space, an expansive window over the kitchen sink, large island, desk and pantry.
- The kitchen also is open to the nook and family room, which combine to make a great space for family living.
- The master suite is a pure delight, with a luxurious whirlpool tub and his-and-hers walk-in closets.
- The room marked for storage could also be an exercise or hobby room.

Plan R-2083

Bedrooms: 3	Baths: 2½
Living Area:	
Upper floor	926 sq. ft.
Main floor	1,447 sq. ft.
Total Living Area:	**2,373 sq. ft.**
Garage	609 sq. ft.
Storage	138 sq. ft.
Exterior Wall Framing:	2x6

Foundation Options:

Crawlspace
(Typical foundation & framing conversion diagram available—see order form.)

BLUEPRINT PRICE CODE:	**C**

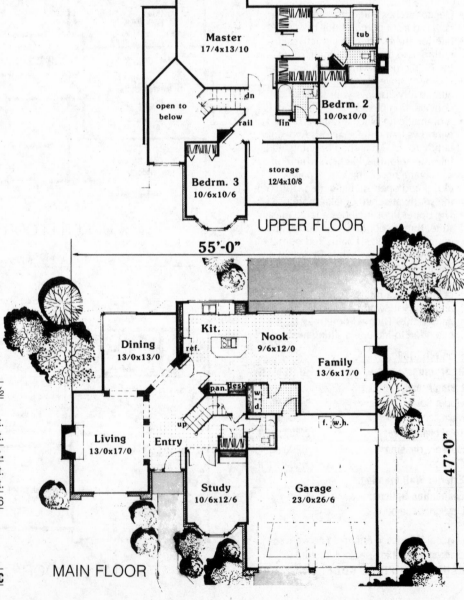

UPPER FLOOR

MAIN FLOOR

TO ORDER THIS BLUEPRINT, CALL TOLL-FREE 1-800-547-5570

Plan R-2083

PRICES AND DETAILS ON PAGES 12-15

Charming Economy

- This plan is economical to construct, but still charming in its visual appeal and restful interior.
- The interior presents abundant space for family or informal entertaining.
- A roomy Great Room adjoining the breakfast nook includes a handsome fireplace.
- A formal dining room is available for dressier occasions.
- The downstairs guest bedroom would make a great home office if not needed for sleeping.
- Note the full bath downstairs, in addition to two baths upstairs.
- The large master suite includes a sumptuous private bath with separate tub and shower.
- Bedrooms 2 and 3 are roomy and share access to a compartmentalized bath.

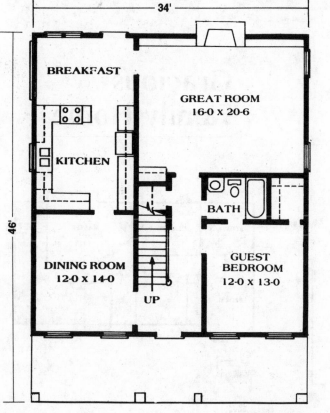

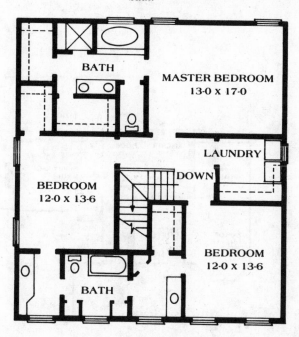

Plan V-2398	
Bedrooms: 3-4	**Baths:** 3
Space:	
Upper floor:	1,174 sq. ft.
Main floor:	1,224 sq. ft.
Total living area:	2,398 sq. ft.
Exterior Wall Framing:	2x6

Ceiling Heights:	
Upper floor:	9'
Main floor:	9'

Foundation options:
Crawlspace only.
(Foundation & framing conversion diagram available — see order form.)

Blueprint Price Code:	C

Gracious Family Home

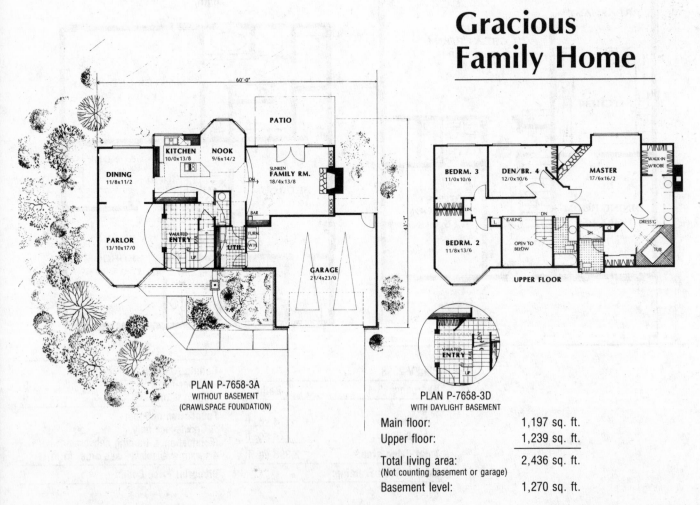

PLAN P-7658-3A
WITHOUT BASEMENT
(CRAWLSPACE FOUNDATION)

PLAN P-7658-3D
WITH DAYLIGHT BASEMENT

Main floor:	1,197 sq. ft.
Upper floor:	1,239 sq. ft.
Total living area: (Not counting basement or garage)	2,436 sq. ft.
Basement level:	1,270 sq. ft.

Blueprint Price Code C

Plans P-7658-3A & -3D

PRICES AND DETAILS
ON PAGES 12-15

Design Exudes Warmth and Comfort

- This plan represents a return to traditional styling with the open-concept interior so much in demand today.
- A vaulted entry and living room with an adjacent dining room make up the formal portion of this plan.
- A spacious hall leads to the large informal entertaining area composed of the kitchen, nook and family room.

- The second floor offers a large master suite and two additional bedrooms with a bonus room that can be left unfinished until needed.
- Exterior rooflines are all gabled for ease of construction and lower framing costs. The brick veneer garage face echoes the brick columns supporting the covered entry.

Plan S-8389	
Bedrooms: 3-4	**Baths:** 2½
Living Area:	
Upper floor	932 sq. ft.
Main floor	1,290 sq. ft.
Bonus room	228 sq. ft.
Total Living Area:	**2,450 sq. ft.**
Standard basement	1,290 sq. ft.
Garage	429 sq. ft.
Exterior Wall Framing:	2x6
Foundation Options:	
Standard basement	
Crawlspace	
Slab	
(Typical foundation & framing conversion diagram available—see order form.)	
BLUEPRINT PRICE CODE:	C

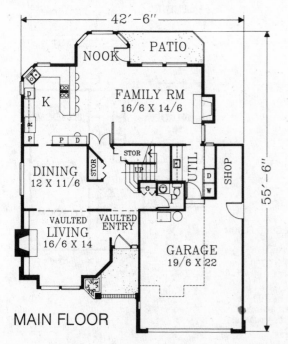

MAIN FLOOR

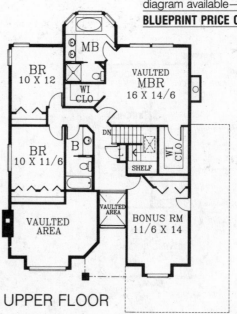

UPPER FLOOR

English Tudor with Contemporary Layout

Inside a traditional exterior is a contemporary layout that includes double garage, two-story section, high ceilinged foyer and living room wing with window bay and two fireplace units.

This three-bedroom Tudor separates formal and informal social areas and nicely isolates the service entry from other parts of the house.

Strong exterior lines and interesting interiors have kept the English Tudor among the most popular classic styles and this three-bedroom version was designed in that tradition. Well-proportioned rooms open off the center hallway, which permits easy separation of traffic to living areas on all sides.

The living room features a massive log-sized fireplace and a large bay window seat.

First floor:	1,452 sq. ft.
Second floor:	999 sq. ft.
Total living area: (Not counting basement or garage)	2,451 sq. ft.

GENERAL USE

UTILITIES

BASEMENT

RECREATION
22' 7" - 14' 9"

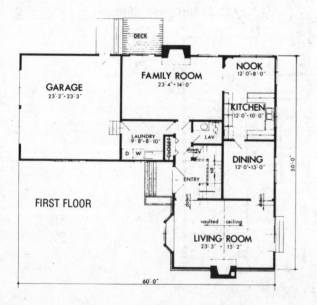

FIRST FLOOR

SECOND FLOOR

PLAN H-3700-2
WITH BASEMENT

PLAN H-3700-2A
WITHOUT BASEMENT
(CRAWLSPACE FOUNDATION)

Blueprint Price Code C
Plans H-3700-2 & -2A

PRICES AND DETAILS ON PAGES 12-15

Elegant Post-Modern Design

- Here's a design that is highly fashionable today and that will undoubtedly stay in style for decades.
- A wagon roof porch with paired columns lends sophistication to an elegant design.
- Half-round transom windows and gable vents unify the facade.
- Inside, a diagonal stairway forms the keystone of an exciting, angular design.
- The foyer leads visitors past the den into the sunken living room with vaulted ceiling and fireplace.
- Square columned arcades separate the living room from the dining room.
- A sunny bay window defines the breakfast area, which includes a sliding glass door to the deck.
- The thoroughly modern kitchen includes an islet cooktop and pantry.
- The generously sized family room also sports a vaulted ceiling and offers easy access to the outdoor deck.
- Upstairs, a stylish master suite features a private bath and large closet.

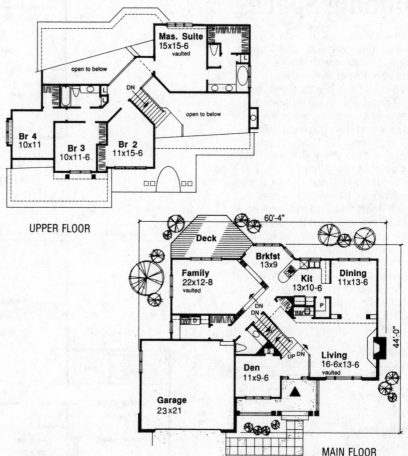

UPPER FLOOR

MAIN FLOOR

Plan B-89005

Bedrooms: 4	Baths: 2½

Space:

Upper floor:	1,083 sq. ft.
Main floor:	1,380 sq. ft.
Total living area:	**2,463 sq. ft.**
Basement:	1,380 sq. ft.
Garage:	483 sq. ft.

Exterior Wall Framing:	2x4

Foundation options:
Standard basement only.
(Foundation & framing conversion diagram available — see order form.)

Blueprint Price Code:	C

TO ORDER THIS BLUEPRINT,
CALL TOLL-FREE 1-800-547-5570

Plan B-89005

PRICES AND DETAILS
ON PAGES 12-15

115

Fantastic Facade, Stunning Spaces

- Matching dormers and a generous covered front porch give this home its fantastic facade. Inside, the open living spaces are just as stunning.

- A two-story foyer bisects the formal living areas. The living room offers three bright windows, an inviting fireplace and sliding French doors to the Great Room. The formal dining room overlooks the front porch and has easy access to the kitchen.

- The Great Room is truly grand, featuring a fireplace and TV center flanked by French doors that lead to a large deck.

- A circular dinette joins the Great Room to the spacious kitchen, which is handy to a mudroom and a powder room.

- The main-floor master suite boasts a cathedral ceiling, a walk-in closet and a fabulous bath with a whirlpool tub.

- Upstairs, the center-hall floor plan efficiently accommodates four large bedrooms and another whirlpool bath.

Plan AHP-9397

Bedrooms: 5	Baths: 2½
Living Area:	
Upper floor	928 sq. ft.
Main floor	1,545 sq. ft.
Total Living Area:	**2,473 sq. ft.**
Standard basement	1,165 sq. ft.
Garage and storage	432 sq. ft.
Exterior Wall Framing:	2x4 or 2x6

Foundation Options:

Standard basement

Crawlspace

Slab

(All plans can be built with your choice of foundation and framing. A generic conversion diagram is available. See order form.)

BLUEPRINT PRICE CODE:　　　　C

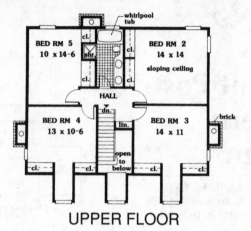

UPPER FLOOR

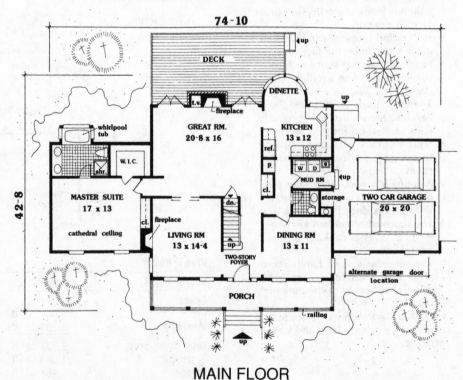

MAIN FLOOR

TO ORDER THIS BLUEPRINT, CALL TOLL-FREE 1-800-547-5570　　　Plan AHP-9397　　　**PRICES AND DETAILS ON PAGES 12-15**

FRONT VIEW

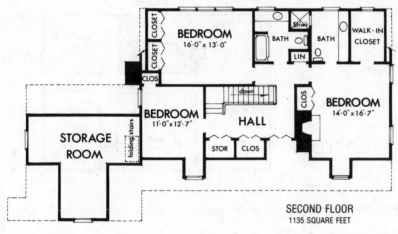

BEDROOM
16'-0" x 13'-0"

BATH

Shwr

BATH

WALK-IN CLOSET

LIN

CLOSET

CLOSET

CLOS

BEDROOM
11'-0" x 12'-7"

folding stairs

STORAGE ROOM

HALL

STOR

CLOS

CLOS

BEDROOM
14'-0" x 16'-7"

SECOND FLOOR
1135 SQUARE FEET

Authentic Colonial Styling, Functional Design

We are offering here another example of authentic Colonial styling. These features include the steeply pitched roof; the large chimney, preferably located as near the center of the dwelling as possible; and the traditional arrangement of windows. Likewise, the windows are divided by muntin bars into small panes, and the shutters are part of the design.

Also notice that one side of the garage roof extends closer to the grade level than on the other side of the gable, reminiscent of colonial "saltbox" designs.

First floor:	1,383 sq. ft.
Second floor:	1,135 sq. ft.
Total living area: (Not counting basement or garage)	2,518 sq. ft.

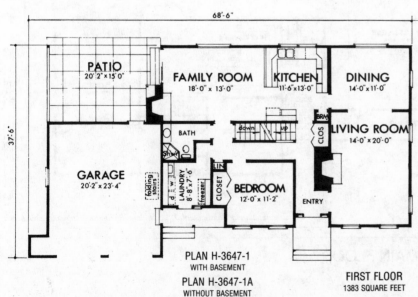

68'-6"

37'-6"

PATIO
20'-2" x 15'-0"

FAMILY ROOM
18'-0" x 13'-0"

KITCHEN
11'-6" x 13'-0"

DINING
14'-0" x 11'-0"

BATH

Shwr

down

up

BRM

CLOS

LIVING ROOM
14'-0" x 20'-0"

GARAGE
20'-2" x 23'-4"

folding stairs

d w

LAUNDRY
8'-8" x 7'-6"

freezer

LIN

CLOSET

BEDROOM
12'-0" x 11'-2"

ENTRY

PLAN H-3647-1
WITH BASEMENT

PLAN H-3647-1A
WITHOUT BASEMENT
(HAS CRAWLSPACE)

FIRST FLOOR
1383 SQUARE FEET

Blueprint Price Code D

Classic Country-Style

- Almost completely surrounded by an expansive porch, this classic plan exudes warmth and grace.
- The foyer is liberal in size and leads guests to a formal dining room to the left or the large living room to the right.
- A large country kitchen includes a sunny, bay-windowed breakfast nook.
- The main floor also includes a utility area and full bath.
- Upstairs, the master suite is impressive, with its large sleeping area, big closet and magnificent bath.
- Three secondary bedrooms with ample closets share a full bath with double sinks.
- Also note the stairs leading up to an attic, which is useful for storage space.

Plan J-86134

Bedrooms: 4	**Baths:** 3

Living Area:	
Upper floor	1,195 sq. ft.
Main floor	1,370 sq. ft.
Total Living Area	**2,565 sq. ft.**
Basement	1,370 sq. ft.
Garage	576 sq. ft.
Storage	144 sq. ft.
Exterior Wall Framing	2x4

Foundation Options:

Standard basement
Crawlspace
Slab
(Typical foundation & framing conversion diagram available—see order form.)

BLUEPRINT PRICE CODE	D

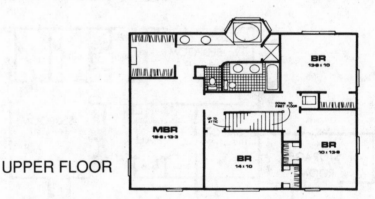

UPPER FLOOR

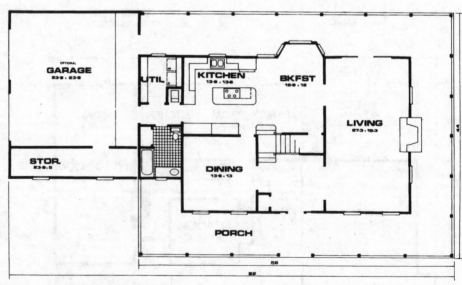

MAIN FLOOR

TO ORDER THIS BLUEPRINT,
CALL TOLL-FREE 1-800-547-5570

Plan J-86134

PRICES AND DETAILS
ON PAGES 12-15

Trendy Transitional Design

- This striking transitional design offers a combination of staggered hip and gable rooflines, arched transoms, brick trim and a three-car garage with decorative facade.
- The dramatic vaulted entry focuses on circular walls and a curved staircase.
- To the right, a large, vaulted living room with fireplace combines with a formal dining room for a spacious setting. The two rooms are separated by a decorative plant shelf and columns.
- Open to the walk-through kitchen are a gazebo breakfast area and a vaulted family room with corner window and second fireplace.
- The main-floor guest room can be used as a den or library.
- The upper-level master bedroom is separated from the three other bedrooms. A private master bath and octagonal sitting area are featured.

Plan AG-9104

Bedrooms: 4-5	Baths: 3
Living Area:	
Upper floor:	1,128 sq. ft.
Main floor	1,456 sq. ft.
Total Living Area:	**2,584 sq. ft.**
Standard basement	1,456 sq. ft.
Garage	832 sq. ft.
Exterior Wall Framing:	2x6

Foundation Options:
Standard basement
(Typical foundation & framing conversion diagram available—see order form.)

BLUEPRINT PRICE CODE:	D

UPPER FLOOR

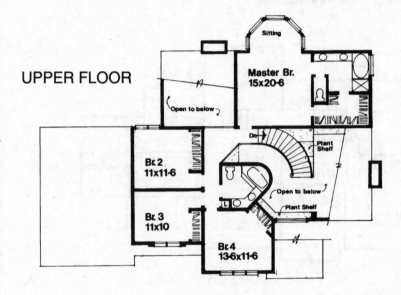

MAIN FLOOR

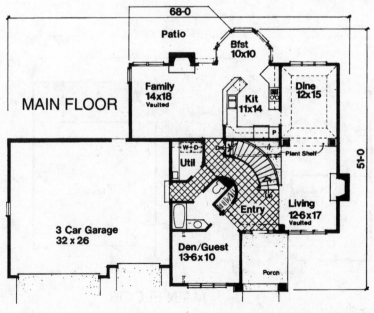

Vertical Elegance

- This spacious two-story has unique features that give it a vertical elegance.
- The two-story-high foyer offers an open-railed stairway that adjoins a second stairway from the family room. The two stairways bridge together before reaching the upper floor.
- Behind high, decorative columns is the formal living room. To the rear is a spacious family room with an exciting fireplace flanked by windows. The kitchen and breakfast room overlook the outdoors, accessed through a French door.
- Three secondary bedrooms share a compartmentalized bath on the upper floor. The luxurious master bedroom features a private sitting room with a stunning two-sided fireplace, a big walk-in closet and a private vaulted bath with a separate tub and shower.

Plan FB-2600

Bedrooms: 4	Baths: 2½
Living Area:	
Upper floor	1,348 sq. ft.
Main floor	1,252 sq. ft.
Total Living Area:	**2,600 sq. ft.**
Daylight basement	1,252 sq. ft.
Garage	448 sq. ft.
Storage	36 sq. ft.
Exterior Wall Framing:	2x4
Foundation Options:	

Daylight basement
Crawlspace
(Typical foundation & framing conversion diagram available—see order form.)

BLUEPRINT PRICE CODE:	D

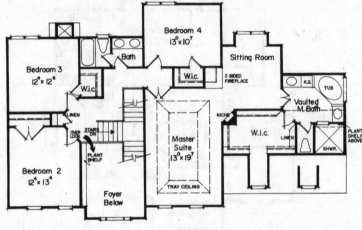

UPPER FLOOR

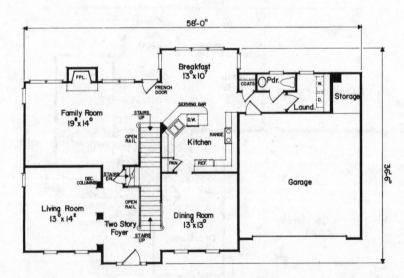

MAIN FLOOR

TO ORDER THIS BLUEPRINT,
CALL TOLL-FREE 1-800-547-5570

Plan FB-2600

PRICES AND DETAILS
ON PAGES 12-15

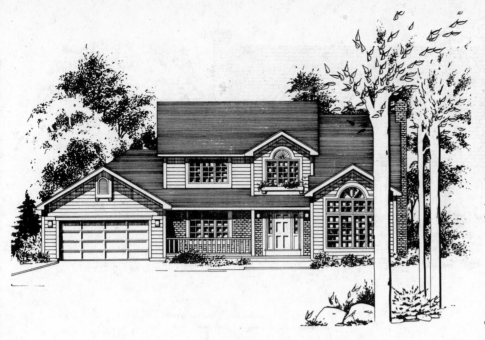

Plenty of Family Room to Roam

- The large family needs room to roam and wants style as well. This traditional two-story delivers, with an efficient rectangular perimeter which is cost-effective to build and a half round window theme with a covered front porch giving it plenty of style.
- The main floor begins with a focal point open stair in the foyer. To the left is the spacious formal dining room overlooking the front porch, and to the right is a sunken living room with a cathedral ceiling and pocket door access to the family room.
- The kitchen overlooks the bay-windowed dinette and beyond to the fireplace in the sunken family room. The main floor also houses a laundry room and an optional den/guest room.
- There are four bedrooms upstairs plus a bonus library/reading loft above the stairwell. The master bedroom features a spacious walk-in closet and private bath.

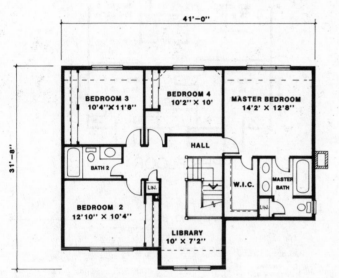

UPPER FLOOR

Plan GL-2472

Bedrooms: 4-5	Baths: 2½
Space:	
Upper floor:	1,098 sq. ft.
Main floor:	1,530 sq. ft.
Total living area:	2,628 sq. ft.
	(with optional den)
Garage:	484 sq. ft.
Exterior Wall Framing:	2x4
Foundation options:	
Standard basement.	
(Foundation & framing conversion diagram available — see order form.)	
Blueprint Price Code:	D

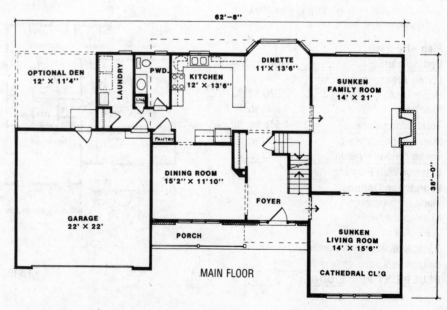

MAIN FLOOR

Innovative Floor Plan

- The wide, covered front porch, arched windows and symmetrical lines of this traditional home conceal the modern, innovative floor plan found within.
- The vaulted foyer guides guests to the formal living and dining rooms. The hotspot of the home is the Great Room, island kitchen and glassed-in eating nook, all of which overlook a large backyard deck. The main floor is also enhanced by 9-ft. ceilings.
- Three fireplaces add to the home's aura of warmth and hospitality, including a fireplace in the master suite. This private oasis also boasts a cathedral ceiling and a delicious bath with a garden tub.
- The largest of the four bedrooms upstairs has a sloped ceiling and a private bath, making it an ideal guest suite. Another full bath is centrally located for the remaining bedrooms.

Plan AHP-9360

Bedrooms: 5	Baths: 3½
Living Area:	
Upper floor	970 sq. ft.
Main floor	1,688 sq. ft.
Total Living Area:	**2,658 sq. ft.**
Standard basement	1,550 sq. ft.
Garage and utility area	443 sq. ft.
Exterior Wall Framing:	2x6

Foundation Options:

Standard basement
Crawlspace
Slab
(Typical foundation & framing conversion diagram available—see order form.)

BLUEPRINT PRICE CODE:	D

UPPER FLOOR

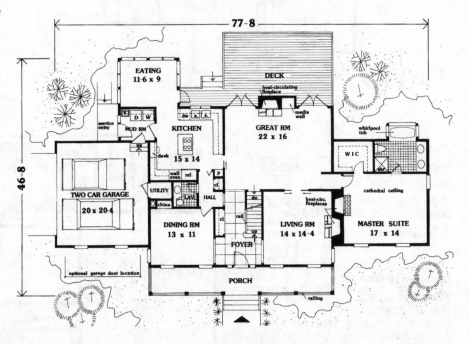

MAIN FLOOR

Plan AHP-9360

Dramatic, Soaring Lines

- This dramatic two-story offers a daylight basement option for hillside settings.
- Note the large island kitchen with adjoining nook and family room.
- Upstairs master suite includes splendid bath, walk-in closet and fireplace.
- Bonus space is available for office, exercise room, extra play space or additional bedroom.

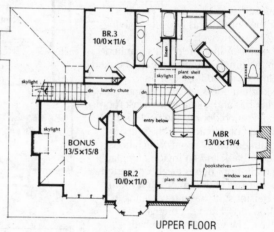

UPPER FLOOR

MAIN FLOOR

Plan CDG-2005

Bedrooms: 3-4	Baths: 2½
Space:	
Upper floor:	1,041 sq. ft.
Main floor:	1,386 sq. ft.
Bonus area:	231 sq. ft.
Total living area:	**2,658 sq. ft.**
Basement:	1,386 sq. ft.
Garage:	419 sq. ft.
Exterior Wall Framing:	2x4
Ceiling Heights:	
Upper floor:	8'
Main floor:	9'

Foundation options:
Daylight basement
Crawlspace.
(Foundation & framing conversion diagram available — see order form.)

Blueprint Price Code:	D

Fantastic Front Entry

- A fantastic arched window presides over the entry of this two-story, giving guests a sunny welcome.
- The spacious living room is separated from the dining room by a pair of boxed columns with built-in shelves.
- The kitchen offers a walk-in pantry, a serving bar and a sunny breakfast room with a French door to the backyard.
- A boxed column accents the entry to the vaulted family room, which boasts a window bank and an inviting fireplace.
- The main-floor den is easily converted into an extra bedroom or guest room.
- The master suite has a tray ceiling, a walk-in closet and decorative plant shelves. The vaulted private bath features an oval tub and two vanities, one with knee space.
- Three additional bedrooms share another full bath near the second stairway to the main floor.

Plan FB-2680

Bedrooms: 4+	Baths: 3
Living Area:	
Upper floor	1,256 sq. ft.
Main floor	1,424 sq. ft.
Total Living Area:	**2,680 sq. ft.**
Daylight basement	1,424 sq. ft.
Garage	496 sq. ft.
Exterior Wall Framing:	2x4

Foundation Options:
Daylight basement
(Typical foundation & framing conversion diagram available–see order form.)

BLUEPRINT PRICE CODE:	D

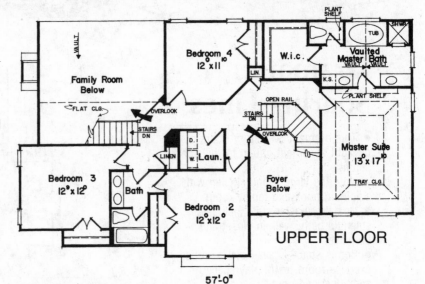

UPPER FLOOR

57'-0"

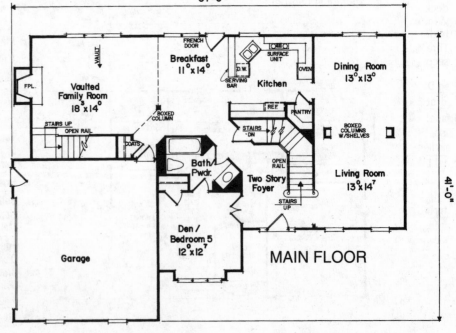

MAIN FLOOR

41'-0"

Bordered in Brick

- Decorative brick borders, front columns and arched windows give a classy look to this two-story palace.
- The entry is flanked by formal dining and living rooms, both with dramatic front windows.
- A fireplace warms the massive family room that stretches to the morning room and the kitchen at the rear of the home. The bayed morning room offers access to an attached deck; the kitchen has an island worktop.
- A unique sun room also overlooks the deck.
- Windows also surround the master bedroom, which has a large bath.
- Three nice-sized bedrooms share a second full bath on the upper level.

Plan DD-2689

Bedrooms: 4	Baths: 2 ½
Space:	
Upper floor	755 sq. ft.
Main floor	1,934 sq. ft.
Total Living Area	**2,689 sq. ft.**
Basement	1,934 sq. ft.
Garage	436 sq. ft.
Exterior Wall Framing	**2×4**

Foundation options:

Standard Basement
Crawlspace
Slab

(Foundation & framing conversion diagram available—see order form.)

Blueprint Price Code	**D**

UPPER FLOOR

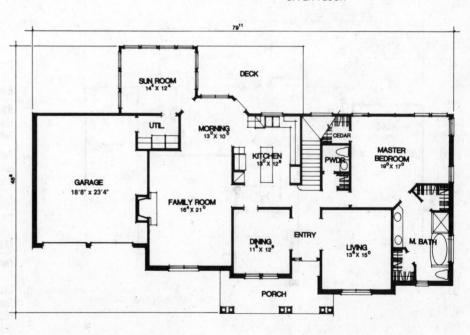

MAIN FLOOR

BEDROOM 3
12⁰ X 12⁰

BATH 2

A/C

MASTER BEDROOM
18⁸ X 14⁰

DOWN

CLOSET

OPEN TO BELOW

MASTER BATH

BEDROOM 2
14⁰ X 12⁴

UPPER FLOOR

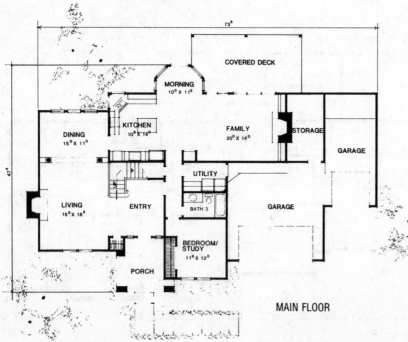

73⁸

COVERED DECK

MORNING
10⁰ X 11⁰

KITCHEN
10⁸ X 14⁰

FAMILY
20⁰ X 14⁰

STORAGE

DINING
15⁰ X 11⁰

GARAGE

47⁴

UTILITY

LIVING
15⁰ X 16⁴

ENTRY

BATH 3

GARAGE

PORCH

BEDROOM/
STUDY
11⁸ X 12⁰

MAIN FLOOR

Executive Excellence

- This executive home with stucco exterior has an open, lighted effect with large expanses of glass and flowing spaces.
- The entry and stairwell are a two-story space opening to the formal living and dining rooms.
- Family gathering spaces are at the rear with plenty of glass opening to a large covered deck.
- A guest bedroom/study with full bath complete the lower level.
- Upstairs is the enormous master suite with a closet big enough for large wardrobes and a lavish master bath. Two more bedrooms and the hall bath are also upstairs.

Plan DD-2725

Bedrooms: 3-4	Baths: 3
Space:	
Upper floor:	1,152 sq. ft.
Main floor:	1,631 sq. ft.
Total living area:	2,783 sq. ft.
Garage:	approx. 600 sq. ft.
Storage:	approx. 100 sq. ft.
Exterior Wall Framing:	2x4
Ceiling Heights:	
Upper floor:	8'
Main floor:	9'

Foundation options:
Basement.
Crawlspace.
Slab.
(Foundation & framing conversion diagram available — see order form.)

Blueprint Price Code:	D

Plan DD-2725

PRICES AND DETAILS ON PAGES 12-15

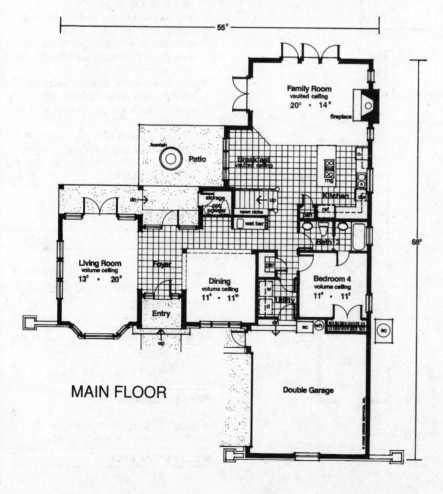

UPPER FLOOR

MAIN FLOOR

Plan HDS-99-163

Grand 1930s Style

- This stunning two-story is the perfect blend of 1930s architecture and 1990s livability.
- The interior is also reminiscent of the grand styling of earlier days with a traditionally large foyer that stretches to the rear fountain patio. A wet bar and an optional powder room are centrally located.
- The huge formal living room boasts attractive French doors.
- The family will enjoy the spacious informal family room, kitchen and breakfast room combination at the rear of the home. All three rooms have a view of the fireplace and the outdoors.
- The luxurious master suite on the upper floor features a private lounging deck, a spectacular see-through fireplace to the spa tub and a big walk-in closet. Two more upper-floor bedrooms, a second bath and an additional main-floor bedroom are also included.

Plan HDS-99-163	
Bedrooms: 4	**Baths:** 3-3½
Living Area:	
Upper floor	1,167 sq. ft.
Main floor	1,624 sq. ft.
Total Living Area:	**2,791 sq. ft.**
Garage	413 sq. ft.

Exterior Wall Framing:
Combination concrete block and 2x4

Foundation Options:
Slab
(Typical foundation & framing conversion diagram available—see order form.)

BLUEPRINT PRICE CODE:	D

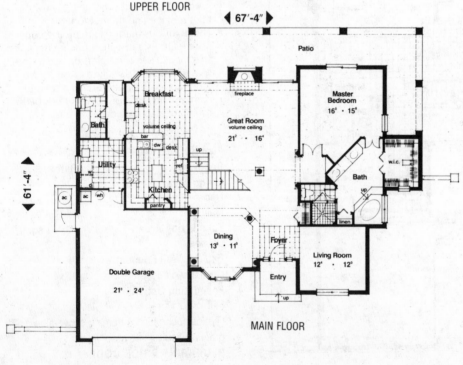

Deck

Great Room
Below

Bedroom 2
13⁸ · 11¹⁰
window seat

Loft
16⁰ · 11⁸

down
rail

Study / Den
14⁸ · 13⁸
rail
Foyer
Below

Bath

storage

window seat

Bedroom 3
12⁰ · 10⁴

UPPER FLOOR

◄ 67'-4" ►

Patio

Breakfast
desk

Master
Bedroom
16⁰ · 15⁸

fireplace

Bath

Great Room
volume ceiling
21⁷ · 16⁴

volume ceiling
bar
dw desk
Utility
ref
up
w.i.c.

Kitchen
pantry

61'-4"

ac   ac   wh

up

linen

Dining
13⁰ · 11⁸

Foyer

Living Room
12⁰ · 12⁰

Double Garage
21⁰ · 24⁰

Entry
up

MAIN FLOOR

Elegant Italian Flavor

- Equally at home on the Mediterranean or in an American suburb, this design bespeaks quality and elegance both inside and out.
- A spacious two-story high Great Room features a fireplace and easy access to the patio.
- The roomy kitchen joins with a sunny, airy breakfast nook; also note the handy utility area off the garage, and convenient bath by the back door.
- The magnificent master bedroom on the main floor includes an opulent bath and enormous walk-in closet.
- Upstairs, you'll find two more bedrooms, a full bath and a study/den which could serve as a fourth bedroom.

Plan HDS-90-803

Bedrooms: 3-4	Baths: 3
Space:	
Upper floor:	978 sq. ft.
Main floor:	1,818 sq. ft.
Total living area:	2,796 sq. ft.
Garage:	504 sq. ft.
Exterior Wall Framing:	2x4
Ceiling Heights:	
Upper floor:	8'
Main floor:	10'
Foundation options:	
Slab only.	
(Foundation & framing conversion diagram available — see order form.)	
Blueprint Price Code:	D

Tudor Style Blends Wood, Brick & Stone

- A warm combination of textures and finishes lends this exterior extra appeal.
- The interior offers plenty of space for a big, busy family.
- The large living room includes an impressive fireplace, and joins the dining room to create a super space for entertaining.
- The spacious family room also includes a fireplace, and is a step down from the dinette/kitchen area.
- A library off the impressive foyer would be great for a home office.
- The master suite, upstairs, provides a large sleeping area plus a luxurious private bath and large walk-in closet.

Plan A-130

Bedrooms: 4	Baths: 2½

Space:	
Upper floor:	1,305 sq. ft.
Main floor:	1,502 sq. ft.

Total living area:	2,807 sq. ft.
Basement:	1,502 sq. ft.
Garage:	576 sq. ft.

Exterior Wall Framing:	2x4

Foundation options:
Standard basement only.
(Foundation & framing conversion diagram available — see order form.)

Blueprint Price Code:	D

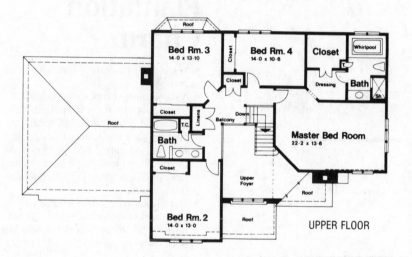

UPPER FLOOR

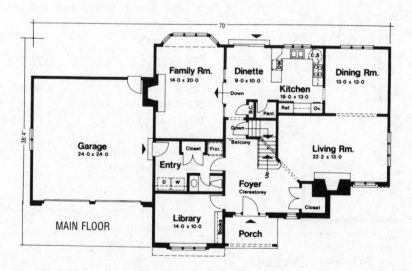

MAIN FLOOR

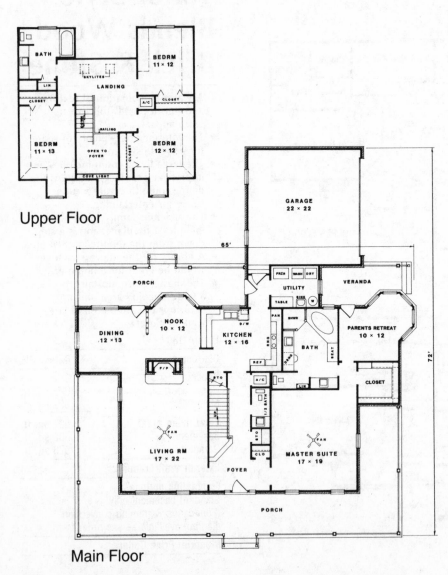

Upper Floor

Main Floor

Plantation Charm

- Yesterday's plantation home has today's luxuries.
- A stand-alone fireplace separates the living room from the formal dining room and bayed breakfast nook, but still ensures easy traffic flow throughout.
- The well-equipped kitchen overlooks the nook and rear porch beyond, and has handy garage access through the utility room.
- The master suite offers a variety of pleasures, including a private bayed retreat with veranda access and a large bath with whirlpool tub and dressing seat.
- Three more nice-sized bedrooms are found upstairs.

Plan VL-2817

Bedrooms: 4	Baths: 2 ½
Space:	
Upper floor	859 sq. ft.
Main floor	1,958 sq. ft.
Total Living Area	**2,817 sq. ft.**
Garage	488 sq. ft.
Exterior Wall Framing	2x4

Foundation options:
Crawlspace
Slab
(Foundation & framing conversion diagram available—see order form.)

Blueprint Price Code	**D**

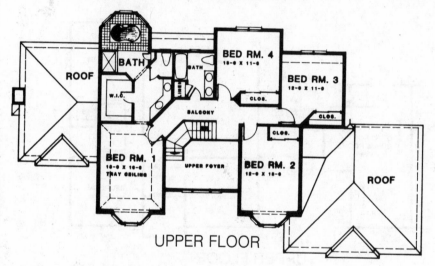

UPPER FLOOR

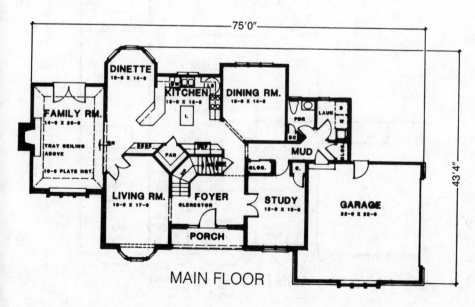

MAIN FLOOR

Meant to Impress

- This home was meant to impress, from inside and out. The exquisite detailing of the exterior is reminiscent of an English manor home. The interior features a floor plan that is designed for elegant entertaining as well as for comfortable family living.
- The kitchen is at the core of the design, between the dining nook and the formal dining room. A breakfast bar faces the bayed dinette for quick meals. An island work center provides extra space while directing traffic flow. A built-in desk, a deluxe walk-in pantry and a lazy Susan are other bonus features.
- The sunken family room is a natural extension of the kitchen and dining areas. A fireplace, a tray ceiling and French doors to the backyard make this room a family favorite.
- The stairway and vaulted foyer are illuminated by a clerestory window above the front door. The master bedroom suite offers a sumptuous spa bath. Three more bedrooms share another full bath.

Plan A-2210-DS

Bedrooms: 4-5	Baths: 2 ½
Space:	
Upper floor	1,208 sq. ft.
Main floor	1,634 sq. ft.
Total Living Area	**2,842 sq. ft.**
Basement	1,634 sq. ft.
Garage	484 sq. ft.
Exterior Wall Framing	2x6
Foundation options:	
Standard Basement	
(Foundation & framing conversion diagram available—see order form.)	
Blueprint Price Code	D

Two-Story Great Room

- A spacious vaulted Great Room, with a fireplace and sliding glass doors to a backyard deck, is the highlight of this distinguished brick home.
- The front dining room and study both feature bay windows; the study can be used as an extra bedroom or as a guest room.
- A second stairway off the breakfast room accesses a home office or bonus space; an optional bath could also be built in.
- The main-floor master suite offers his-and-hers walk-in closets, a splashy master bath and private access to the rear deck.
- Three secondary bedrooms are located off the second-floor balcony that overlooks the Great Room and foyer.

Plan C-9010

Bedrooms: 4+	Baths: 2½-3½
Living Area:	
Upper floor	761 sq. ft.
Main floor	1,637 sq. ft.
Bonus room	347 sq. ft.
Optional bath and closet	106 sq. ft.
Total Living Area:	**2,851 sq. ft.**
Daylight basement	1,637 sq. ft.
Garage	572 sq. ft.
Exterior Wall Framing:	2x4

Foundation Options:

Daylight basement

Crawlspace

(Typical foundation & framing conversion diagram available—see order form.)

BLUEPRINT PRICE CODE: D

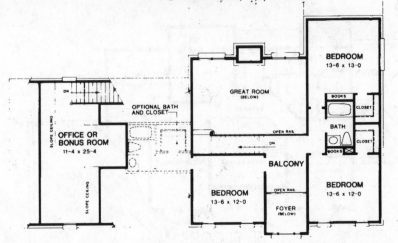

UPPER FLOOR

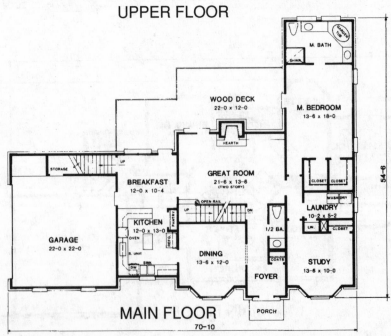

MAIN FLOOR

Take the Plunge!

- From the elegant porte cochere to the striking rooflines, this home's facade is magnificent. But the rear area is equally fine, with its spa, waterfall and pool.
- Double doors lead from the entry into a columned foyer. Beyond the living room is a sunken wet bar that extends into the pool area, allowing guests to swim up to the bar for refreshments.
- The stunning master suite offers views of the pool through a curved window wall, access to the patio and an opulent bath.
- A secluded den, study or guest room is conveniently close to the hall bath.
- The dining room boasts window walls and a tiered pedestal ceiling. The island kitchen easily services both the formal and the informal areas of the home.
- A large breakfast room flows into a warm family room with a fireplace and sliders to the patio and pool.
- A railed staircase leads to the upper floor, where there are two bedrooms, a continental bath and a shared balcony deck overlooking the pool area.
- The observatory features high windows to accommodate an amateur stargazer's telescope. This room could also be used as an activity area for hobbies or games.

Plan HDS-99-154

Bedrooms: 3-4	Baths: 3
Living Area:	
Upper floor	675 sq. ft.
Main floor	2,212 sq. ft.
Total Living Area:	**2,887 sq. ft.**
Garage	479 sq. ft.
Exterior Wall Framing:	2x4

Foundation Options:

Slab

(Typical foundation & framing conversion diagram available—see order form.)

BLUEPRINT PRICE CODE:	D

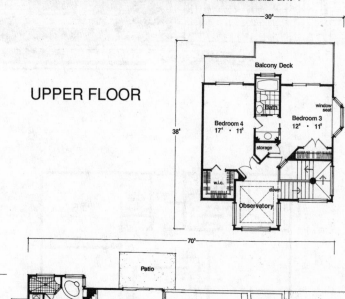

UPPER FLOOR

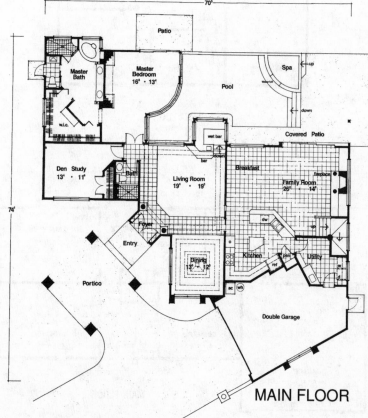

MAIN FLOOR

TO ORDER THIS BLUEPRINT,
CALL TOLL-FREE 1-800-547-5570

Plan HDS-99-154

PRICES AND DETAILS
ON PAGES 12-15

133

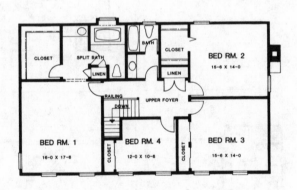

UPPER FLOOR

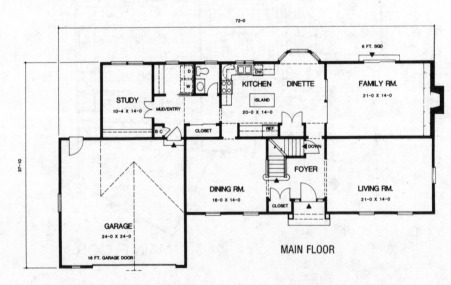

MAIN FLOOR

Early American with Four Bedrooms

- Time-tested traditional shows the symmetry of design that keeps this style always popular.
- Basically rectangular two-story with simple, straight roofline offers big space for economical costs.
- Main floor presents spacious family room and living room.
- Large island kitchen adjoins a bright, bay-windowed dinette area.
- Formal dining room is large enough for a good-sized dinner party.
- A study behind the garage is available for an exercise or hobby room, or perhaps a home office or work room.
- Upstairs, the spacious master suite includes a deluxe bath and large walk-in closet.

Plan A-118-DS

Bedrooms: 4	Baths: 2½
Space:	
Upper floor:	1,344 sq. ft.
Main floor:	1,556 sq. ft.
Total living area:	**2,900 sq. ft.**
Basement:	approx. 1,556 sq. ft.
Garage:	576 sq. ft.
Exterior Wall Framing:	2x4

Foundation options:
Standard basement only.
(Foundation & framing conversion diagram available — see order form.)

Blueprint Price Code:	D

Sprawling French Country

- A hip roof and gable accents give this sprawling home a country, French look.
- The spectacular living room stretches from the entry of the home to the rear. Windows at both ends offer light and a nice breeze.
- Both the living room and the formal dining room have high ceilings with transom lights.
- Angled walls add interest to the roomy island kitchen, which overlooks the covered lanai. The kitchen opens to the adjoining morning room and family room.
- The spacious main-floor master suite is highlighted by a large, bayed sitting area, set apart from the bedroom with columns and dividers. The master bath features dual walk-in closets and vanities, a large spa tub and a separate shower.
- Three extra bedrooms and two more baths share the upper level.

Plan DD-2889

Bedrooms: 4	**Baths:** 3 ½

Space:	
Upper floor	819 sq. ft.
Main floor	2,111 sq. ft.
Total Living Area	**2,930 sq. ft.**
Basement	2,111 sq. ft.
Garage	622 sq. ft.
Exterior Wall Framing	2x4

Foundation options:

Standard Basement

Crawlspace

Slab

(Foundation & framing conversion diagram available—see order form.)

Blueprint Price Code	D

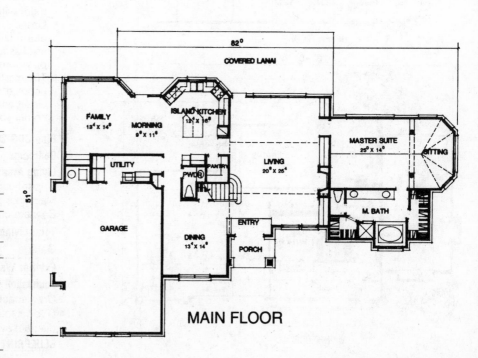

UPPER FLOOR

MAIN FLOOR

Nostalgic but New

- Triple dormers, a covered front porch and half-round windows lend a nostalgic country feel to this exciting two-story home.
- A dramatic two-story foyer makes an elegant introduction, leading into the vaulted living room with a fireplace, a window seat and round-top windows.
- The formal dining room, which features a tray ceiling, opens to the living room through an arch supported by stylish columns.
- The island kitchen has an open view into the breakfast nook and the family room with rear patio beyond.
- Upstairs, there are three bedrooms, plus a large bonus room that could be used as a fourth bedroom or as a playroom.
- The master suite dazzles with double doors, a sitting bay, a huge walk-in closet and an angled bath with a corner spa tub beneath windows.

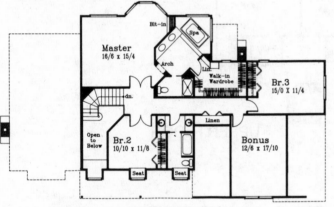

UPPER FLOOR

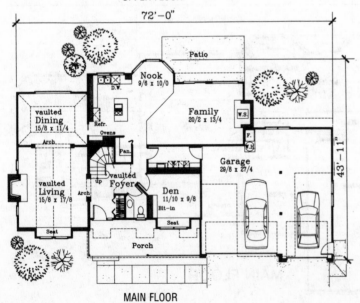

MAIN FLOOR

Plan CDG-2031

Bedrooms: 3-5	Baths: 2½
Living Area:	
Upper floor	1,203 sq. ft.
Main floor	1,495 sq. ft.
Bonus room	238 sq. ft.
Total Living Area:	**2,936 sq. ft.**
Garage	811 sq. ft.
Exterior Wall Framing:	2x6

Foundation Options:

Crawlspace
(Typical foundation & framing conversion diagram available—see order form.)

BLUEPRINT PRICE CODE:	D

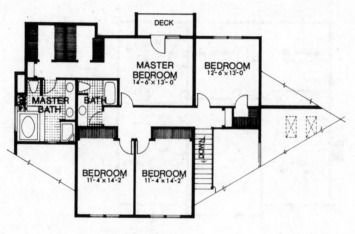

UPPER FLOOR

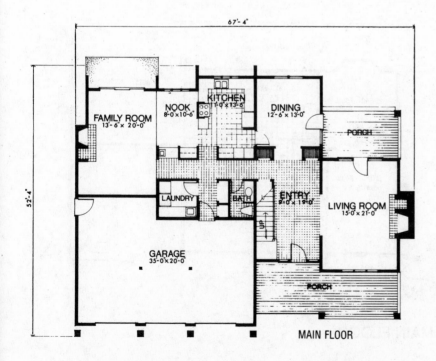

MAIN FLOOR

Room to Grow in the 90's

- Front and rear porches add a comforting touch to this lovely two-story.
- Spacious formal living and informal family rooms each feature focal point fireplaces.
- Attributes include a U-shaped kitchen sandwiched between a formal dining room and a nook for casual meals.
- Upper level features a master bedroom with private deck, "his 'n hers" closets, and a large bath.

Plans H-3745-1 & -1A

Bedrooms: 4	Baths: 2½
Space:	
Upper floor:	1,344 sq. ft.
Main floor:	1,680 sq. ft.
Total living area:	**3,024 sq. ft.**
Basement:	approx. 1,680 sq. ft.
Garage:	700 sq. ft.
Porches:	446 sq. ft.
Exterior Wall Framing:	2x6

Foundation options:
Standard basement (Plan H-3745-1).
Crawlspace (Plan H-3745-1A).
(Foundation & framing conversion diagram available — see order form.)

Blueprint Price Code:	E

Elegant Two-Story

- This elegant two-story home is available with a durable brick or stucco exterior.
- Past the columned entry is an oversized foyer with dual coat closets and a dramatic curved stairway.
- Double doors open to a study or extra bedroom. In the opposite direction are the formal living areas. The living room features a fireplace; the adjoining dining room boasts a lovely bay window.
- The island kitchen and breakfast room form a comfortable and spacious informal setting with the family room. The sunken family room offers a vaulted ceiling and a second fireplace. Rear doors access the outdoor spaces.
- The handy main-floor laundry room is located near the garage entrance.
- The upper floor houses four nice-sized bedrooms and two full baths, each with dual dressing areas. The master bath also includes a garden tub and a separate shower.

Plan CH-280-A

Bedrooms: 4	Baths: 2½
Living Area:	
Upper floor	1,262 sq. ft.
Main floor	1,797 sq. ft.
Total Living Area:	**3,059 sq. ft.**
Basement	1,797 sq. ft.
Garage	462 sq. ft.
Exterior Wall Framing:	2x4

Foundation Options:
Daylight basement
Standard basement
Crawlspace
(Typical foundation & framing conversion diagram available—see order form.)

BLUEPRINT PRICE CODE: E

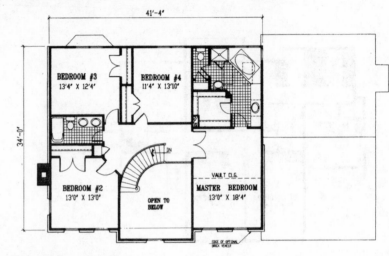

UPPER FLOOR

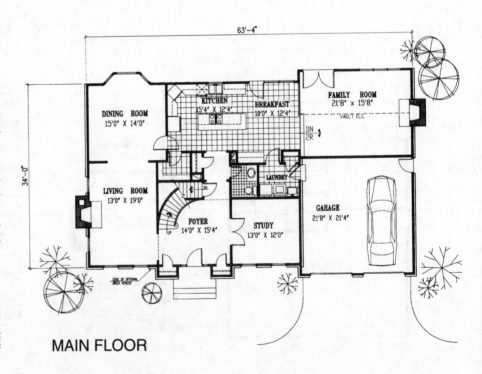

MAIN FLOOR

BEDROOM 12'-0"x17'-6"

DRESS

BATH

CLOSET

RAIL

STORAGE 18'-0"x10'-4"

DN

STOR

BEDROOM 13'-0"x11'-10"

BEDROOM 12'-8"x11'-10"

CLOSET

SITTING 8'-0"x10'-8"

CLOSET

28'-6"

65'-6"

UPPER FLOOR

Bay Windows Enhance a Country Home

A large master bedroom suite includes a deluxe bath with separate shower, garden tub, twin vanities and two large walk-in closets. Kitchen has direct access to both the breakfast nook and the dining room, which features a large bay window. Three bedrooms, a sitting area and storage or bonus room combine to form the second level.

First floor: 2,005 sq. ft.

Second floor: 1,063 sq. ft.

Total living area: 3,068 sq. ft.
(Not counting basement or garage)

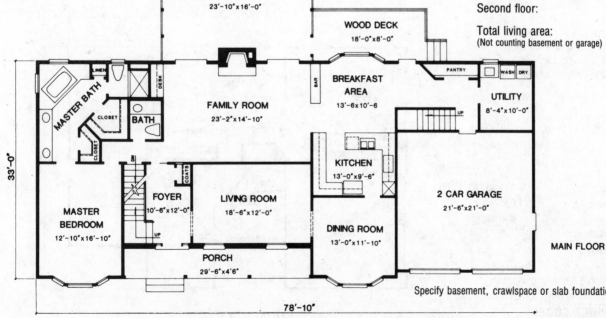

SCREENED PORCH 23'-10"x16'-0"

WOOD DECK 18'-0"x8'-0"

MASTER BATH

LINEN

DESK

BAR

BREAKFAST AREA 13'-6x10'-6

PANTRY

WASH **DRY**

UTILITY 8'-4"x10'-0"

CLOSET

BATH

FAMILY ROOM 23'-2"x14'-10"

UP

CLOSET

DN

COATS

KITCHEN 13'-0"x9'-6"

FOYER 10'-6"x12'-0"

LIVING ROOM 18'-6"x12'-0"

2 CAR GARAGE 21'-6"x21'-0"

MASTER BEDROOM 12'-10"x16'-10"

UP

DINING ROOM 13'-0"x11'-10"

PORCH 29'-6"x4'-6"

MAIN FLOOR

33'-0"

78'-10"

Specify basement, crawlspace or slab foundation.

Large and Luxurious

- This two-story home offers large, luxurious living areas and a variety of options to tailor the home to your needs.
- The oversized, two-story foyer shows off an angled stairway and, to the right, elegant formal living spaces.
- A den or fifth bedroom sits to the left of the foyer and could be accessed through French doors. The hall bath can be privately entered from the den.
- The family will enjoy the huge vaulted family room, which is separated from the breakfast room and kitchen by an open railing. The sunken family room offers a wet bar and a warm fireplace.
- The gourmet kitchen boasts a cooktop island with a handy serving bar and a walk-in pantry.
- The upper floor has a convenient laundry room and space for four bedrooms. The fourth bedroom could serve as a playroom or a hobby room.

Plan FB-3071

Bedrooms: 3-5	Baths: 4
Living Area:	
Upper floor	1,419 sq. ft.
Main floor	1,652 sq. ft.
Total Living Area:	**3,071 sq. ft.**
Daylight basement	1,652 sq. ft.
Garage	456 sq. ft.
Exterior Wall Framing:	2x4

Foundation Options:

Daylight basement

(Typical foundation & framing conversion diagram available—see order form.)

BLUEPRINT PRICE CODE:	E

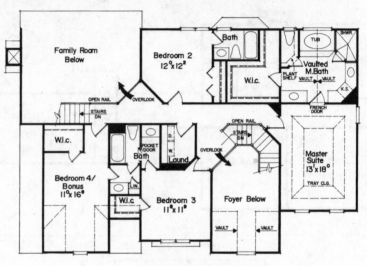

UPPER FLOOR

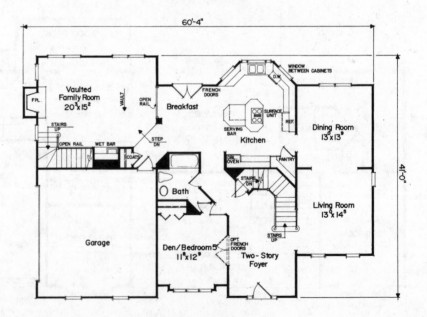

MAIN FLOOR

Impressive Home for Sloping Lot

PLAN Q-3080-1A
WITHOUT BASEMENT
(SLAB-ON-GRADE FOUNDATION)

First floor:	1,505 sq. ft.
Second floor:	1,575 sq. ft.
Total living area:	3,080 sq. ft.
(Not counting garage)	

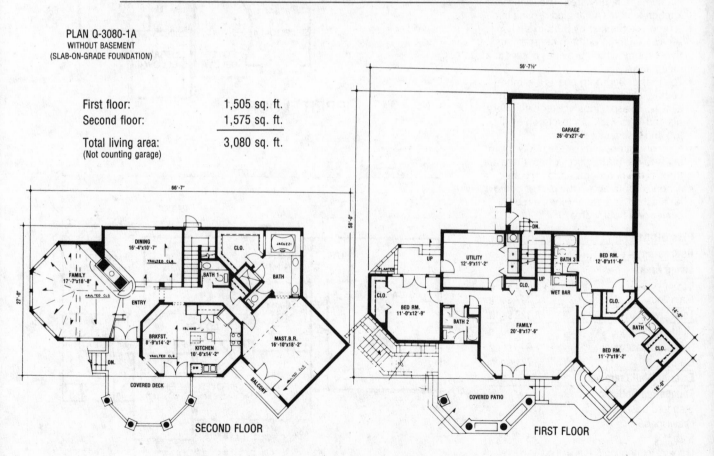

SECOND FLOOR

FIRST FLOOR

NOTE: This house was designed for a lot sloping down in the direction of the arrow.

Blueprint Price Code E

Plan Q-3080-1A

Tall Two-Story

- This gorgeous two-story is highlighted by a spectacular curved staircase leading to a balcony that overlooks the living room and the foyer.
- Off of the foyer is an open two-story-high library for reading or study.
- A formal dining room opposite the library opens to the fabulous airy kitchen and family area. The island kitchen features an angled serving bar.
- A fireplace flanked by built-in shelving serves as a focal point in the spacious living room, which provides access to a nice patio.
- The master bedroom boasts a gambrel ceiling, a sunny bay window and patio access. The spacious master bath offers his-and-hers walk-in closets, an oval tub and a separate shower.
- A second stairway near the utility room leads to the upper floor, where there are three more bedrooms and two baths.
- A bonus room above the garage could be finished as a game room, a media center or a hobby area.

Plan DD-3125

Bedrooms: 4+	Baths: 3½
Living Area:	
Upper floor	982 sq. ft.
Main floor	2,147 sq. ft.
Total Living Area:	**3,129 sq. ft.**
Unfinished Bonus	196 sq. ft.
Standard basement	1,996 sq. ft.
Garage	771 sq. ft.
Exterior Wall Framing:	2x4

Foundation Options:

Standard basement
Crawlspace
Slab
(Typical foundation & framing conversion diagram available—see order form.)

BLUEPRINT PRICE CODE:	E

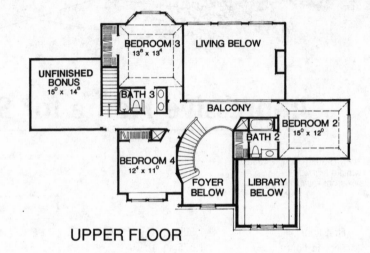

UPPER FLOOR

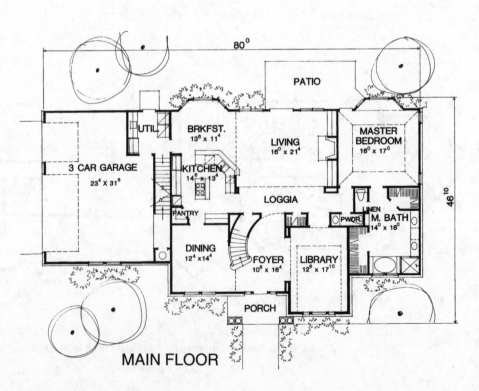

MAIN FLOOR

TO ORDER THIS BLUEPRINT,
CALL TOLL-FREE 1-800-547-5570

Plan DD-3125

PRICES AND DETAILS
ON PAGES 12-15

Stunning Country-Style

- A lovely front porch that encases bay windows provides a friendly welcome to this stunning country-style home.
- Inside, the main living areas revolve around the large country kitchen and dinette, complete with island worktop, a roomy built-in desk and access to the backyard deck.
- A raised-hearth fireplace, French doors, and a cathedral ceiling highlight the casual setting of the family room.
- The formal dining room is open to the living room and features an inviting window seat and a tray ceiling. A French door in the bay-windowed living room opens to the relaxing porch. A den and a large laundry area/mud room complete the main floor.
- The upper floor showcases a super master suite with a bay window, a tray ceiling, two walk-in closets and a private bath with a garden tub.
- Three additional bedrooms share a full bath designed for multiple users.

Plan A-538-R

Bedrooms: 4+	Baths: 2½
Living Area:	
Upper floor:	1,325 sq. ft.
Main floor:	1,728 sq. ft.
Total Living Area:	**3,053 sq. ft.**
Garage:	576 sq. ft.
Basement:	1,728 sq. ft.
Exterior Wall Framing:	2x4
Foundation options:	

Standard Basement
(Foundation & framing conversion diagram available – see order form.)

BLUEPRINT PRICE CODE:	E

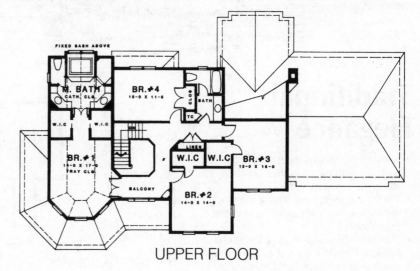

UPPER FLOOR

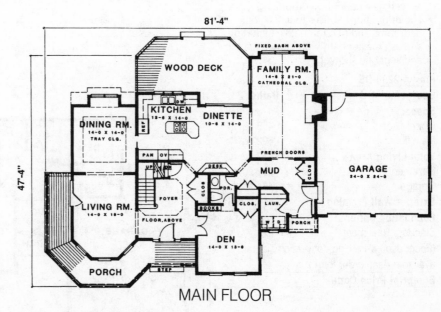

MAIN FLOOR

TO ORDER THIS BLUEPRINT,
CALL TOLL-FREE 1-800-547-5570

Plan A-538-R

PRICES AND DETAILS
ON PAGES 12-15

143

Traditional Elegance

- A stately traditional exterior is enhanced by brick with quoin corner details and a stunning two-story entry.
- The formal living and dining rooms flank the entry foyer at the front of the main floor.
- The informal living areas of the island kitchen, dinette bay, and sunken family room with fireplace face the rear yard.
- The main floor also includes a handy mud room with laundry and powder room accessible from a second entrance as well as a den/5th bedroom.
- The upper floor houses four spacious bedrooms and two full baths, including a lavish master bath with corner spa tub and separate shower.

Plan A-2230-DS

Bedrooms: 4-5	Baths: 2 ½
Space:	
Upper floor	1,455 sq. ft.
Main floor	1,692 sq. ft.
Total Living Area	**3,147 sq. ft.**
Basement	1,692 sq. ft.
Garage	484 sq. ft.
Exterior Wall Framing	**2x6**
Foundation options:	
Standard Basement	
(Foundation & framing conversion diagram available—see order form.)	
Blueprint Price Code	**E**

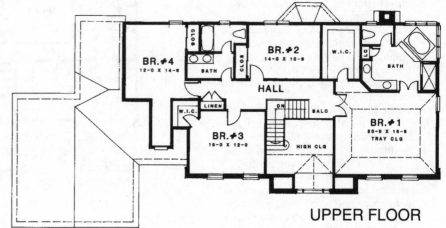

UPPER FLOOR

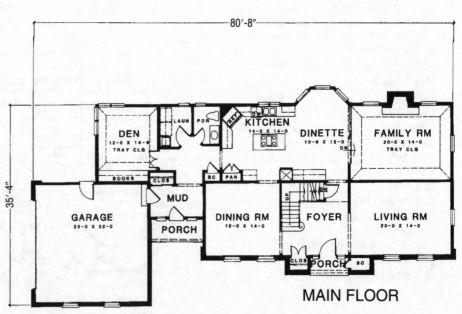

MAIN FLOOR

Plan A-2230-DS

PRICES AND DETAILS
ON PAGES 12-15

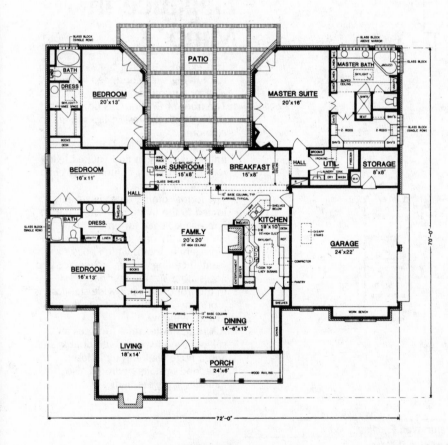

PLAN E-3102
WITHOUT BASEMENT

Exterior walls are 2x6 construction.
Specify crawlspace or slab foundation.

Ranch-Style Designed for Entertaining

- This all-brick home offers both formal living and dining rooms.
- The family room is large scale with 13' ceilings, formal fireplace and an entertainment center. An adjoining sun room reveals a tucked away wet bar.
- The master suite has private patio access and its own fireplace. An adjoining bath offers abundant closet and linen storage, a separate shower and garden tub with glass block walls.
- The home contains three additional bedrooms and two baths. Each bath has glass block above the tubs and separate dressing rooms.
- The master bedroom ceiling is sloped to 14' high. Both the sun room and the breakfast room have sloped ceilings with skylights. Typical ceiling heights are 9'.
- The home is energy efficient.

Heated area:	3,158 sq. ft.
Unheated area:	767 sq. ft.
Total area:	3,925 sq. ft.

TO ORDER THIS BLUEPRINT,
CALL TOLL-FREE 1-800-547-5570

Blueprint Price Code E
Plan E-3102

PRICES AND DETAILS
ON PAGES 12-15

145

Designed with Elegance in Mind

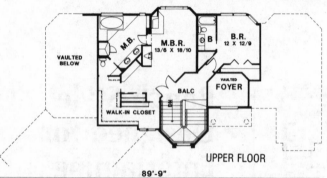

UPPER FLOOR

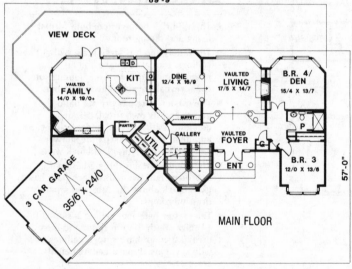

89'-9"

57'-0"

MAIN FLOOR

- This expansive home boasts 3,220 sq. ft. of living space designed with elegance in mind.
- The front of the home is finished in stucco, with the rest in lap siding for economy.
- The vaulted foyer leads directly into an impressive sunken and vaulted living room, guarded by columns that echo the exterior treatment.
- The formal dining room is visually joined to the living room to make an impressive space for entertaining.
- An unusually fine kitchen opens to a large family room, which boasts a vaulted ceiling, a corner fireplace and access to a sizable rear deck.
- In the front, the extra-wide staircase is a primary attraction, with its dramatic feature window.
- A terrific master suite includes a splendid master bath with double sinks and a huge walk-through closet.
- A second upstairs bedroom also includes a private bath.

Plan LRD-11388

Bedrooms: 3-4	Baths: 3

Living Area:

Upper floor:	1,095 sq. ft.
Main floor	2,125 sq. ft.
Total Living Area:	**3,220 sq. ft.**
Standard basement	2,125 sq. ft.
Garage	802 sq. ft.

Exterior Wall Framing:	2x6

Foundation Options:
Standard basement
Crawlspace
Slab
(Typical foundation & framing conversion diagram available—see order form.)

BLUEPRINT PRICE CODE: E

Graceful Elegance

This graceful French country home with ageless brick veneer, corner quoins, and interesting roofline typifies elegance.

Double front doors welcome visitors to a foyer accentuated by beautiful spiral stairs and case openings leading to the living area. The centrally located kitchen is especially well designed with modern appliances, triple sinks and handy garbage compactor. The kitchen flows together with the nook and dining room for easy traffic flow.

Everything is big in the family room: the windows, the raised hearth fireplace and the room itself. Bay windows flanking the main entry delightfully detail the study and the living room.

Four bedrooms are located on the second floor, allowing extra privacy from the rest of the living area. The master bedroom has excellent space usage with walk-in closet and a private bath. A double bowl vanity is included in the second bath for the three other bedrooms. Linen and closet space is plentiful.

The double garage has side entrance and immediate access to the laundry area, which also includes abundant cabinetry. Exterior walls, behind the brick facade, are framed with 2x6 studs for energy efficiency. Basement plan included.

First floor:	1,884 sq. ft.
Second floor:	1,348 sq. ft.
Total living area:	3,232 sq. ft.

(Not counting basement or garage)

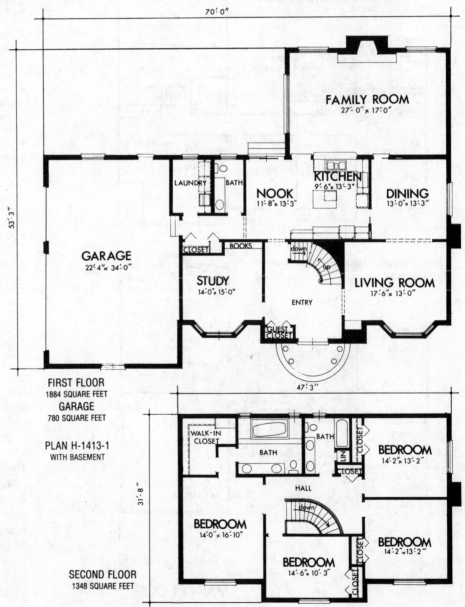

FIRST FLOOR
1884 SQUARE FEET
GARAGE
780 SQUARE FEET

PLAN H-1413-1
WITH BASEMENT

SECOND FLOOR
1348 SQUARE FEET

TO ORDER THIS BLUEPRINT,
CALL TOLL-FREE 1-800-547-5570

Blueprint Price Code E
Plan H-1413-1

PRICES AND DETAILS
ON PAGES 12-15

147

UPPER FLOOR

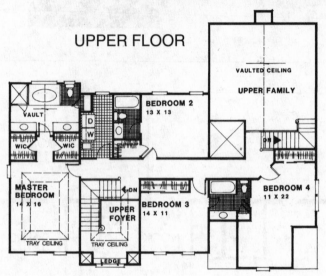

VAULTED CEILING

UPPER FAMILY

VAULT

D W

BEDROOM 2
13 X 13

WIC WIC

MASTER BEDROOM
14 X 16

UPPER FOYER

BEDROOM 3
14 X 11

DN

BEDROOM 4
11 X 22

TRAY CEILING

TRAY CEILING

LEDGE

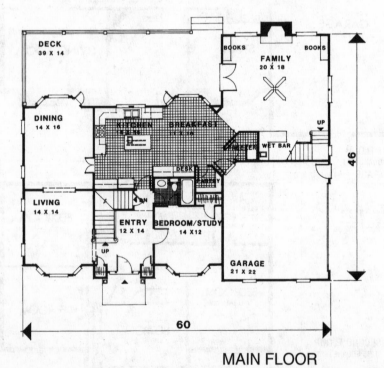

DECK
39 X 14

BOOKS

FAMILY
20 X 18

BOOKS

DINING
14 X 16

KITCHEN

BREAKFAST

UP

WET BAR

DESK

PANTRY

LIVING
14 X 14

ENTRY
12 X 14

BEDROOM/STUDY
14 X12

DN

UP

GARAGE
21 X 22

60

46

MAIN FLOOR

European Enticement

- This exciting European stucco home exudes elegance with its stunning entry, brick steps, copper-topped bay windows and shuttered windows.
- The dramatic two-story foyer opens to a lovely bayed study or fifth bedroom on one side. Opposite is the formal living room, also with a front bay.
- To the rear is an equally spacious dining room, fitting for formal occasions. Double doors access the spacious kitchen and breakfast room where you'll find a handy work island, a built-in desk, a walk-in pantry and a separate freezer room.
- Access to the huge rear deck is possible from the dining room, breakfast room and family room. The family room also offers a fireplace, an L-shaped wet bar, built-in bookcases and an alternate stairway to the upper floor.
- The upper floor houses four bedrooms, two with private baths. An oversized laundry room is conveniently located on this floor as well.

Plan APS-3203	
Bedrooms: 4-5	**Baths:** 4
Living Area:	
Upper floor	1,525 sq. ft.
Main floor	1,735 sq. ft.
Total Living Area:	**3,260 sq. ft.**
Partial daylight basement	1,170 sq. ft.
Garage	462 sq. ft.
Exterior Wall Framing:	2x4
Foundation Options:	
Partial daylight basement	
(Typical foundation & framing conversion diagram available—see order form.)	
BLUEPRINT PRICE CODE:	**E**

Plan APS-3203

PRICES AND DETAILS
ON PAGES 12-15

Time-Tested Traditional Design

- The traditional exterior of this home encloses an up-to-date, interesting interior.
- The unique family room/nook/kitchen combination includes a fireplace and an island cooktop/snack bar.
- The sumptuous master bedroom suite features a deluxe bath and a huge walk-in closet.
- The bonus room above the garage offers plenty of space for a home office, a playroom or an extra bedroom.
- The entire main floor boasts 9-ft. ceilings, with standard 8-ft. ceilings on the upper floor.

Plan CDG-2012

Bedrooms: 4	Baths: 2 full, 2 half
Living Area:	
Upper floor	1,435 sq. ft.
Main floor	1,525 sq. ft.
Bonus room	348 sq. ft.
Total Living Area:	**3,308 sq. ft.**
Partial daylight basement	1,092 sq. ft.
Garage	620 sq. ft.
Exterior Wall Framing:	2x6

Foundation Options:
Partial daylight basement
Crawlspace
(Typical foundation & framing conversion diagram available—see order form.)

BLUEPRINT PRICE CODE: E

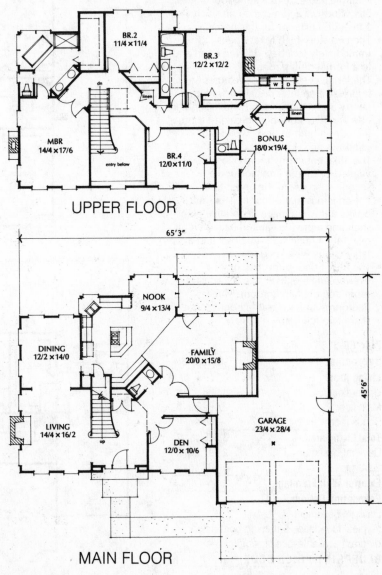

UPPER FLOOR

MAIN FLOOR

TO ORDER THIS BLUEPRINT,
CALL TOLL-FREE 1-800-547-5570

Plan CDG-2012

PRICES AND DETAILS
ON PAGES 12-15
149

Unique Kitchen/ Breakfast Area

- Multiple gables, captivating roof angles, bay windows and a stucco finish create a beautiful exterior for this home.
- The two-story-high foyer opens immediately to a bayed living room and to a formal dining room.
- The large, central kitchen features an impressive counter design, a walk-in pantry and a range island with a serving bar. The two-story-high breakfast room includes a built-in desk, wonderful windows and outdoor access.
- The adjacent family room offers a vaulted ceiling, a fireplace and a second staircase to the upper floor.
- The spacious main-floor master suite boasts a tray ceiling, a decorative plant shelf and a private vaulted bath with an oval tub, a huge walk-in closet and a large vanity with knee space.
- The upper floor offers balconies overlooking the foyer, the breakfast room and the family room. Three bedrooms and a versatile bonus room share two full baths.

Plan FB-3135

Bedrooms: 4+	Baths: 3½
Living Area:	
Upper floor	1,038 sq. ft.
Main floor	2,097 sq. ft.
Bonus room	240 sq. ft.
Total Living Area:	**3,375 sq. ft.**
Daylight basement	2,097 sq. ft.
Garage	462 sq. ft.
Exterior Wall Framing:	2x4

Foundation Options:

Daylight basement
(Typical foundation & framing conversion diagram available–see order form.)

BLUEPRINT PRICE CODE: E

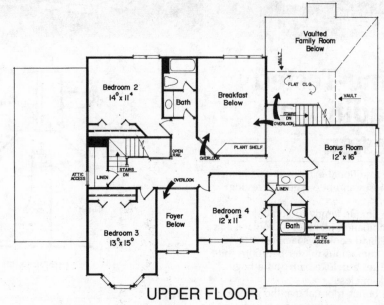

UPPER FLOOR

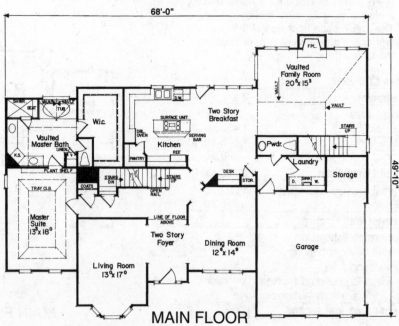

MAIN FLOOR

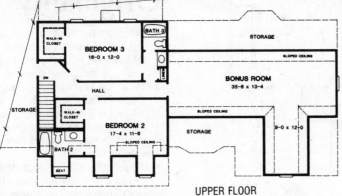

UPPER FLOOR

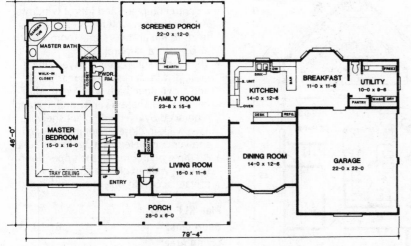

MAIN FLOOR

Deluxe Main-Floor Master Suite

- Traditional-style exterior with modern floor plan. Dormers and stone add curb appeal to this home.
- Formal entry with staircase leads to formal living or large family room.
- Large kitchen is conveniently located between formal dining room and secluded breakfast nook with bay window.
- Private master suite has tray ceiling and walk-in closet. Master bath has corner tub, shower, and dual vanities.
- Large screened porch off family room is perfect for outdoor living.
- Large utility room with pantry and toilet are conveniently located off the garage.
- Second floor features two large bedrooms with walk-in closets and two full baths.
- Optional bonus room (624 sq. ft.) can be finished as a large game room, bedroom, office, etc.

Plan C-8915

Bedrooms: 3	Baths: 3½

Space:

Upper floor:	832 sq. ft.
Main floor:	1,927 sq. ft.
Bonus area:	624 sq. ft.
Total living area:	**3,383 sq. ft.**
Basement:	1,674 sq. ft.
Garage:	484 sq. ft.

Exterior Wall Framing:	2x4

Ceiling Heights:

First floor:	9'
Second floor:	8'

Foundation options:
Daylight basement.
Crawlspace.
(Foundation & framing conversion diagram available — see order form.)

Blueprint Price Code:	E

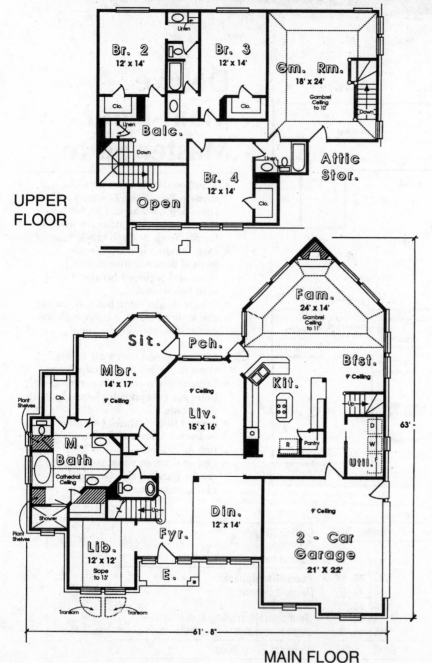

UPPER FLOOR

Br. 2
12' x 14'

Br. 3
12' x 14'

Gm. Rm.
18' x 24'
Gambrel Ceiling to 10'

Linen

Clo.

Clo.

Balc.

Linen

Down

Br. 4
12' x 14'

Open

Clo.

Linen

Attic Stor.

MAIN FLOOR

Sit.

Pch.

Fam.
24' x 14'
Gambrel Ceiling to 11'

Bfst.
9' Ceiling

Mbr.
14' x 17'
9' Ceiling

Kit.

Plant Shelves

Clo.

Liv.
15' x 16'

9' Ceiling

Up

M. Bath
Cathedral Ceiling

Pantry

D

W

Utii.

Shower

Plant Shelves

Up

Din.
12' x 14'

9' Ceiling

Lib.
12' x 12'
Slope to 13'

Fyr.

E.

2 - Car Garage
21' X 22'

Transom

Transom

61' - 8"

63'

Luxury and Originality

- Rich brick detailing, arched windows and a combination of hipped and gabled roofs mark the exterior of this luxurious traditional home.
- Inside, the keynotes are a stunningly unusual family room and an un-believable first-floor master suite.
- The two-story foyer focuses on the formal living and dining rooms and the winding staircase.
- The gourmet kitchen faces the spectacular triangular-shaped family room, highlighted by a gambrel ceiling, a central fireplace and lots of windows. Another stairway off the breakfast area leads to the upstairs game room, which also sports a gambrel ceiling.
- The master suite offers a bayed sitting area, private access to the rear porch and a dynamite bath with a cathedral ceiling, a U-shaped vanity and a spa tub embraced by overhead plant shelves. Two walk-in closets and an oversized shower complete this magnificent suite.
- All three bedrooms on the upper floor include walk-in closets and enjoy private access to one of two full baths.

Plan KLF-9217	
Bedrooms: 4	**Baths:** 3½
Living Area:	
Upper floor	1,194 sq. ft.
Main floor	2,209 sq. ft.
Total Living Area:	**3,403 sq. ft.**
Garage	519 sq. ft.
Exterior Wall Framing:	2x4
Foundation Options:	
Slab	
(Typical foundation & framing conversion diagram available—see order form.)	
BLUEPRINT PRICE CODE:	E

TO ORDER THIS BLUEPRINT, CALL TOLL-FREE 1-800-547-5570

Plan KLF-9217

PRICES AND DETAILS ON PAGES 12-15

Master Suite Showpiece

- The traditional exterior of this upscale home features arched windows accented by decorative keystones.
- Arches also embellish the entrance to the formal dining room, while elegant French doors in the formal living room open to a delightful porch.
- The heartbeat of the home is the vaulted family room, the octagonal breakfast nook and the gourmet kitchen. This open area hosts many built-ins, including bookshelves, a wet bar, a plant ledge and a serving bar.
- Two separate stairways lead to the upper floor, where a balcony hall overlooks the family room and the foyer.
- The real showpiece is the marvelous master suite, featuring a two-sided fireplace, built-in bookshelves and a vaulted sitting room. The plush bath adjoins a huge walk-in closet.
- The two corner bedrooms have private access to a full bath, while the central bedroom enjoys a bath of its own.

Plan FB-5051-MART

Bedrooms: 4+	Baths: 4
Living Area:	
Upper floor	1,677 sq. ft.
Main floor	1,851 sq. ft.
Total Living Area:	**3,528 sq. ft.**
Daylight basement	1,851 sq. ft.
Garage	455 sq. ft.
Exterior Wall Framing:	2x4

Foundation Options:

Daylight basement
(Typical foundation & framing conversion diagram available—see order form.)

BLUEPRINT PRICE CODE: F

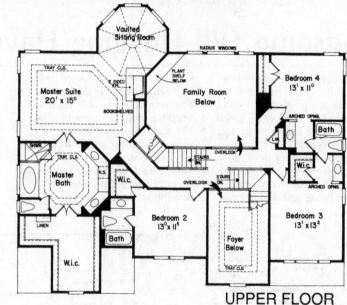

UPPER FLOOR

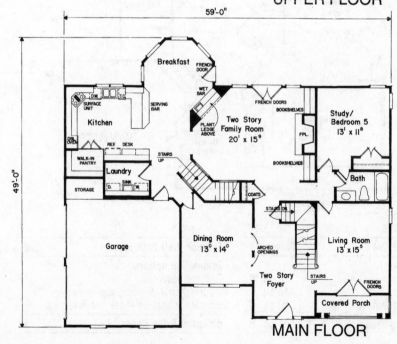

MAIN FLOOR

Handsome Hill-Hugging Haven

- Multiple octagonal rooms allow this dramatic home to take full advantage of surrounding views.
- A dazzling two-story entry greets guests from the three-car garage motor courtyard.
- Once inside the front door, a soaring dome ceiling catches the eye past the octagonal stairway.
- A sunken living and dining room

with cathedral and domed ceiling face out to the rear deck and views.
- The octagonal island kitchen and breakfast nook are sure to please.
- The main floor den features a second fireplace and front-facing window seat.
- The entire second floor houses the master bedroom suite with a sensational master bath.

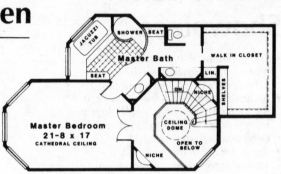

UPPER FLOOR

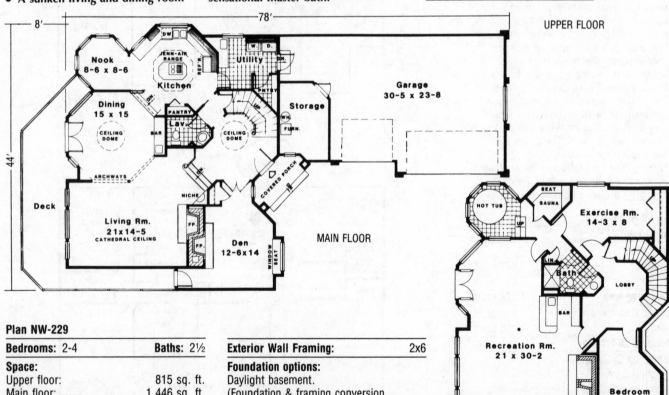

MAIN FLOOR

BASEMENT

Plan NW-229

Bedrooms: 2-4	Baths: 2½

Space:		Exterior Wall Framing:	2x6
Upper floor:	815 sq. ft.	**Foundation options:**	
Main floor:	1,446 sq. ft.	Daylight basement.	
Daylight basement:	1,330 sq. ft.	(Foundation & framing conversion	
		diagram available — see order form.)	
Total living area:	**3,591 sq. ft.**	**Blueprint Price Code:**	F

TO ORDER THIS BLUEPRINT,
CALL TOLL-FREE 1-800-547-5570

Plan NW-229

PRICES AND DETAILS
ON PAGES 12-15

Elegant Arches

- Gracious arched windows and entry portico create a rhythm and style on this brick-clad exterior.
- An elegant curved staircase with balcony bridge overhead lend interest to the raised entry foyer.
- Two steps down to the left of the foyer lies the cathedral — vaulted living room with fireplace and formal dining room defined with column separation.
- The quiet main floor master wing features another bay window, coved ceiling, walk-in closets, and well-planned private bath.
- The island kitchen overlooks the bay-windowed breakfast wall of the adjacent family room.

Plan DD-3639

Bedrooms: 4 +	**Baths:** 3½

Space:	
Upper floor:	868 sq. ft.
Main floor:	2,771 sq. ft.

Total living area:	3,639 sq. ft.
Basement:	2,771 sq. ft.
Garage:	approx. 790 sq. ft.

Exterior Wall Framing:	2x4

Ceiling Heights:	
Upper floor:	8'
Main floor:	9'

Foundation options:
Standard basement
Crawlspace
Slab
(Foundation & framing conversion diagram available — see order form.)

Blueprint Price Code:	F

UPPER FLOOR

BEDROOM 3
17'0" X 12'5"

FAMILY BELOW

BALCONY

BEDROOM 4
13'4" X 12'0"

BEDROOM 2
13'0" X 14'0"

FOYER BELOW

MAIN FLOOR

85'-0"

54'-8"

DECK

BREAKFAST
17'0" X 11'4"

UTILITY

FAMILY ROOM
26'0" X 16'0"

MASTER BEDROOM
15'0" X 20'0"

KITCHEN
17'0" X 12'0"

3 CAR GARAGE

POWDER

HALL

DINING ROOM
15'0" X 12'0"

STUDY
13'0" X 16'0"

MASTER BATH

FOYER

LIVING ROOM
17'0" X 18'0"

PORCH

TO ORDER THIS BLUEPRINT,
CALL TOLL-FREE 1-800-547-5570

Plan DD-3639

PRICES AND DETAILS
ON PAGES 12-15

155

Ultimate Elegance

- The gracious foyer of this distinguished Southern home reveals a sweeping staircase and a direct view to the pool environment beyond.
- The grand parlour at center has a two-story ceiling, high-fixed glass, ale bar and fireplace.
- Open to the equally large gathering room is the gourmet island kitchen with menu desk, walk-in pantry and octagonal morning room which offers a second route to the upper level.
- Bright and luxurious, the master suite features a convenient morning kitchen, sunny octagonal sitting area that overlooks the covered veranda and optional pool, and a lavish bath.
- Three bedroom suites are located off the circular staircase and hall·bridge that overlooks the parlour; a sunset deck adjoins two of them.

Plan EOF-3

Bedrooms: 4-5	Baths: 5 ½
Space:	
Upper floor	1,150 sq. ft.
Main floor	3,045 sq. ft.
Total Living Area	**4,195 sq. ft.**
Garage	814 sq. ft.
Exterior Wall Framing	2x6
Foundation options:	
Slab	
(Foundation & framing conversion diagram available—see order form.)	
Blueprint Price Code	**G**

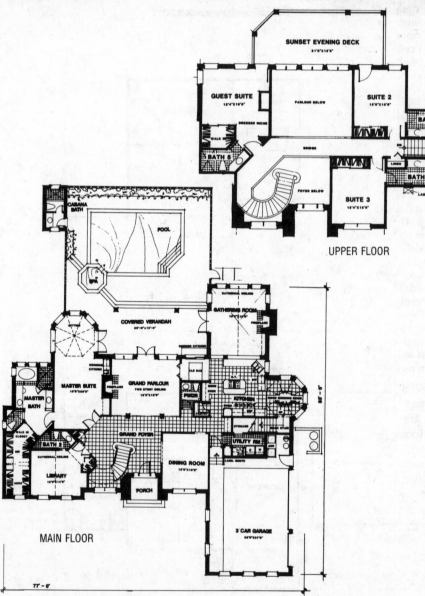

UPPER FLOOR

MAIN FLOOR

Plan EOF-3

Design Leaves out Nothing

- This design has it all, from the elegant detailing of the exterior to the exciting, luxurious spaces of the interior.
- High ceilings, large, open rooms and lots of glass are found throughout the home. Nearly all of the main living areas, as well as the master suite, overlook the veranda.
- Unusual features include a built-in ale bar in the formal dining room, an art niche in the Grand Room and a TV niche in the Gathering Room. The Gathering Room also features a fireplace framed by window seats, a wall of windows facing the backyard and a half-wall open to the morning room. The island kitchen is open to all of the main living areas.
- The delicious master suite includes a raised lounge, a three-sided fireplace and French doors that open to the veranda. The spiral stairs nearby lead to the "evening deck" above. The master bath boasts two walk-in closets, a sunken shower and a Roman tub.
- The upper floor hosts two complete suites and a loft, plus a vaulted bonus room reached via a separate stairway.

Plan EOF-61

Bedrooms: 3-5	Baths: 4½
Living Area:	
Upper floor	877 sq. ft.
Main floor	3,094 sq. ft.
Bonus room	280 sq. ft.
Total Living Area:	**4,251 sq. ft.**
Garage	774 sq. ft.
Exterior Wall Framing:	2x6

Foundation Options:

Slab

(Typical foundation & framing conversion diagram available—see order form.)

BLUEPRINT PRICE CODE:	**G**

UPPER FLOOR

MAIN FLOOR

Plan DD-4300-B

Bedrooms: 4	**Baths:** 4½

Space:

Upper floor	868 sq. ft.
Main floor	3,416 sq. ft.
Total Living Area	**4,284 sq. ft.**
Basement	3,416 sq. ft.
Garage	633 sq. ft.
Storage	approx. 50 sq. ft.
Exterior Wall Framing	2x4 or 2x6

Ceiling Heights:

Upper floor	9'
Main floor	10'

Foundation options:

Standard Basement
Crawlspace
Slab
(Foundation & framing conversion diagram available—see order form.)

Blueprint Price Code	**G**

Colonial Recall

- The symmetry, massing, materials, and colonnaded entry porch all recall the best of colonial design on this estate home.
- The formal dining and parlor rooms, each with high glass windows, flank the entry's graceful curved staircase.
- The informal living spaces are oriented to the rear greenspaces. They include a two-story volumed family room with fireplace, transom windows and an adjoining library room, as well as a large island kitchen with breakfast eating area.
- The main-floor master suite presses all the right buttons with its fireplace wall, his and her walk-in closets, and private bath with platform tub, separate shower, compartmented tub and double vanities.
  - The three additional bedrooms each boast full private baths.

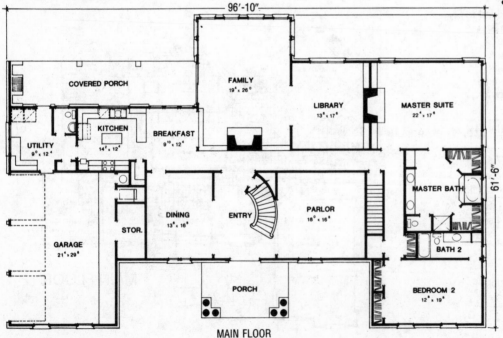

MAIN FLOOR

Plan DD-4300-B

PRICES AND DETAILS
ON PAGES 12-15

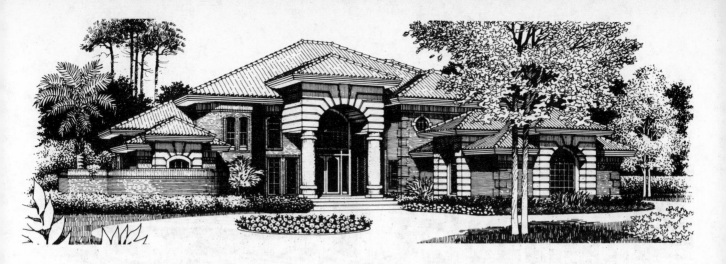

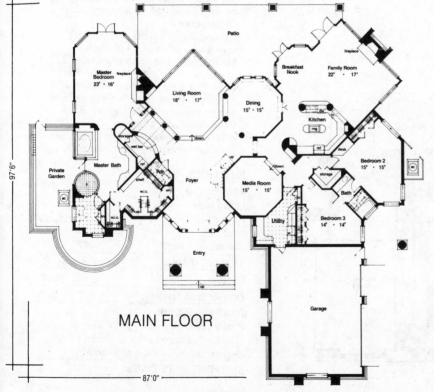

UPPER FLOOR

MAIN FLOOR

Plan HDS-90-819

Grand Style

- The grand style of this luxurious residence exudes elegance and grace.
- The gothic contemporary architecture draws the eye to a stately 2½-story entry portico.
- Equally stunning is the interior with its high, open spaces, interesting angles, coffered ceilings and dramatic columns.
- The formal spaces include an octagonal dining room and a huge sunken living room under corner window walls. A curved wet bar is a nice extra!
- The informal zone consists of an island kitchen with a snack bar, a sunken media room, a bayed breakfast nook and a spacious family room with patio access and an inviting fireplace.
- The elegant master suite is removed from the secondary bedrooms, which share a full bath. The master bedroom boasts a warming fireplace and an oversized bay with outdoor access. The master bath is surrounded by a private garden and features a step-up tub, a circular shower and a toilet room.
- Throughout the home, ceilings are at least 9 ft. high, making every room seem spacious.

Plan HDS-90-819	
Bedrooms: 4+	**Baths:** 3½
Living Area:	
Upper floor	765 sq. ft.
Main floor	3,770 sq. ft.
Total Living Area:	**4,535 sq. ft.**
Garage	750 sq. ft.
Exterior Wall Framing:	2x4
Foundation Options:	
Slab	
(Typical foundation & framing conversion diagram available—see order form.)	
BLUEPRINT PRICE CODE:	**G**

Elegance at Every Turn

- For a home that is truly outstanding in both beauty and space, this design is hard to beat!
- Elegance is found in every corner, from the spectacular curved stairways in the foyer to the luxurious master suite.
- The huge central living room features a vaulted ceiling, decorative entry columns and a dramatic fireplace.
- The gourmet kitchen and breakfast nook are hidden behind double doors. The kitchen has a cooktop island, a walk-in pantry and a snack counter. The octagon-shaped nook opens to the backyard and adjoins a large sunken family room.
- Up one flight of stairs is the master suite and a quiet den with built-in bookshelves. The master bedroom is entered through elegant double doors and offers a sunny sitting area and a skylighted private bath with an exciting garden tub, a separate shower and a toilet room with a bidet.
- A second stairway accesses two more bedrooms, each with a private bath.

UPPER FLOOR

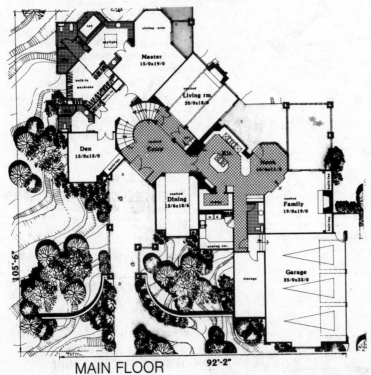

MAIN FLOOR   92'-2"

Plan R-4029

Plan R-4029	
Bedrooms: 3	**Baths:** 4½
Living Area:	
Upper floor	972 sq. ft.
Main floor	3,346 sq. ft.
Partial basement	233 sq. ft.
Total Living Area:	**4,551 sq. ft.**
Garage	825 sq. ft.
Exterior Wall Framing:	2x6
Foundation Options:	
Partial basement	
(Typical foundation & framing conversion diagram available—see order form.)	
BLUEPRINT PRICE CODE:	**G**

Plan R-4029

Charming Three-Bedroom

- A covered front porch and shuttered windows lend an authentic charm to this two-story home.
- The main-floor living areas are oriented around stairways that access the basement and the upper floor. The spacious family room shows off a dramatic centered fireplace and an array of surrounding windows. A French door opens to the backyard.
- The nice-sized kitchen is nestled between the sunny vaulted breakfast room and the formal dining room.
- A convenient main-floor laundry closet is neatly positioned off the breakfast room and near the garage entrance.
- The upper floor houses three bedrooms, including a large master bedroom with a tray ceiling, a huge walk-in closet and a private vaulted bath with an oval tub.

Plan FB-5013-LYNW

Bedrooms: 3	Baths: 2½
Living Area:	
Upper floor	681 sq. ft.
Main floor	771 sq. ft.
Total Living Area:	**1,452 sq. ft.**
Daylight basement	771 sq. ft.
Garage	420 sq. ft.
Storage	20 sq. ft.
Exterior Wall Framing:	2x4

Foundation Options:

Daylight basement
(Typical foundation & framing conversion diagram available—see order form.)

BLUEPRINT PRICE CODE: A

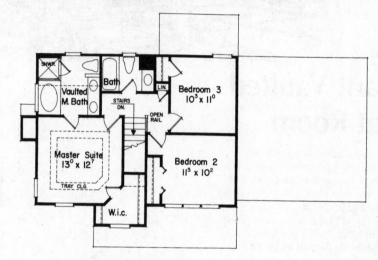

UPPER FLOOR

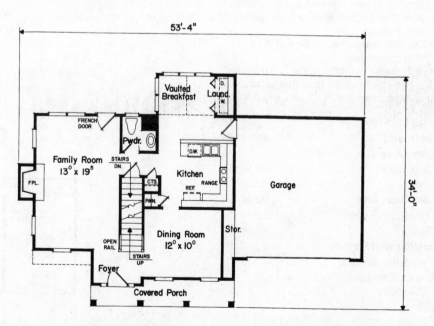

MAIN FLOOR

Elegant Vaulted Great Room

- This affordable home is equally appealing in the city or the country.
- The home is shown with an exterior of wood shingles, but lap siding is another possibility and is equally attractive.
- The open Great Room is the focal point of the floor plan. The raised-hearth fireplace extends the full height of the vaulted ceiling.
- A boxed-out dining room can be extended further to increase the dining area. The kitchen offers a large island snack counter.
- The two bedrooms on the first floor share a hall bath.
- A dramatic overlook to the Great Room is possible from the luxurious second-floor master suite.

Plan LRD-4692

Bedrooms: 3	Baths: 2
Living Area:	
Upper floor	380 sq. ft.
Main floor	1,082 sq. ft.
Total Living Area:	**1,462 sq. ft.**
Standard basement	1,082 sq. ft.
Garage	348 sq. ft.
Exterior Wall Framing:	2x6

Foundation Options:
Standard basement
Crawlspace
Slab
(Typical foundation & framing conversion diagram available—see order form.)

BLUEPRINT PRICE CODE:	A

UPPER FLOOR

MAIN FLOOR

Plan LRD-4692

FRONT VIEW

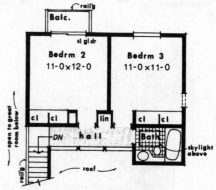

REAR VIEW

More for Less

- Big in function but small in square footage, this two-story passive-solar plan puts every inch of space to efficient use. It is also designed so that it can be built as a single-family unit or as part of a multiple-unit complex.
- The floor plan flows visually from its open foyer to its high-ceilinged Great Room, ending with a brilliant south-facing sun room that overlooks a backyard patio or terrace.
- The spacious Great Room boasts a high-efficiency fireplace flanked by glass, along with an informal dining area that opens to a side terrace.
- A handy laundry closet and a half-bath are located near the master suite and the entrance from the garage.
- The master bedroom includes a deluxe private bath and two roomy closets.
- Upstairs, a skylighted bath serves two more bedrooms, one with a private, rear-facing balcony.

Plan K-507-S

Bedrooms: 3	Baths: 2½
Living Area:	
Upper floor	397 sq. ft.
Main floor	915 sq. ft.
Sun room	162 sq. ft.
Total Living Area:	**1,474 sq. ft.**
Standard basement	915 sq. ft.
Garage	400 sq. ft.
Exterior Wall Framing:	2x4 or 2x6

Foundation Options:

Standard basement

Slab

(All plans can be built with your choice of foundation and framing. A generic conversion diagram is available. See order form.)

BLUEPRINT PRICE CODE: **A**

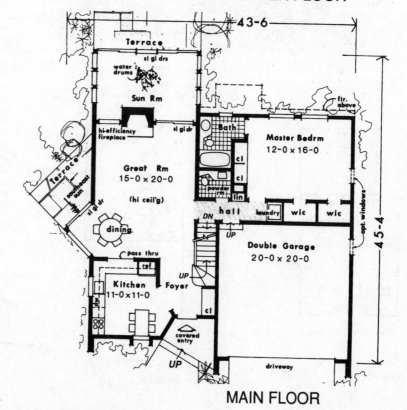

UPPER FLOOR

MAIN FLOOR

TO ORDER THIS BLUEPRINT,
CALL TOLL-FREE 1-800-547-5570

Plan K-507-S

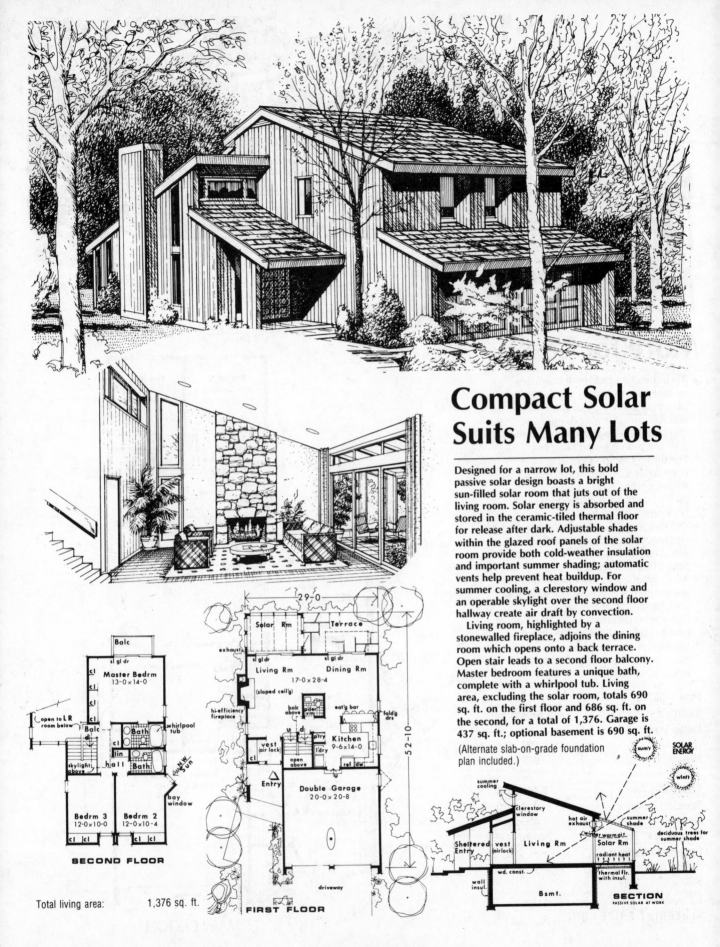

Compact Solar Suits Many Lots

Designed for a narrow lot, this bold passive solar design boasts a bright sun-filled solar room that juts out of the living room. Solar energy is absorbed and stored in the ceramic-tiled thermal floor for release after dark. Adjustable shades within the glazed roof panels of the solar room provide both cold-weather insulation and important summer shading; automatic vents help prevent heat buildup. For summer cooling, a clerestory window and an operable skylight over the second floor hallway create air draft by convection.

Living room, highlighted by a stonewalled fireplace, adjoins the dining room which opens onto a back terrace. Open stair leads to a second floor balcony. Master bedroom features a unique bath, complete with a whirlpool tub. Living area, excluding the solar room, totals 690 sq. ft. on the first floor and 686 sq. ft. on the second, for a total of 1,376. Garage is 437 sq. ft.; optional basement is 690 sq. ft.

(Alternate slab-on-grade foundation plan included.)

SOLAR ENERGY

Total living area: 1,376 sq. ft.

SECOND FLOOR

FIRST FLOOR

SECTION
PASSIVE SOLAR AT WORK

TRADITIONAL

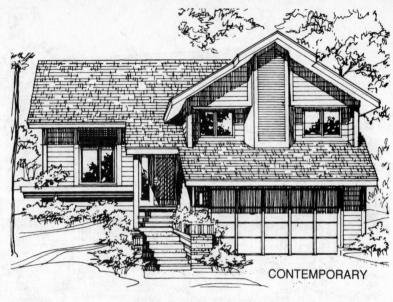

CONTEMPORARY

Split-Level with Flexibility

- Choose a contemporary or a traditional facade for this roomy split-level plan. Both options are included in the blueprints.
- A covered entry opens into the Great Room, which boasts a vaulted ceiling, a fireplace and access to a rear deck.
- The open kitchen offers a snack counter and a handy pantry. It also has a view of the Great Room as well as a window overlooking the charming plant shelf.
- The master bedroom features built-in shelves, a walk-in closet and a private bath. Two more bedrooms share another full bath.
- The bonus space on the lower level is ideal as a playroom, study, office or entertainment area. A convenient half-bath is nearby.

Plan B-8321

Bedrooms: 2+	Baths: 2½
Living Area:	
Main floor	1,096 sq. ft.
Lower floor	400 sq. ft.
Total Living Area:	**1,496 sq. ft.**
Partial basement	405 sq. ft.
Garage	400 sq. ft.
Exterior Wall Framing:	2x4

Foundation Options:

Partial basement

(All plans can be built with your choice of foundation and framing. A generic conversion diagram is available. See order form.)

BLUEPRINT PRICE CODE: A

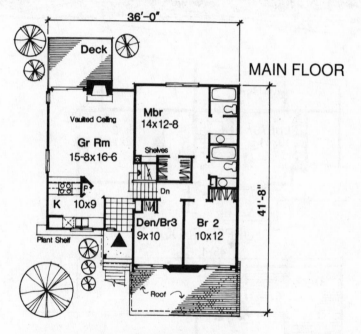

MAIN FLOOR

36'-0"

41'-8"

Deck

Vaulted Ceiling

Mbr 14x12-8

Gr Rm 15-8x16-6

Shelves

K 10x9

Plant Shelf

Dn

Den/Br3 9x10

Br 2 10x12

Roof

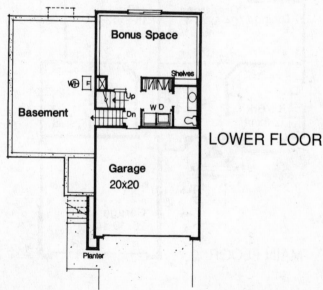

LOWER FLOOR

Bonus Space

Shelves

Basement

Up

Dn

WD

Garage 20x20

Planter

UPPER FLOOR

Loft/Br 3
10x11-6

Br 2
12x11-6

dn

open to below

MAIN FLOOR

45'-4"

46'-0"

Deck

Dining

Greatroom
24-8x13-4
vaulted

MBr
15-8x13-4
vaulted

Kit/Brk
12-8x14

up   dn

Garage
20x19-4

A Lot to Like

- An exciting assortment of features gives this modest-sized design the volume and impact of a much larger home.
- The highly detailed, custom-looking exterior wraps this handsome package.
- The big foyer opens to a charming bayed breakfast area and highly organized kitchen.
- A balconied stairway overlooks the vaulted Great Room and dining area. The Great Room enjoys a dramatic fireplace and view of the outdoors through a corner window wall. You can access the rear deck through sliders in the dining area.
- Adding to the appeal of the home is a luxurious vaulted master bedroom on the main level. The master bath features a large walk-in closet, a windowed corner tub and a separate shower.
- Another full bath and room for two additional bedrooms are provided on the upper level.

Plan B-917

Bedrooms: 2-3	Baths: 2½
Living Area:	
Upper floor	460 sq. ft.
Main floor	1,105 sq. ft.
Total Living Area:	**1,565 sq. ft.**
Standard basement	1,105 sq. ft.
Garage	387 sq. ft.
Exterior Wall Framing:	2x4

Foundation Options:
Standard basement
(Typical foundation & framing conversion diagram available—see order form.)

BLUEPRINT PRICE CODE:	B

Panoramic Prow View

- A glass-filled prow gable design is almost as spectacular as the panoramic view from inside. The two-story window-wall floods the living room with light and views.
- The open-feeling corner kitchen has the right angle to enjoy the dining room and the family room, including views of the front and rear decks.
- Two main level bedrooms share a full bath.
- The entire upper floor is a private master bedroom suite with large bath, dressing area and balcony opening to the two-story glass wall, a real "good morning" view.

Plan NW-196

Bedrooms: 3	Baths: 2

Space:	
Upper floor	394 sq. ft.
Main floor:	1,317 sq. ft.

Total living area:	1,711 sq. ft.

Exterior Wall Framing:	2x6

Foundation options:
Crawlspace.
(Foundation & framing conversion diagram available — see order form.)

Blueprint Price Code:	B

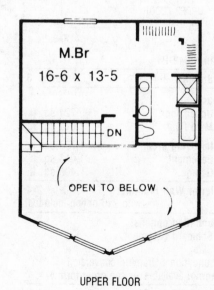

MAIN FLOOR

UPPER FLOOR

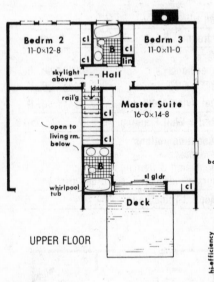

UPPER FLOOR

Plan K-649-P

Bedrooms: 3-4	Baths: 3

Space:

Upper floor:	724 sq. ft.
Main floor:	1,013 sq. ft.
Total living area:	**1,737 sq. ft.**
Basement:	1,013 sq. ft.
Garage:	400 sq. ft.

Exterior Wall Framing: 2x4
(with 2x6 option included)

Foundation options:
Standard basement.
Slab.
(Foundation & framing conversion diagram available — see order form.)

Blueprint Price Code: B

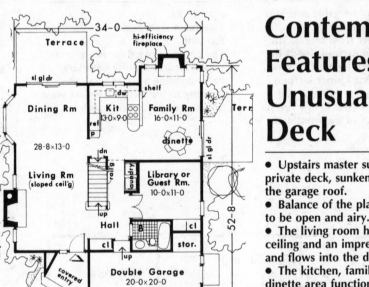

MAIN FLOOR

Contemporary Features Unusual Roof Deck

● Upstairs master suite includes a private deck, sunken into a cavity in the garage roof.
● Balance of the plan is also designed to be open and airy.
● The living room has a sloped ceiling and an impressive fireplace, and flows into the dining area.
● The kitchen, family room and dinette area function well together for family dining and other activities.
● A library or guest bedroom with a full bath also offers the option of becoming a home office.

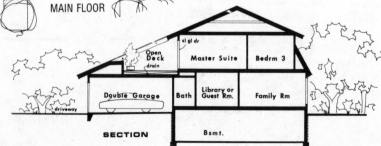

SECTION

Vaulted Living Room
Features Large Windows

Plan S-31086

Bedrooms: 3	**Baths:** 2½

Finished space:
Upper floor: 860 sq. ft.
Main floor: 924 sq. ft.

Total living area: 1,784 sq. ft.
Basement: 924 sq. ft.
Garage: 431 sq. ft.

Features:
Large kitchen includes walk-in pantry.
Vaulted living room.
Master suite is large and luxurious.
Family/dining/kitchen area is open and convenient.

Exterior Wall Framing: 2x6

Foundation options: (Specify)
Standard basement.
Crawlspace.
Slab.
(Foundation & framing conversion diagram available — see order form.)

Blueprint Price Code: B

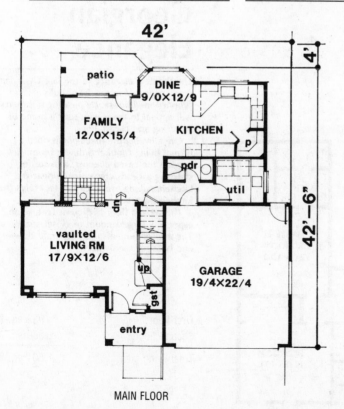

MAIN FLOOR

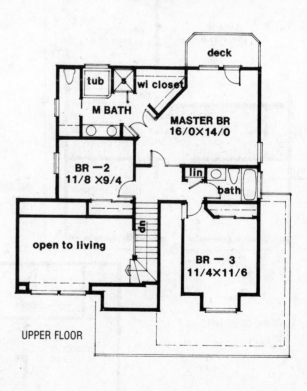

UPPER FLOOR

TO ORDER THIS BLUEPRINT,
CALL TOLL-FREE 1-800-547-5570

Plan S-31086

PRICES AND DETAILS
ON PAGES 12-15

169

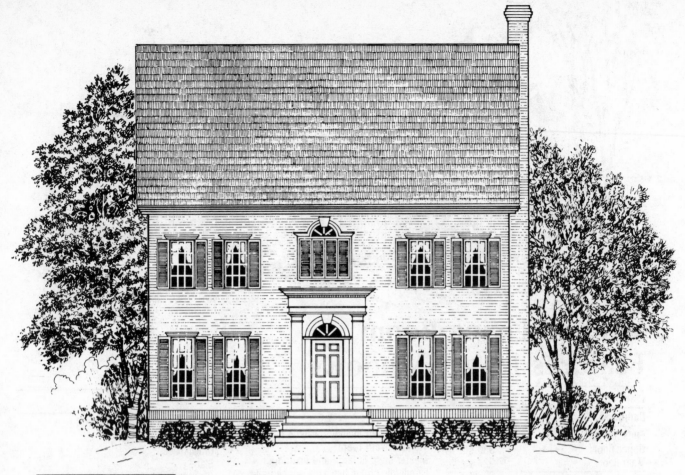

Timeless Georgian Elegance

The timeless elegance of the late Georgian era is captured in this beautifully proportioned house. Its pleasing symmetry will appeal to those who seek a home of enduring and classic lines.

Once inside, the foyer opens onto a formal living room and dining room. Just beyond the cased opening, a beautiful stairway ascends conveniently near the kitchen. A long breakfast bar separates the kitchen from the cozy Great Room.

The second floor bedrooms feature an especially large amount of closet space. The master suite also has separate shower and bath for the owners.

GARAGE 19-6 x 21-0

GREAT ROOM 13-0 x 14-6

UP

KITCHEN

LIVING ROOM 11-0 x 13-0

DINING ROOM 11-0 x 13-0

42'

36'

Ceiling height first floor 9'

Ceiling height second floor 8'

BATH

MASTER BEDROOM 12-0 x 13-0

DOWN

BEDROOM 11-0 x 13-0

BATH

BEDROOM 11-0 x 13-0

First floor: 932 sq. ft.
Second floor: 869 sq. ft.

Total living area: 1,801 sq. ft.

Blueprint Price Code B
Plan V-1801

TO ORDER THIS BLUEPRINT, CALL TOLL-FREE 1-800-547-5570

PRICES AND DETAILS ON PAGES 12-15

Dramatic Heights

- Brick lends a rich look to this two-story traditional home.
- Interior highlights begin with a dramatic two-story foyer with a decorative corner niche. The formal spaces are located on either side of the foyer, with the living room showing off a lovely bay window.
- The informal spaces are incorporated into a large activity area at the back of the home. A handsome corner fireplace and a window wall are featured in the spectacular two-story family room.
- The roomy kitchen offers an angled snack bar and a pantry closet. The sunny adjoining breakfast room opens to the outdoors.
- The upper floor houses three bedrooms and is accessed from stairs in the family room. The large master bedroom features a tray ceiling and the option of an added sitting room. A huge walk-in closet and a luxurious vaulted bath with an oval tub and his-and-hers dressing areas are also included.

Plan FB-5014-SOME

Bedrooms: 3	Baths: 2½
Living Area:	
Upper floor	963 sq. ft.
Main floor	915 sq. ft.
Total Living Area:	**1,878 sq. ft.**
Daylight basement	915 sq. ft.
Garage	240 sq. ft.
Storage	63 sq. ft.
Exterior Wall Framing:	2x4

Foundation Options:
Daylight basement
(Typical foundation & framing conversion diagram available—see order form.)

BLUEPRINT PRICE CODE:	B

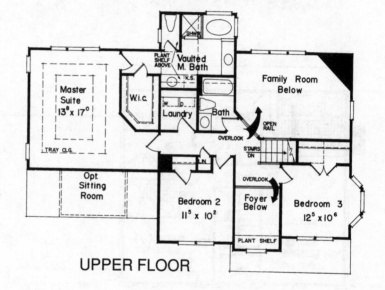

UPPER FLOOR

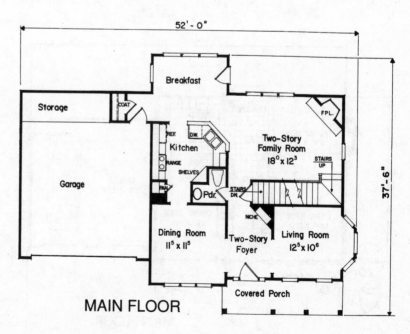

MAIN FLOOR

TO ORDER THIS BLUEPRINT,
CALL TOLL-FREE 1-800-547-5570

Plan FB-5014-SOME

PRICES AND DETAILS
ON PAGES 12-15

171

Exemplary Colonial

- Inside this traditionally designed home is an exciting floor plan for today's lifestyles.
- The classic center-hall arrangement of this Colonial allows easy access to all living areas.
- Plenty of views are possible from the formal rooms at the front of the home, as well as from the informal areas at the rear.
- The spacious kitchen offers lots of counter space, a handy work island, a laundry closet and a sunny bayed breakfast nook.
- The adjoining family room shows off a fireplace and elegant double doors to the rear. An optional set of double doors offers easy access to the living room.
- The beautiful master suite on the upper level boasts a vaulted ceiling, two closets, twin vanities, a garden tub and a separate shower.

Plan CH-100-A

Bedrooms: 4	Baths: 2 ½
Space:	
Upper floor	923 sq. ft.
Main floor	965 sq. ft.
Total Living Area	**1,888 sq. ft.**
Basement	952 sq. ft.
Garage	462 sq. ft.
Exterior Wall Framing	2x4

Foundation options:
Standard Basement
Daylight Basement
(Foundation & framing conversion diagram available—see order form.)

Blueprint Price Code	B

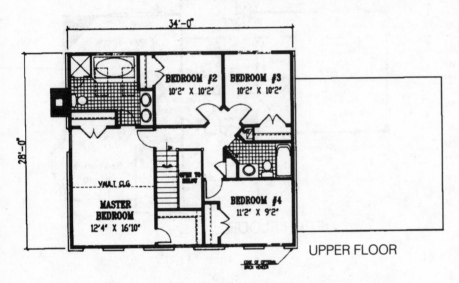

UPPER FLOOR

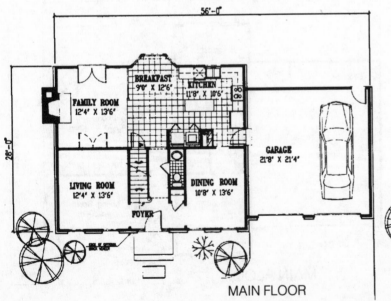

MAIN FLOOR

TO ORDER THIS BLUEPRINT, CALL TOLL-FREE 1-800-547-5570 Plan CH-100-A *PRICES AND DETAILS ON PAGES 12-15*

Spacious and Open

- A brilliant, sunken family room with rear fireplace, backyard access and vaulted ceiling is found at the center of this open floor plan.
- A cozy dinette with rear sliders and roomy island kitchen merge with the family room, creating a spacious, open atmosphere.
- Formal dining and living rooms share the front of the home.
- The main-floor master bedroom has tray ceiling, large walk-in closet and lavish bath designed for two.
- Two additional bedrooms share the upper level with a second full bath; the balcony landing overlooks the family room and foyer.

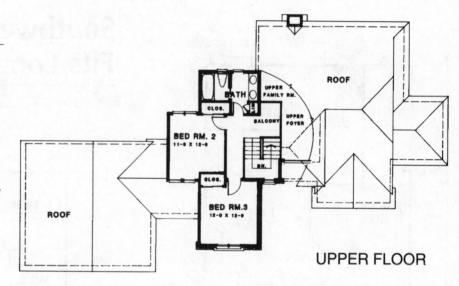

UPPER FLOOR

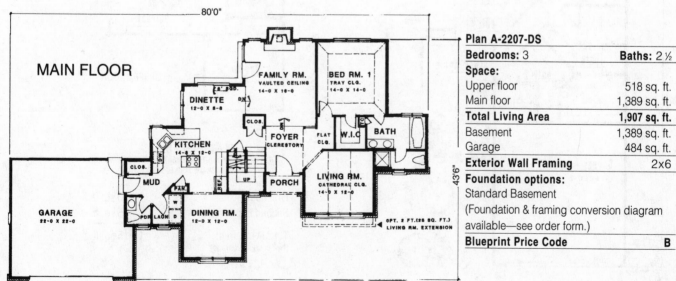

MAIN FLOOR

Plan A-2207-DS	
Bedrooms: 3	**Baths:** 2 ½
Space:	
Upper floor	518 sq. ft.
Main floor	1,389 sq. ft.
Total Living Area	**1,907 sq. ft.**
Basement	1,389 sq. ft.
Garage	484 sq. ft.
Exterior Wall Framing	2x6
Foundation options:	
Standard Basement	
(Foundation & framing conversion diagram	
available—see order form.)	
Blueprint Price Code	B

**TO ORDER THIS BLUEPRINT,
CALL TOLL-FREE 1-800-547-5570**

Plan A-2207-DS

**PRICES AND DETAILS
ON PAGES 12-15**

173

Southwest Design
Fits Long, Narrow Lot

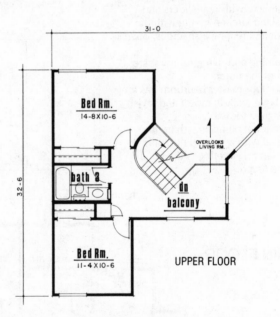

MAIN FLOOR

31-0

70-0

covered patio

Family
12-8 x 17-0

Kitchen
10-8 x 9-0

CATH CLG

CATH CLG

Dining
10-8 x 7-8

Mast. B.R.
15-0 x 14-8

Living
15-4 x 12-4

VAULTED CLG.

up

Entry

bath 1

bath 2

CLOSET

Study / opt. b.r.
10-8 x 10-6

utility

Garage
19-4 x 20-2

UPPER FLOOR

31-0

32-6

Bed Rm.
14-8 X 10-6

bath 3

OVERLOOKS LIVING RM.

dn
balcony

Bed Rm.
11-4 X 10-6

PLAN Q-1915-1A
WITHOUT BASEMENT
(SLAB-ON-GRADE FOUNDATION)

First floor:	1,400 sq. ft.
Second floor:	515 sq. ft.
Total living area: (Not counting garage)	1,915 sq. ft.

Blueprint Price Code B

Plan Q-1915-1A

Indoor/Outdoor Living on A Sloping Lot

- The wood siding, the front deck, and the multi-paned exterior of this Northwest contemporary will beckon you up to the entry stairs and inside.
- The two-story entry opens up to a vaulted living room with tall windows, exposed beam ceiling and adjoining dining area which accesses the hand-railed deck.
- An updated kitchen offers a walk-in

pantry, eating bar and breakfast nook with sliders to a rear deck.
- A fireplace and rear patio highlight the attached family room.
- A washer/dryer in the upper level bath is convenient to all three bedrooms, making laundry a breeze.

UPPER FLOOR

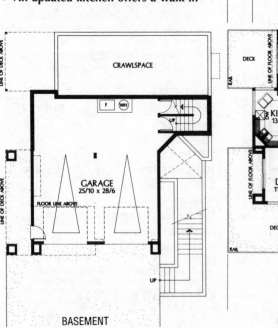

BASEMENT

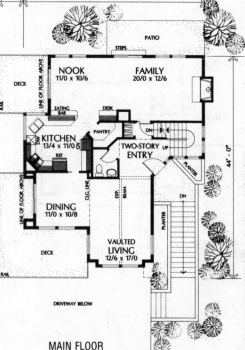

MAIN FLOOR

Plan P-7737-4D

Bedrooms: 3	Baths: 2½
Space:	
Upper floor:	802 sq. ft.
Main floor:	1,158 sq. ft.
Total living area:	1,960 sq. ft.
Garage/basement:	736 sq. ft.
Exterior Wall Framing:	2x6

Foundation options:
Crawlspace.
(Foundation & framing conversion diagram available — see order form.)

Blueprint Price Code:	B

TO ORDER THIS BLUEPRINT,
CALL TOLL-FREE 1-800-547-5570

Plan P-7737-4D

PRICES AND DETAILS
ON PAGES 12-15

175

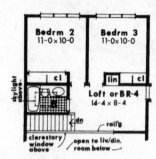

UPPER FLOOR

Bedrm 2
11-0 x 10-0

Bedrm 3
11-0 x 10-0

Loft or BR-4
14-4 x 8-4

clerestory
window
above

open to liv/din.
room below

rail'g

dn

cl

lin

cl

skylight
above

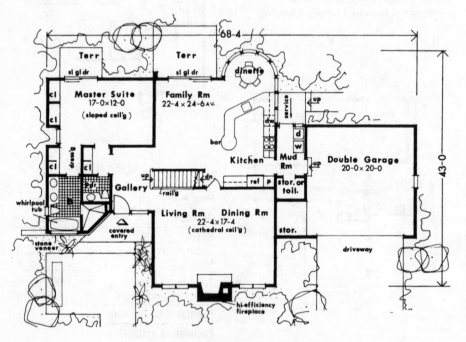

MAIN FLOOR

68-4

43-0

Terr

Terr

sl gl dr

sl gl dr

dinette

Master Suite
17-0 x 12-0
(sloped ceil'g)

Family Rm
22-4 x 24-6 AV.

service

up

cl

cl

bar

dw

d

w

Kitchen

Mud
Rm

up

Double Garage
20-0 x 20-0

dress'g

cl

cl

Gallery

up

rail'g

dn

ref

p

stor. or
toil.

whirlpool
tub

Pdr

Living Rm   Dining Rm
22-4 x 17-4
(cathedral ceil'g)

stor.

driveway

stone
veneer

covered
entry

hi-efficiency
fireplace

Light-Filled Interior

- A stylish contemporary exterior and an open, light-filled interior define this two-level home.
- The covered entry leads to a central gallery. A huge living room and dining room combine to generate a spacious ambience that is enhanced by a cathedral ceiling and an energy-saving fireplace.
- Oriented to the rear and overlooking the terrace and backyard landscaping are the informal spaces. The family room, sunny semi-circular dinette and modern kitchen share a snack counter and a private terrace.
- The main-floor master suite boasts a sloped ceiling, a private terrace and a personal bath with a dressing area and a whirlpool tub.
- Two to three extra bedrooms share a skylighted bath on the upper floor.

Plan K-683-D

Bedrooms: 3+	Baths: 2½+
Living Area:	
Upper floor	491 sq. ft.
Main floor	1,475 sq. ft.
Total Living Area:	**1,966 sq. ft.**
Standard basement	1,425 sq. ft.
Garage and storage	487 sq. ft.
Exterior Wall Framing:	2x4 or 2x6

Foundation Options:

Standard basement

Slab

(All plans can be built with your choice of foundation and framing. A generic conversion diagram is available. See order form.)

BLUEPRINT PRICE CODE:	B

Updated Colonial

- This home is thoroughly Colonial on the outside, but it offers an updated, ultra-modern floor plan inside.
- Guests are welcomed into a formal gallery that leads to all of the main-floor living areas. A large living room and a formal dining room flank the gallery. Optional folding doors open the living room to the adjoining family room.
- The family room features an inviting fireplace as its hub and sliding-door access to a backyard terrace.
- The kitchen is located to easily service the formal dining room as well as the bayed dinette. A mudroom and a half-bath are nearby.
- Upstairs, the master suite boasts a private bath and a wall of closets. Three unique secondary bedrooms share a hall bath.

Plan K-274-M

Bedrooms: 4	Baths: 2½
Living Area:	
Upper floor	990 sq. ft.
Main floor	1,025 sq. ft.
Total Living Area:	**2,015 sq. ft.**
Standard basement	983 sq. ft.
Garage and storage	520 sq. ft.
Exterior Wall Framing:	2x4 or 2x6

Foundation Options:

Standard basement
Slab

(All plans can be built with your choice of foundation and framing. A generic conversion diagram is available. See order form.)

BLUEPRINT PRICE CODE:	C

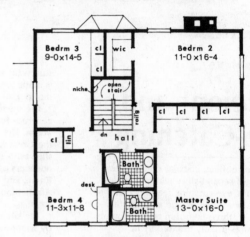

UPPER FLOOR

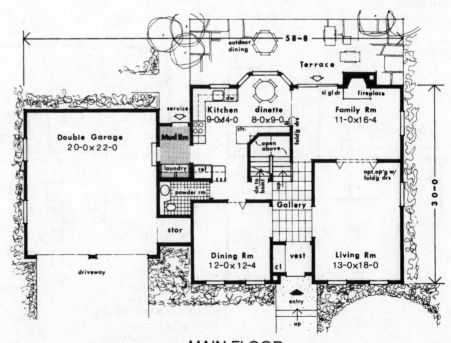

MAIN FLOOR

Energy-Efficient and Eye-Catching

The tiered roofline, circular dining room, and fanlight second-story window are just a few of the eye-catching features found in this two-story home. Inside and out, this 2,022-sq.-ft. three-bedroom home abounds with features usually found only in custom-designed houses.

The house is designed to funnel light into the interior, while the 2x6 exterior

stud walls keep the weather out. Provision is made for R-38 and R-30 insulation in the roof and R-19 in floors and walls.

The sidelight entry door opens onto a generous foyer that faces the sunken Great Room. The dining room is separated from the Great Room by 3-ft.-high built-in shelves. A skylight emphasizes the openness of the vaulted-ceilinged Great Room, and the corner fireplace and Atrium door bring added richness to the room.

The kitchen, with a corner sink framed by windows, boasts many built-ins, including a desk, table, and two pantry closets. The combination of a Great Room plus a family room gives the owner the

option of using the Great Room as one huge family room/living room, while the family room could be a fourth bedroom, a den, or a playroom.

The first-level bathroom and laundry area are conveniently located off the garage. The laundry can thus serve as a mudroom too, and the bathroom is handy for cleanup.

The skylighted stairway leading to the second floor is open to the Great Room below. The master bedroom, brightened by the large fanlight window, has a walk-in closet and its own bath. A full bath with tub/shower unit separates the remaining bedrooms, one of which features a built-in desk illuminated by two skylights.

First floor:	1,289 sq. ft.
Second floor:	733 sq. ft.
Total living area:	2,022 sq. ft.

(Not counting basement or garage)

SECOND FLOOR

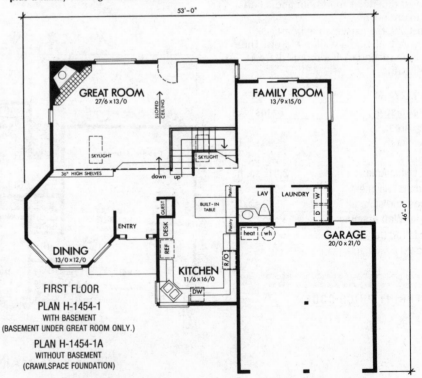

FIRST FLOOR

PLAN H-1454-1
WITH BASEMENT
(BASEMENT UNDER GREAT ROOM ONLY.)

PLAN H-1454-1A
WITHOUT BASEMENT
(CRAWLSPACE FOUNDATION)

Blueprint Price Code C

Plans H-1454-1 & -1A

Impressive Foyer, Deluxe Master Suite

- A dignified design and brick exterior lend an air of permanence and stability to this design.
- Inside, the impressive foyer leads to a sunken family room with fireplace on one side or a formal, sunken living room on the other.
- The formal dining room adjoins the living room to create a large space for entertaining.
- The kitchen and nook combine to make space for family living, and the utility area and half-bath are also conveniently located.
- A first-rate master suite upstairs includes a compartmentalized bath and large walk-in closet.
- Bedrooms 2 & 3 share a second full bath and each has a large closet.

UPPER FLOOR

DECK

TUB

DRESSING

TUB

S

BDRM. 2
12/2 x 11/6

RAILING   DN

DESK

MASTER
15/6 x 18/0

BDRM. 3
13/2 x 13/2

FOYER BELOW

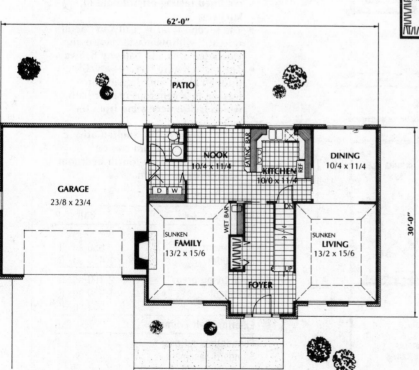

62'-0"

PATIO

GARAGE
23/8 x 23/4

NOOK
10/4 x 11/4

EATING BAR

KITCHEN
10/0 x 11/4

REF

DINING
10/4 x 11/4

D   W

30'-0"

SUNKEN
FAMILY
13/2 x 15/6

WET BAR

DN

SUNKEN
LIVING
13/2 x 15/6

UP

FOYER

MAIN FLOOR

U-87-205

Bedrooms: 3	Baths: 2½

Space:

Upper floor:	966 sq. ft.
Main floor:	1,086 sq. ft.

Total living area:	2,052 sq. ft.
Basement:	1,086 sq. ft.
Garage:	552 sq. ft.

Exterior Wall Framing:	2x4 & 2x6

Foundation options:
Standard basement.
Crawlspace.
Slab.
(Foundation & framing conversion diagram available — see order form.)

Blueprint Price Code:	C

TO ORDER THIS BLUEPRINT,
CALL TOLL-FREE 1-800-547-5570

Plan U-87-205

PRICES AND DETAILS
ON PAGES 12-15

179

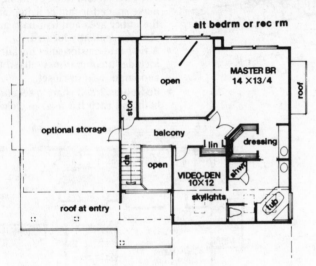

alt bedrm or rec rm

MASTER BR
14 × 13/4

roof

open

stor

optional storage

balcony

lin

dressing

dn

open

VIDEO-DEN
10×12

shwr

roof at entry

skylights

tub

52'

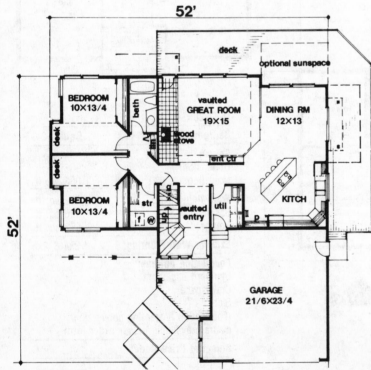

deck

optional sunspace

BEDROOM
10×13/4

bath

vaulted
GREAT ROOM
19×15

DINING RM
12×13

desk

desk

wood
stove

ent ctr

BEDROOM
10×13/4

52'

str

vaulted
entry

util

KITCH

f   w

GARAGE
21/6×23/4

Convenient Contemporary Design

- A thoroughly contemporary front elevation includes a sheltered porch as a traditional, homey touch.
- A vaulted Great Room makes this home look extra spacious.
- A large, open kitchen gives plenty of working space and avoids the confined feeling often found in kitchens.
- The second floor is really an "adult retreat," with its master bedroom, video/den area and balcony hallway.
- The master suite features a walk-through closet and dressing area leading to a generous master bath, which is also accessible from the video room.
- As an alternate, the vaulted area over the Great Room can be enclosed to make a fourth bedroom or upstairs rec room.

Plan S-72485

Bedrooms: 3-4	Baths: 2

Space:

Upper floor:	650 sq. ft.
Main floor:	1,450 sq. ft.

Total living area:	**2,100 sq. ft.**
Basement:	1,450 sq. ft.
Garage:	502 sq. ft.

Exterior Wall Framing:	**2x6**

Foundation options:
Standard basement.
Crawlspace.
(Foundation & framing conversion diagram available — see order form.)

Blueprint Price Code:	C

TO ORDER THIS BLUEPRINT, CALL TOLL-FREE 1-800-547-5570

Plan S-72485

PRICES AND DETAILS ON PAGES 12-15

Comfortable Country Home

- A central gable and a wide, welcoming front porch with columns give this design comfortable country charm.
- The large living room is open to the dining room, which features a tray ceiling and views to the backyard.
- The kitchen offers an oversized island counter with a snack bar. The adjoining breakfast area has a sliding glass door to the backyard and a half-wall that separates it from the family room. This inviting room includes a fireplace and a bay window with a cozy seat.
- Upstairs, the master suite boasts three windows, including a lovely arched window, that overlook the front yard. The private bath offers a whirlpool tub and a separate shower.
- Three more bedrooms, a second full bath and a multipurpose den make this a great family-sized home.

Plan OH-165

Bedrooms: 4+	Baths: 2½
Living Area:	
Upper floor	1,121 sq. ft.
Main floor	1,000 sq. ft.
Total Living Area:	**2,121 sq. ft.**
Standard basement	1,000 sq. ft.
Garage	400 sq. ft.
Exterior Wall Framing:	2x4

Foundation Options:

Standard basement
(Typical foundation & framing conversion diagram available—see order form.)

BLUEPRINT PRICE CODE:	C

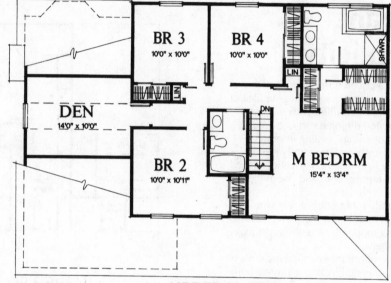

UPPER FLOOR

BR 3
10'0" x 10'0"

BR 4
10'0" x 10'0"

DEN
14'0" x 10'0"

BR 2
10'0" x 10'11"

M BEDRM
15'4" x 13'4"

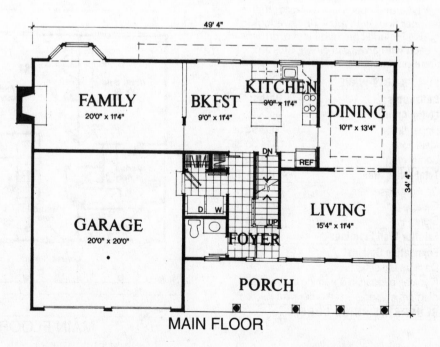

MAIN FLOOR

49' 4"

34' 4"

FAMILY
20'0" x 11'4"

BKFST
9'0" x 11'4"

KITCHEN
9'0" x 11'4"

DINING
10'1" x 13'4"

GARAGE
20'0" x 20'0"

FOYER

LIVING
15'4" x 11'4"

PORCH

Elegant Simplicity

- From the covered front porch to the main-floor master suite, this simple yet elegant home is filled with surprises.
- The vaulted dining room is graced by arched openings leading from the vaulted foyer and the family room.
- A sunny breakfast nook overlooks the vaulted family room and floods the kitchen with light.
- The family room offers a rear window wall, an inviting fireplace and built-in shelving topped by attention-getting plant shelves.
- The main-floor master suite includes an elegant tray ceiling and a vaulted bath with an oval whirlpool tub and an adjacent shower.
- A beautiful open staircase leads to the upper floor with a balcony overlook. Also included are two large bedrooms, each with a walk-in closet, plus an optional bonus space.

Plan FB-5019-WAVE

Bedrooms: 3	Baths: 2½
Living Area:	
Upper floor	502 sq. ft.
Main floor	1,414 sq. ft.
Bonus room	208 sq. ft.
Total Living Area:	**2,124 sq. ft.**
Daylight basement	1,414 sq. ft.
Garage	420 sq. ft.
Storage	28 sq. ft.
Exterior Wall Framing:	2x4

Foundation Options:

Daylight basement
(Typical foundation & framing conversion diagram available—see order form.)

BLUEPRINT PRICE CODE: C

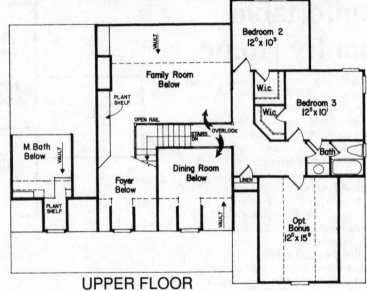

UPPER FLOOR

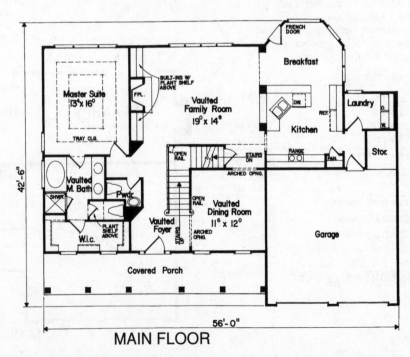

MAIN FLOOR

Plan FB-5019-WAVE

PRICES AND DETAILS ON PAGES 12-15

English Elegance

- Tradition takes on new meaning in this elegant brick and cedar two-story home, starting with the covered front entry and extending to the gracious open stairway.
- A large custom window adds light to the dramatic two-story foyer and draws visitors into a home designed for formal entertaining and casual family living.
- The spacious family room features a brick fireplace, a wall of windows overlooking the backyard and an adjoining kitchen and nook area.
- Designed for convenience, the extra-large kitchen includes an island counter, a built-in pantry and desk, and a convenient buffet counter for serving guests in the adjoining formal dining room and the informal dinette.
- All four bedrooms are on the second floor. The master suite includes a separate dressing area and a private bath with a double vanity.

Plan A-2293-DS

Bedrooms: 4	Baths: 2½
Living Area:	
Upper floor	941 sq. ft.
Main floor	1,192 sq. ft.
Total Living Area:	**2,133 sq. ft.**
Standard basement	1,192 sq. ft.
Garage	484 sq. ft.
Exterior Wall Framing:	2x6

Foundation Options:

Standard basement
(Typical foundation & framing conversion diagram available—see order form.)

BLUEPRINT PRICE CODE:	C

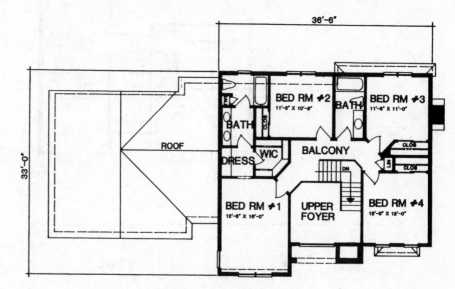

UPPER FLOOR

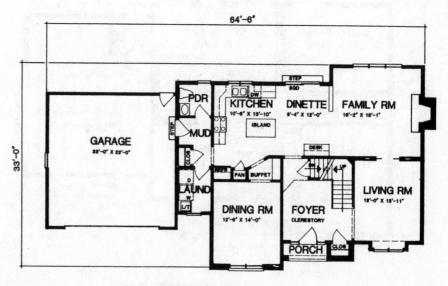

MAIN FLOOR

TO ORDER THIS BLUEPRINT,
CALL TOLL-FREE 1-800-547-5570

Plan A-2293-DS

PRICES AND DETAILS
ON PAGES 12-15

183

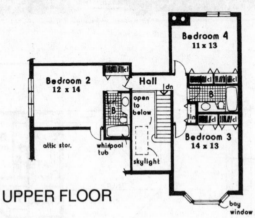

UPPER FLOOR

Vertical Lines Command Attention

- This upstanding home design commands attention with its two-tiered bay windows and triangular transoms.
- Flanking the soaring two-story foyer are the formal living areas. The oversized living room features a brick fireplace.
- A spacious setting is created with the combination of the rear-oriented family room and kitchen. French doors frame a stone fireplace and open to a private rear terrace.
- The main-floor master suite features a cathedral ceiling in addition to its own terrace and private bath.
- Three additional bedrooms and two more baths are located on the upper level.

Plan AHP-9135

Bedrooms: 4	**Baths: 3½**
Space:	
Upper floor	746 sq. ft.
Main floor	1,411 sq. ft.
Total Living Area	**2,157 sq. ft.**
Basement	1,411 sq. ft.
Garage	546 sq. ft.
Exterior Wall Framing	2x4 or 2x6

Foundation options:
Standard Basement
Crawlspace
Slab
(Foundation & framing conversion diagram available—see order form.)

Blueprint Price Code	C

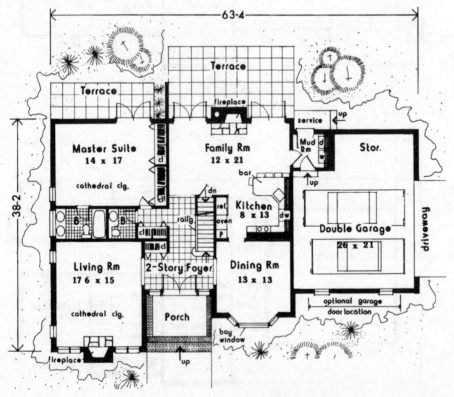

MAIN FLOOR

*TO ORDER THIS BLUEPRINT,
CALL TOLL-FREE 1-800-547-5570* · Plan AHP-9135 · *PRICES AND DETAILS
ON PAGES 12-15*

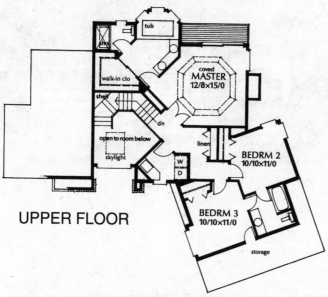

UPPER FLOOR

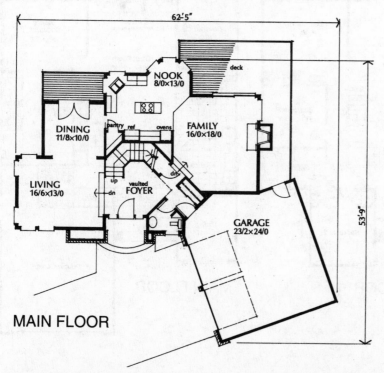

MAIN FLOOR

Master Suite Privacy Deck

- The classic styling of this transitional design creates dramatic street appeal.
- Step-down living areas flank either side of the foyer, and a coat closet and a powder room lie between the foyer and the garage entrance.
- The formal living and dining rooms adjoin to the left. This expansive entertaining area is enhanced with a 12-ft. ceiling and French doors that open to the rear deck.
- A handsome fireplace and a wraparound deck highlight the spacious sunken family room to the right of the foyer.
- Separating the formal spaces from the informal spaces is a gourmet kitchen, which features a convenient cooktop island, a walk-in pantry and an octagonal breakfast nook.
- The spectacular master bedroom on the upper floor boasts a 9-ft. coved ceiling, a private deck and a luxurious bath with a spa tub set in a windowed alcove.

Plan CDG-2042	
Bedrooms: 3	**Baths:** 2½
Living Area:	
Upper floor	1,046 sq. ft.
Main floor	1,129 sq. ft.
Total Living Area:	**2,175 sq. ft.**
Partial daylight basement	739 sq. ft.
Garage	556 sq. ft.
Exterior Wall Framing:	2x6
Foundation Options:	
Partial daylight basement	
(Typical foundation & framing conversion diagram available—see order form.)	
BLUEPRINT PRICE CODE:	C

TO ORDER THIS BLUEPRINT,
CALL TOLL-FREE 1-800-547-5570

Plan CDG-2042

PRICES AND DETAILS
ON PAGES 12-15

185

Striking Stucco

- This striking stucco design has everything for the young family or empty-nester.
- The elegant double-door entry opens to a spectacular Great Room with an inviting fireplace flanked by windows, an optional media center and built-in shelving.
- For quiet, candlelight dinners, the formal dining room tucked away to the front of the home is ideal.
- The roomy kitchen is nestled between the dining room and the breakfast nook, which overlooks a nice covered patio and the Great Room.
- The master bedroom suite is easily accessed on the main floor. The spacious master bath features a unique closet design for the best use of space. A private toilet, a dual-sink vanity, a soaking tub and a separate shower are other conveniences.
- The upper level can accommodate two or three bedrooms.
- You may also choose from two different elevations, both of which are included in the blueprints.

Plan HDS-99-150

Bedrooms: 3+	Baths: 2½
Living Area:	
Upper floor	697 sq. ft.
Main floor	1,485 sq. ft.
Total Living Area:	**2,182 sq. ft.**
Garage	502 sq. ft.
Exterior Wall Framing:	2x4

Foundation Options:

Slab

(All plans can be built with your choice of foundation and framing. A generic conversion diagram is available. See order form.)

BLUEPRINT PRICE CODE	C

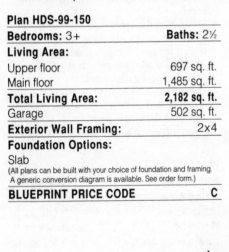

UPPER FLOOR

MAIN FLOOR

Plan HDS-99-150

PRICES AND DETAILS ON PAGES 12-15

Bright Traditional

- Designed to take advantage of natural light, this attractive home offers plenty of windows to take in the front and backyard views.
- Visitors are welcomed in the two-story foyer and ushered into the spacious living and dining rooms that adjoin it.
- A fireplace flanked by large windows highlights the vaulted family room at the back of the home. The adjacent breakfast room features a vaulted ceiling, overhead plant shelves, a handsome bay window and a pantry.
- The kitchen continues the open, airy feeling of the home and is separated from the breakfast room by a serving bar. A convenient powder room and laundry room are removed to the side.
- The main-floor master suite features a tray ceiling and a vaulted bath with an oval tub, a separate shower, a high plant shelf and a dual-sink vanity with knee space.
- A bridge connects the two bedrooms on the upper floor and overlooks the family room and the foyer.

Plan FB-5062-MATT

Bedrooms: 3	Baths: 2½
Living Area:	
Upper floor	560 sq. ft.
Main floor	1,660 sq. ft.
Total Living Area:	**2,220 sq. ft.**
Daylight basement	1,660 sq. ft.
Garage	419 sq. ft.
Exterior Wall Framing:	2x4

Foundation Options:
Daylight basement
(Typical foundation & framing conversion diagram available–see order form.)

BLUEPRINT PRICE CODE: C

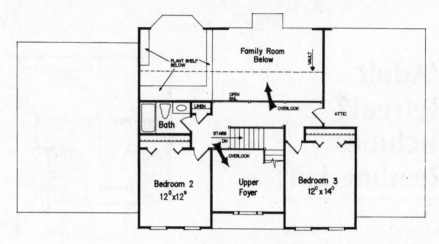

UPPER FLOOR

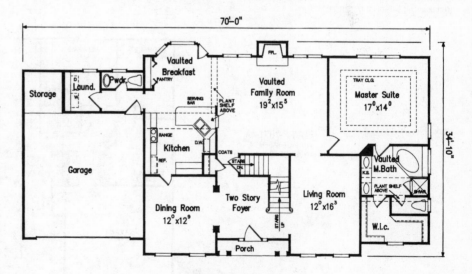

MAIN FLOOR

"Adult Retreat" Includes Reading Loft

Main floor:	1,610 sq. ft.
Upper floor:	715 sq. ft.
Total living area:	2,325 sq. ft.

(Not counting basement or garage)

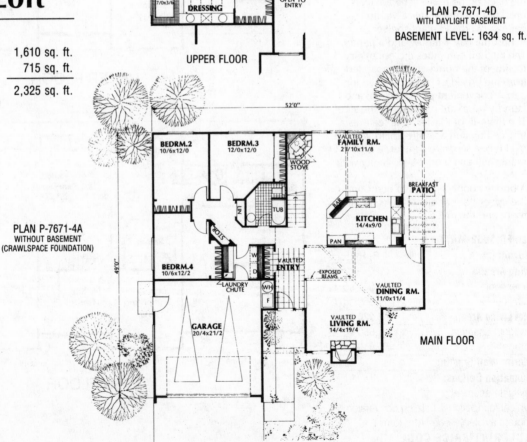

UPPER FLOOR

READING LOFT 12/0x11/0

DN

MASTER SUITE 13/0x17/2

BOOKS

LINEN

SH

TUB 7/0x3/6

SKYLIGHTS

WALK IN WARDROBE

DRESSING

OPEN TO ENTRY

PLAN P-7671-4D
WITH DAYLIGHT BASEMENT
BASEMENT LEVEL: 1634 sq. ft.

FAMILY ROOM

PLAN P-7671-4A
WITHOUT BASEMENT
(CRAWLSPACE FOUNDATION)

MAIN FLOOR

52'0"

49'0"

BEDRM.2 10/6x12/0

BEDRM.3 12/0x12/0

WOOD STOVE

VAULTED FAMILY RM. 21/10x11/8

BREAKFAST PATIO

LIN

TUB

KITCHEN 14/4x9/0

PAN

BAR

BEDRM.4 10/6x12/2

LAUNDRY CHUTE

W D

WH F

VAULTED ENTRY

EXPOSED BEAMS

VAULTED DINING RM. 11/0x11/4

GARAGE 20/4x21/2

VAULTED LIVING RM. 14/4x19/4

Blueprint Price Code C
Plan P-7671-4A & -4D

PRICES AND DETAILS
ON PAGES 12-15

A Horizontal Emphasis

- A metal roof with 4' overhangs offer this unique home energy savings and distinction; a horizontal emphasis is created with the use of blocks.
- The foyer opens to a spacious living and dining room arrangement with see-thru fireplace.
- The family room, on the other side, has vaulted ceiling and rear window wall overlooking the patio.
- The island kitchen is open to the family room and breakfast nook, which offers a second fireplace.
- The main-floor master suite features his 'n her walk-in closets, access to the adjoining patio and a luxury bath.
- Two additional bedrooms share the upper level.

Plan DW-2394	
Bedrooms: 3	**Baths:** 2 ½
Space:	
Upper floor	501 sq. ft.
Main floor	1,893 sq. ft.
Total Living Area	**2,394 sq. ft.**
Basement	1,893 sq. ft.
Garage	390 sq. ft.
Exterior Wall Framing	2x4
Foundation options:	
Standard Basement	
Crawlspace	
Slab	
(Foundation & framing conversion diagram available—see order form.)	
Blueprint Price Code	C

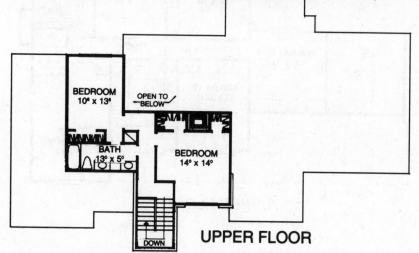

UPPER FLOOR

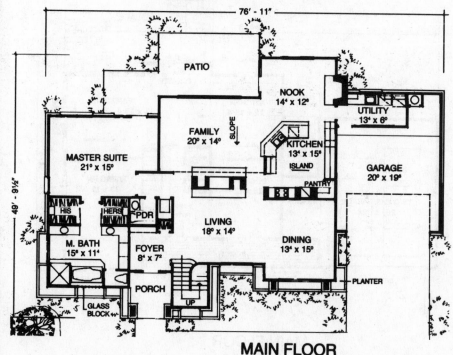

MAIN FLOOR

Five-Bedroom Traditional

- This sophisticated traditional home makes a striking statement both inside and out.
- The dramatic two-story foyer is flanked by the formal living spaces. The private dining room overlooks the front porch, while the spacious living room has outdoor views on two sides.
- A U-shaped kitchen with a snack bar, a sunny dinette area and a large family room flow together at the back of the home. The family room's fireplace warms the open, informal expanse, while sliding glass doors in the dinette access the backyard terrace.
- The second floor has five roomy bedrooms and two skylighted bathrooms. The luxurious master suite has a high ceiling with a beautiful arched window, a dressing area and a huge walk-in closet. The private bath offers dual sinks, a whirlpool tub and a separate shower.
- Attic space is located above the garage.

Plan AHP-9392

Bedrooms: 5	Baths: 2½
Living Area:	
Upper floor	1,223 sq. ft.
Main floor	1,193 sq. ft.
Total Living Area:	**2,416 sq. ft.**
Standard basement	1,130 sq. ft.
Garage	509 sq. ft.
Storage	65 sq. ft.
Exterior Wall Framing:	2x4 or 2x6

Foundation Options:
Standard basement
Crawlspace
Slab
(Typical foundation & framing conversion diagram available—see order form.)

BLUEPRINT PRICE CODE:	C

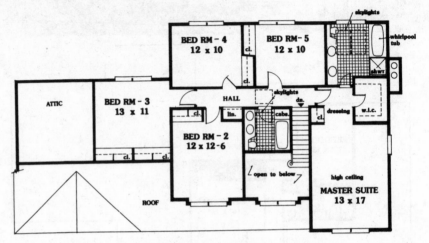

UPPER FLOOR

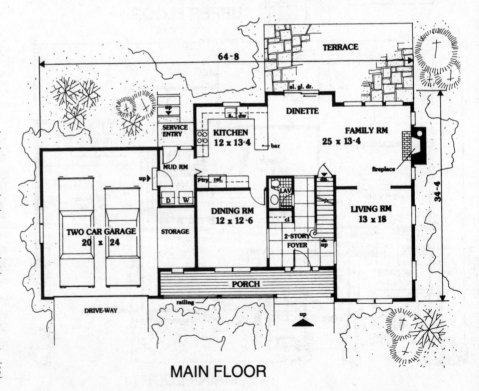

MAIN FLOOR

TO ORDER THIS BLUEPRINT, CALL TOLL-FREE 1-800-547-5570

Plan AHP-9392

PRICES AND DETAILS ON PAGES 12-15

Street Appeal Times Three

- Three optional elevations are offered to frame this attractive contemporary two-story. Please specify your elevation preference when ordering.
- The beautiful vaulted entryway opens to formal living areas and to a study or extra bedroom with vaulted ceiling, window-wall and French doors.
- The roomy kitchen adjoins a breakfast nook and family room, for uninterrupted family activities; the fireplace and the rear deck can both be seen from the kitchen.
- The spectacular master suite features a volume ceiling, generous closet space, dual vanities and a separate tub and shower.

ELEVATION A

ELEVATION B

ELEVATION C

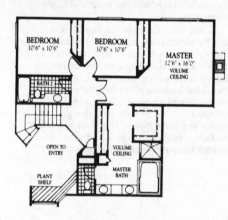

UPPER FLOOR

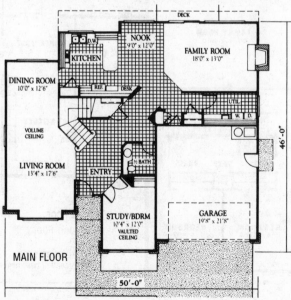

MAIN FLOOR

Plan R-2152

Bedrooms: 3-4	**Baths:** 2½

Living Area:

Upper floor:	955 sq. ft.
Main floor	1,470 sq. ft.
Total Living Area:	**2,425 sq. ft.**
Garage	426 sq. ft.
Exterior Wall Framing:	2x6

Foundation Options:
Crawlspace
(Typical foundation & framing conversion diagram available—see order form.)

BLUEPRINT PRICE CODE:	**C**

Rear of Home As Attractive As Front

The rear of this rustic/contemporary home features a massive stone fireplace and a full-length deck which make it ideal for mountain, golf course, lake or other locations where both the front and rear offer scenic views.

Sliding glass doors in the family room and breakfast nook open onto the deck. The modified A-Frame design combines a 20'6" cathedral ceiling over the sunken family room with a large studio over the two front bedrooms. An isolated master suite features a walk-in closet and compartmentalized bath with double vanity and linen closet. The front bedrooms include ample closet space and share a unique bath-and-a-half arrangement.

On one side of the U-shaped kitchen and breakfast nook is the formal dining room which opens onto the foyer. On the other side is a utility room which can be entered from either the kitchen or garage.

The exterior features a massive stone fireplace, large glass areas and a combination of vertical wood siding and stone.

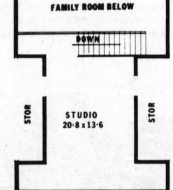

FAMILY ROOM BELOW

DOWN

STOR | STUDIO 20·8 x 13·6 | STOR

SECOND FLOOR

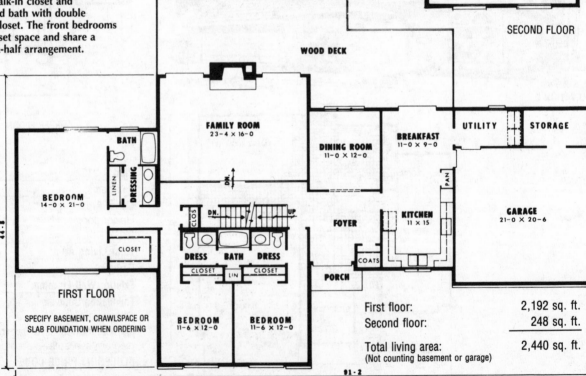

FIRST FLOOR

SPECIFY BASEMENT, CRAWLSPACE OR SLAB FOUNDATION WHEN ORDERING

First floor:	2,192 sq. ft.
Second floor:	248 sq. ft.
Total living area:	2,440 sq. ft.
(Not counting basement or garage)	

Blueprint Price Code C

Plan C-7710

Photo by Mark Englund/HomeStyles

Exciting, Economical Design

Exciting but economical, this 1,895 sq. ft., three-bedroom house is arranged carefully for maximum use and enjoyment on two floors, and is only 42 feet wide to minimize lot size requirements. The multi-paned bay windows of the living room and an upstairs bedroom add contrast to the hip rooflines and lead you to the sheltered front entry porch.

The open, vaulted foyer is brightened by a skylight as it sorts traffic to the downstairs living areas or to the upper bedroom level. A few steps to the right puts you in the vaulted living room and the adjoining dining area. Sliding doors in the dining area and the nook, and a pass-through window in the U-shaped kitchen, make the patio a perfect place for outdoor activities and meals.

A large fireplace warms the spacious family room, which has a corner wet bar for efficient entertaining. A utility room leading to the garage and a powder room complete the 1,020 sq. ft. main floor.

An open stairway in the foyer leads to the 875 sq. ft. upper level. The master bedroom has a large walk-in wardrobe, twin vanity, shower and bathroom. The front bedroom has a seat in the bay window and the third bedroom has a built-in seat overlooking the vaulted living room. A full bath with twin vanity serves these bedrooms.

The daylight basement version of the plan adds 925 sq. ft. of living space.

Main floor:	1,020 sq. ft.
Upper floor:	875 sq. ft.
Total living area:	1,895 sq. ft.
(Not counting basement or garage)	

PLAN P-7681-3D
BASEMENT LEVEL: 925 sq. ft.

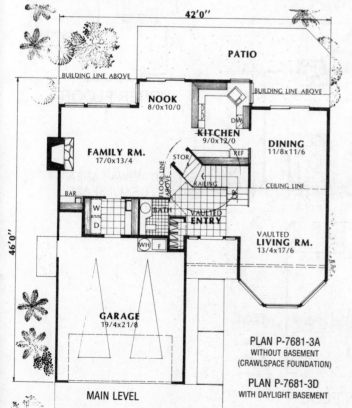

42'0"

PATIO

BUILDING LINE ABOVE

NOOK
8/0x10/0

BUILDING LINE ABOVE

KITCHEN
9/0x12/0

DINING
11/8x11/6

FAMILY RM.
17/0x13/4

STOR

REF

CEILING LINE

BAR

RAILING

BATH

VAULTED ENTRY

VAULTED LIVING RM.
13/4x17/6

WH F

46'0"

GARAGE
19/4x21/8

MAIN LEVEL

PLAN P-7681-3A
WITHOUT BASEMENT
(CRAWLSPACE FOUNDATION)

PLAN P-7681-3D
WITH DAYLIGHT BASEMENT

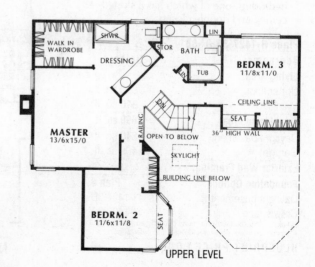

WALK IN WARDROBE

SHWR

STOR

BATH

LIN

DRESSING

TUB

BEDRM. 3
11/8x11/0

CEILING LINE

MASTER
13/6x15/0

RAILING

DN

OPEN TO BELOW

SEAT

36" HIGH WALL

SKYLIGHT

BUILDING LINE BELOW

BEDRM. 2
11/6x11/8

SEAT

UPPER LEVEL

TO ORDER THIS BLUEPRINT,
CALL TOLL-FREE 1-800-547-5570

Blueprint Price Code B
Plans P-7681-3A & 3D

PRICES AND DETAILS
ON PAGES 12-15

193

Instant Impact

- Bold rooflines, interesting angles and unusual window treatments give this stylish home lots of impact.
- Inside, high ceilings and an open floor plan maximize the home's square footage. At only 28 ft. wide, the home also is ideal for a narrow lot.
- A covered deck leads to the main entry, which features a sidelighted door, angled glass walls and a view of the striking open staircase.
- The Great Room is stunning, with its vaulted ceiling, energy-efficient woodstove and access to a large deck.
- A flat ceiling distinguishes the dining area, which shares an angled snack bar/cooktop with the step-saving kitchen. A laundry/mudroom is nearby.
- Upstairs, the master suite offers a sloped ceiling and a clerestory window. A walk-through closet leads to the private bath, which is enhanced by a skylighted, sloped ceiling.
- Linen and storage closets line the hallway leading to the smaller bedrooms, one of which has a sloped ceiling and double closets.

Plans H-1427-3A & -3B

Bedrooms: 3	Baths: 2½
Living Area:	
Upper floor	880 sq. ft.
Main floor	810 sq. ft.
Total Living Area:	**1,690 sq. ft.**
Daylight basement	810 sq. ft.
Garage	409 sq. ft.
Exterior Wall Framing:	2x4
Foundation Options:	**Plan #**
Daylight basement	H-1427-3B
Crawlspace	H-1427-3A

(All plans can be built with your choice of foundation and framing. A generic conversion diagram is available. See order form.)

BLUEPRINT PRICE CODE:	**B**

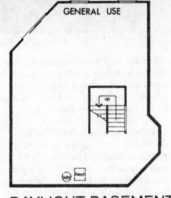

DAYLIGHT BASEMENT

UPPER FLOOR

STAIRWAY AREA IN CRAWLSPACE VERSION

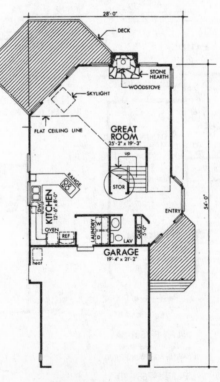

MAIN FLOOR

TO ORDER THIS BLUEPRINT, CALL TOLL-FREE 1-800-547-5570

Plans H-1427-3A & -3B

PRICES AND DETAILS ON PAGES 12-15

UPPER FLOOR

MASTER
11/10x15/0

SHWR

DRESSING

OPEN TO KITCHEN BELOW

WALK IN WARDROBE

LIN

DN

OPEN TO ENTRY BELOW

BEDRM. 2
10/0x11/0

BATH

TUB

KITCHEN

DN

ENTRY

PLAN P-7689-3D
WITH DAYLIGHT BASEMENT

61'0''

DECK

SKYLIGHTS

DECK

VAULTED
NOOK
11/0x11/0

BAR
DN

FAMILY RM.
17/4x13/6

OPEN TO FAMILY RM.

VAULTED
KITCHEN
10/6x13/9

REF

VAULTED
DINING
9/10x12/0

36" HIGH WALL

41'0''

BATH

SH

UTILITY

W

D

VAULTED
LIVING RM.
16/0x13/0

SKYLIGHT

ENTRY

DEN/
BEDRM. 3
11/4x10/6

F

WH

GARAGE
23/2x23/2

PLANTER

MAIN FLOOR

PLAN P-7689-3A
WITHOUT BASEMENT
(CRAWLSPACE FOUNDATION)

Main floor:	1,358 sq. ft.
Upper floor:	576 sq. ft.
Total living area:	1,934 sq. ft.
(Not counting basement or garage)	
Basement level:	1,358 sq. ft.

Blueprint Price Code B

TO ORDER THIS BLUEPRINT,
CALL TOLL-FREE 1-800-547-5570

Plans P-7689-3A & -3D

**PRICES AND DETAILS
ON PAGES 12-15**

195

Excellent Family Design

- Long sloping rooflines and bold design features make this home attractive for any neighborhood.
- Inside, a vaulted entry takes visitors into an impressive vaulted Great Room with a wood stove and window-wall facing the house-spanning rear deck.
- Clerestory windows flanking the stove area and large windows front and rear flood the Great Room with natural light.
- The magnificent kitchen includes a stylish island and opens to the informal dining area which in turn flows into the Great Room.
- Two bedrooms on the main floor share a full bath, and bedroom #2 boasts easy access to the rear deck which spans the width of the house.
- The upstairs comprises an "adult retreat," with a roomy master suite, luxurious bath with double sinks, and a large walk-in closet.
- A daylight basement version adds another 1,410 sq. ft. of space for entertaining and recreation, plus a fourth bedroom and a large shop/storage area.

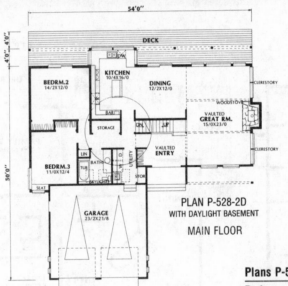

PLAN P-528-2D
WITH DAYLIGHT BASEMENT

MAIN FLOOR

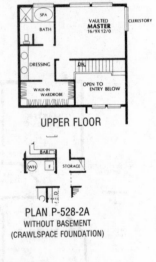

UPPER FLOOR

PLAN P-528-2A
WITHOUT BASEMENT
(CRAWLSPACE FOUNDATION)

BASEMENT

Plans P-528-2A & -2D

Bedrooms: 3-4	Baths: 2-3

Space:	
Upper floor:	498 sq. ft.
Main floor:	1,456 sq. ft.

Total living area:	1,954 sq. ft.
Basement:	1,410 sq. ft.
Garage:	502 sq. ft.

Exterior Wall Framing:	2x6

Foundation options:
Daylight basement (Plan P-528-2D).
Crawlspace (Plan P-528-2A).
(Foundation & framing conversion diagram available — see order form.)

Blueprint Price Code:	
Without basement:	B
With basement:	E

Plans P-528-2A & -2D

PRICES AND DETAILS ON PAGES 12-15

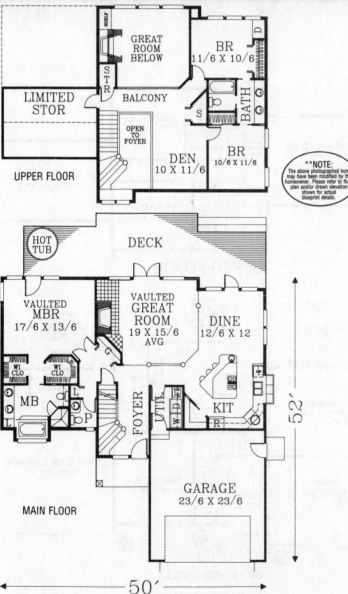

GREAT ROOM BELOW

BR 11/6 X 10/6

LIMITED STOR

BALCONY

STR

SHELF

OPEN TO FOYER

BATH

S

UPPER FLOOR

DEN 10 X 11/6

BR 10/6 X 11/6

NOTE: The above photographed home may have been modified by the homeowner. Please refer to floor plan and/or drawn elevation shown for actual blueprint details.

HOT TUB

DECK

VAULTED MBR 17/6 X 13/6

VAULTED GREAT ROOM 19 X 15/6 AVG

DINE 12/6 X 12

WI CLO

WI CLO

MB

L

P

FOYER

UTIL

W D

KIT

R

MAIN FLOOR

GARAGE 23/6 X 23/6

52'

50'

Vaulted Great Room

- While the exterior has traditional overtones, this plan is thoroughly modern both inside and out.
- The vaulted Great Room with adjacent kitchen and dining room gives the home an open and spacious feeling.
- The vaulted master suite on the first floor includes walk-in closets and a sumptuous master bath.
- The upper floor includes two more bedrooms, which share a continental bath.
- Also note the den and balcony overlooking the foyer and Great Room below.
- A huge deck with a hot tub can be reached easily from the master suite, the Great Room or the dining room.

Plan S-2100	
Bedrooms: 3	**Baths:** 2½
Living Area:	
Upper floor:	660 sq. ft.
Main floor	1,440 sq. ft.
Total Living Area:	**2,100 sq. ft.**
Standard basement	1,440 sq. ft.
Garage	552 sq. ft.
Exterior Wall Framing:	2x6

Foundation Options:
Standard basement
Crawlspace
Slab
(Typical foundation & framing conversion diagram available—see order form.)

BLUEPRINT PRICE CODE:	C

Alluring Two-Story

- This dramatic contemporary is adorned with staggered rooflines that overlap and outline large expanses of glass.
- The interior features a floor plan that is both practical and functional, with individual rooms equally exciting.
- Flanking the two-story-high foyer are a formal dining room and a sunken living room. The living room boasts a cathedral ceiling and unfolds to a sunken family room with a fireplace and a patio overlook.
- A bright breakfast area and a U-shaped kitchen adjoin the family room.
- The second level features a spacious master bedroom with dual closets and a private bath. Two secondary bedrooms, another bath and an optional expansion room above the garage are also included.

Plan AX-8596-A

Bedrooms: 3+	Baths: 2½
Living Area:	
Upper floor	738 sq. ft.
Main floor	1,160 sq. ft.
Bonus room	226 sq. ft.
Total Living Area:	**2,124 sq. ft.**
Standard basement	1,160 sq. ft.
Garage	465 sq. ft.
Exterior Wall Framing:	2x4

Foundation Options:

Standard basement

(All plans can be built with your choice of foundation and framing. A generic conversion diagram is available. See order form.)

BLUEPRINT PRICE CODE: C

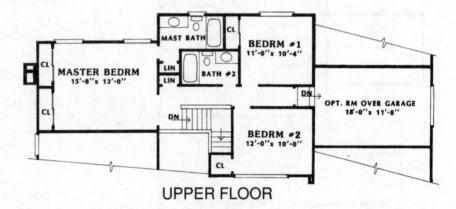

UPPER FLOOR

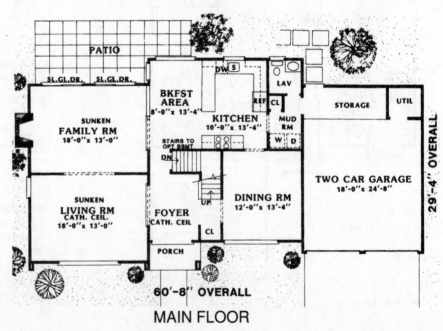

MAIN FLOOR

TO ORDER THIS BLUEPRINT, CALL TOLL-FREE 1-800-547-5570

Plan AX-8596-A

PRICES AND DETAILS ON PAGES 12-15

Contemporary Elegance

- This striking contemporary design combines vertical siding with elegant traditional overtones.
- Inside, an expansive activity area is created with the joining of the vaulted living room, the family/dining room and the kitchen. The openness of the rooms creates a spacious, dramatic feeling, which extends to an exciting two-story sun space and a patio beyond.

- A convenient utility/service area near the garage includes a clothes-sorting counter, a deep sink and ironing space.
- Two main-floor bedrooms share a bright bath.
- The master suite includes a sumptuous skylighted bath with two entrances. The tub is uniquely positioned on an angled wall, while the shower and toilet are secluded behind a pocket door. An optional overlook provides views down into the sun space, which is accessed by a spiral staircase.
- A versatile loft area and a bonus room complete this design.

Plan LRD-1971

Bedrooms: 3+	Baths: 2
Living Area:	
Upper floor	723 sq. ft.
Main floor	1,248 sq. ft.
Sun space	116 sq. ft.
Bonus room	225 sq. ft.
Total Living Area:	**2,312 sq. ft.**
Standard basement	1,248 sq. ft.
Garage	483 sq. ft.
Exterior Wall Framing:	2x6

Foundation Options:

Standard basement

Crawlspace

(All plans can be built with your choice of foundation and framing. A generic conversion diagram is available. See order form.)

BLUEPRINT PRICE CODE:	C

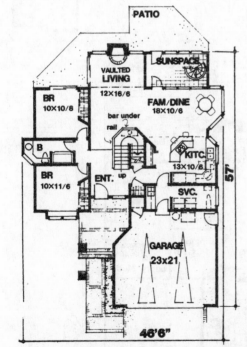

MAIN FLOOR

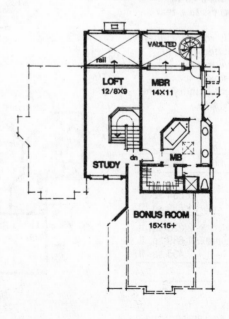

UPPER FLOOR

Photo by Mark Englund

Fantastic Floor Plan!

- This is the famous house shown on the PBS "Hometime" television series.
- Impressive floor plan includes a deluxe master suite with a private courtyard, magnificent bath and large closet.
- The large island kitchen/nook combination includes a corner pantry and easy access to a rear deck.
- The spacious family room includes a fireplace and vaulted ceiling.
- The two upstairs bedrooms share a bath with double sinks.
- Note the convenient laundry room in the garage entry area.

Plan B-88015

Bedrooms: 3	Baths: 2½
Space:	
Upper floor:	534 sq. ft.
Main floor:	1,689 sq. ft.
Total living area:	**2,223 sq. ft.**
Basement:	approx. 1,689 sq. ft.
Garage:	455 sq. ft.
Exterior Wall Framing:	2x4

Foundation options:
Standard basement only.
(Foundation & framing conversion diagram available — see order form.)

Blueprint Price Code:	C

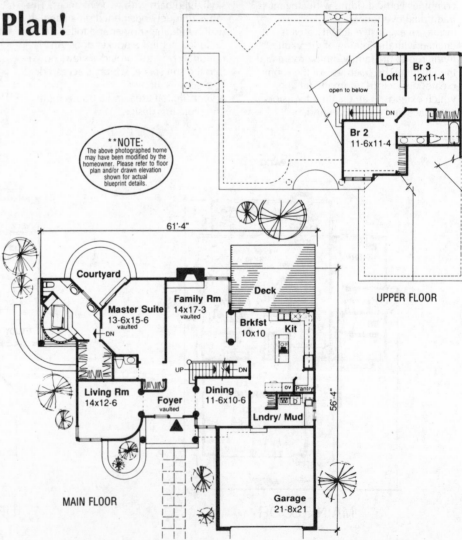

**NOTE:
The above photographed home may have been modified by the homeowner. Please refer to floor plan and/or drawn elevation shown for actual blueprint details.

UPPER FLOOR

Br 3
12x11-4

Loft

open to below

DN

Br 2
11-6x11-4

61'-4"

Courtyard

Master Suite
13-6x15-6
vaulted

DN

Family Rm
14x17-3
vaulted

Deck

Brkfst
10x10

Kit

Living Rm
14x12-6

UP

DN

Dining
11-6x10-6

ov Pantry

W D

Lndry/ Mud

Foyer
vaulted

56'-4"

Garage
21-8x21

MAIN FLOOR

**TO ORDER THIS BLUEPRINT,
CALL TOLL-FREE 1-800-547-5570**

Plan B-88015

**PRICES AND DETAILS
ON PAGES 12-15**

Photo by Mark Englund/HomeStyles

NOTE:
The above photographed home may have been modified by the homeowner. Please refer to floor plan and/or drawn elevation shown for actual blueprint details.

Four-Bedroom Contemporary Style

Steeply pitched, multi-level gable rooflines accented by diagonal board siding and tall windows add imposing height to this contemporary, 2,289 sq. ft. home. With most of the 1,389 sq. ft. main floor devoted to the living, dining and family rooms, and a long patio or wood deck accessible off the nook, the home lends itself ideally to family activities and gracious entertaining.

Directly off the spacious foyer is the vaulted-ceiling living room and dining area, brightened with high windows and warmed by a log-sized fireplace. The wide U-shaped kitchen, nook and family room, with wood stove, join and extend across the back half of the main floor. With doors off the nook and utility room leading to a large patio, this area combines for large, informal activities. Also off the front entry hall is a full bathroom, a den or fourth bedroom, and the open stairway, brightened by a skylight, leading to the upper floor.

The master bedroom suite, occupying about half of the upper floor, has a wide picture window, walk-in dressing room/ wardrobe, and a skylighted bathroom with sunken tub and separate shower. The other two bedrooms share the hall bathroom. A daylight basement version of the plan further expands the family living and recreation areas of this home.

Main floor:	1,389 sq. ft.
Upper floor:	900 sq. ft.
Total living area:	2,289 sq. ft.
(Not counting basement or garage)	
Basement level:	1,389 sq. ft.

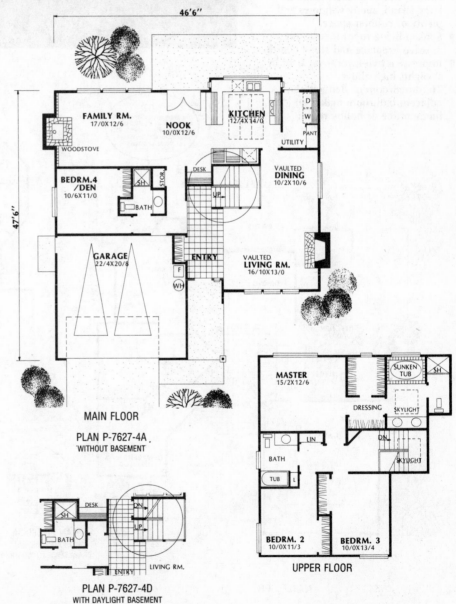

MAIN FLOOR

PLAN P-7627-4A
WITHOUT BASEMENT

PLAN P-7627-4D
WITH DAYLIGHT BASEMENT

UPPER FLOOR

Blueprint Price Code C

Plans P-7627-4A & -4D

**PRICES AND DETAILS
ON PAGES 12-15**

Dramatic Interior Makes a Best-Seller

- An incredible master suite takes up the entire 705 sq. ft. second floor, and includes deluxe bath, huge closet and skylighted balcony.
- Main floor design utilizes angles and shapes to create dramatic interior.
- Extra-spacious kitchen features large island, sunny windows and plenty of counter space.
- Sunken living room focuses on massive fireplace and stone hearth.
- Impressive two-level foyer is lit by skylights high above.
- Third bedroom or den with an adjacent bathroom makes an ideal home office or hobby room.

Photo by Karlis Grants

**NOTE:
The above photographed home may have been modified by the homeowner. Please refer to floor plan and/or drawn elevation shown for actual blueprint details.

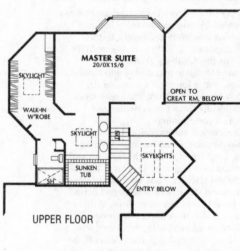

UPPER FLOOR

MASTER SUITE 20/0X15/0

SKYLIGHT

WALK-IN W'ROBE

SKYLIGHT

SUNKEN TUB

OPEN TO GREAT RM. BELOW

SKYLIGHTS

ENTRY BELOW

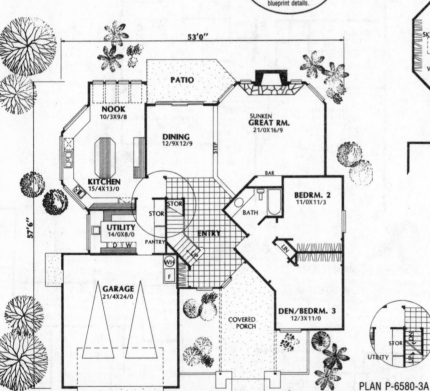

53'0"

57'6"

PATIO

NOOK 10/3X9/8

DINING 12/9X12/9

SUNKEN GREAT RM. 21/0X16/9

KITCHEN 15/4X13/0

BAR

STOR

STOR

BATH

BEDRM. 2 11/0X11/3

UTILITY 14/0X8/0

ENTRY

PANTRY

LIN

WH F

GARAGE 21/4X24/0

COVERED PORCH

DEN/BEDRM. 3 12/3X11/0

STOR

UTILITY

PLAN P-6580-3A
WITHOUT BASEMENT
(CRAWLSPACE FOUNDATION)

MAIN FLOOR

Plans P-6580-3A & -3D

Bedrooms: 2-3	Baths: 2
Space:	
Upper floor:	705 sq. ft.
Main floor:	1,738 sq. ft.
Total living area:	2,443 sq. ft.
Basement:	1,738 sq. ft.
Garage:	512 sq. ft.
Exterior Wall Framing:	2x4

Foundation options:
Daylight basement (Plan P-6580-3D).
Crawlspace (Plan P-6580-3A).
(Foundation & framing conversion diagram available — see order form.)

Blueprint Price Code:	C

Photo by Mark Englund/HomeStyles

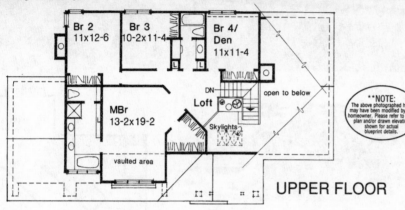

Br 2
11x12-6

Br 3
10-2x11-4

Br 4/
Den
11x11-4

MBr
13-2x19-2

Loft

DN

open to below

Skylights

vaulted area

UPPER FLOOR

**NOTE: The above photographed home may have been modified by the homeowner. Please refer to floor plan and/or drawn elevation shown for actual blueprint details.

Two-Story for Today

- The charm and character of yesterday are re-created in this two-story design for today. The quaint exterior is highlighted by half-round windows, planter boxes and a covered front porch.
- The dramatic skylighted entry preludes a formal, sunken living room with a stunning corner fireplace and an adjoining formal dining room with a built-in hutch. Both rooms are also enhanced by vaulted ceilings.
- A large kitchen with a built-in desk and a pantry opens to a sunny breakfast room and a large, sunken family room at the rear of the home. The family room features an exciting fireplace wall and French doors that open to the rear deck.
- The upstairs loft leads to a luxurious master bedroom with a vaulted ceiling, angled walk-in closet and private bath. Two to three additional bedrooms and a second bath are also included.

Plan B-159-86

Bedrooms: 3-4		**Baths:** 2½
Living Area:		
Upper floor		1,155 sq. ft.
Main floor		1,290 sq. ft.
Total Living Area:		**2,445 sq. ft.**
Standard basement		1,290 sq. ft.
Garage		683 sq. ft.
Exterior Wall Framing:		2x4
Foundation Options:		

Standard basement
(Typical foundation & framing conversion diagram available—see order form.)

BLUEPRINT PRICE CODE:	C

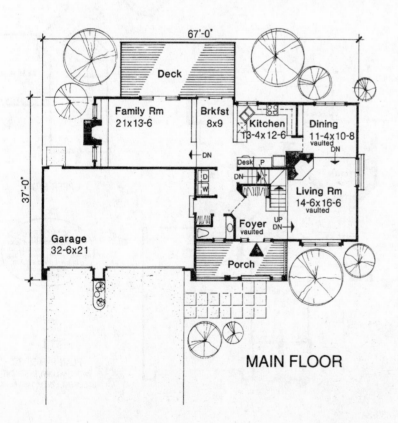

67'-0"

37'-0"

Deck

Family Rm
21x13-6

Brkfst
8x9

Kitchen
13-4x12-6

Dining
11-4x10-8
vaulted

DN

Desk P

Desk
D
W

Living Rm
14-6x16-6
vaulted

Foyer
vaulted

UP
DN

Garage
32-6x21

Porch

MAIN FLOOR

TO ORDER THIS BLUEPRINT,
CALL TOLL-FREE 1-800-547-5570

Plan B-159-86

PRICES AND DETAILS
ON PAGES 12-15

203

Luxury Home with Outdoor Orientation

- Courtyards, patios and a sun room orient this multi-level home to the outdoors.
- Interior design is carefully zoned for informal family living and formal entertaining.
- Expansive kitchen includes large island and plenty of counter space, and a sunny nook adjoins the kitchen.
- Soaring entry area leads visitors to the vaulted living room with fireplace, or to the more casual family room.
- An optional fourth bedroom off the foyer would make an ideal home office.
- Upstairs master suite includes luxury bath and big walk-in closet.
- Daylight basement version adds nearly 1,500 more square feet of space.

Plans P-7659-3A & -3D

Bedrooms: 3-4	Baths: 3
Space:	
Upper floor:	1,050 sq. ft.
Main floor:	1,498 sq. ft.
Total living area:	2,548 sq. ft.
Basement:	1,490 sq. ft.
Garage:	583 sq. ft.
Exterior Wall Framing:	2x4

Foundation options:
Daylight basement, Plan P-7659-3D.
Crawlspace, Plan P-7659-3A.
(Foundation & framing conversion diagram available — see order form.)

Blueprint Price Code:	D

Photo courtesy of Piercy & Barclay Designers, Inc.

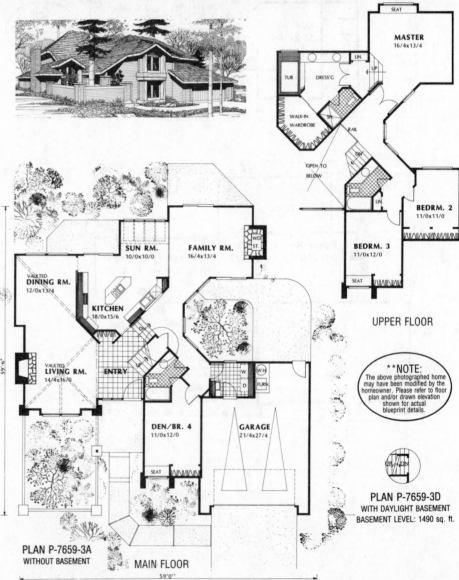

UPPER FLOOR

**NOTE:
The above photographed home may have been modified by the homeowner. Please refer to floor plan and/or drawn elevation shown for actual blueprint details.

PLAN P-7659-3D
WITH DAYLIGHT BASEMENT
BASEMENT LEVEL: 1490 sq. ft.

PLAN P-7659-3A
WITHOUT BASEMENT

MAIN FLOOR

TO ORDER THIS BLUEPRINT,
CALL TOLL-FREE 1-800-547-5570

Plans P-7659-3A & -3D

PRICES AND DETAILS
ON PAGES 12-15

Gracious Open-Concept Floor Plan

- A striking and luxurious contemporary, this home offers great space and modern styling.
- A covered entry leads to a spacious foyer, which flows into the sunken dining and Great Room area.
- The vaulted Great Room boasts a spectacular two-story-high fireplace, dramatic window walls and access to a rear deck or patio.
- A bright nook adjoins the open kitchen, which includes a corner window above the sink.
- The den, which could be a guest bedroom, features a bay window overlooking the deck.
- The majestic master bedroom on the second floor offers a 10-ft.-high coved ceiling, a splendid bath, a large closet and a private deck.
- Two other upstairs bedrooms share a second bath and a balcony hallway overlooking the Great Room and entry below.

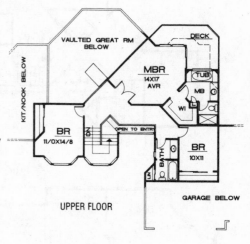

UPPER FLOOR

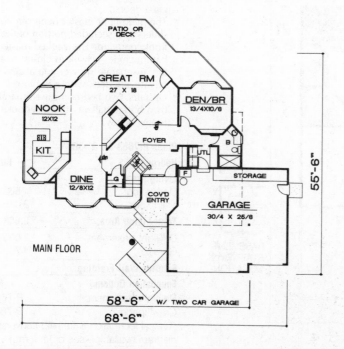

MAIN FLOOR

Plan S-41587

Bedrooms: 3-4	Baths: 3
Living Area:	
Upper floor:	1,001 sq. ft.
Main floor	1,550 sq. ft.
Total Living Area:	**2,551 sq. ft.**
Basement	1,550 sq. ft.
Garage (three-car)	773 sq. ft.
Exterior Wall Framing:	2x6

Foundation Options:
Daylight basement
Standard basement
Crawlspace
Slab
(Typical foundation & framing conversion diagram available—see order form.)

BLUEPRINT PRICE CODE:	D

Photo by Kevin Haslip

Privacy and Luxury

- This home's large roof planes and privacy fences enclose a thoroughly modern, open floor plan.
- A beautiful courtyard greets guests on their way to the secluded entrance. Inside, a vaulted entry area leads directly into the living and dining rooms, which also boast a vaulted ceiling, plus floor-to-ceiling windows, a fireplace and a wall-length stone hearth.
- A sun room next to the spacious, angular kitchen offers passive solar heating and natural brightness.
- The vaulted family room features access to a rear patio through sliding glass doors.
- The main-floor master bedroom boasts sliders to a secluded portion of the front courtyard. The vaulted master bath includes a walk-in closet, a raised tub, a separate shower and access to a private sun deck with a hot tub.
- Upstairs, two bedrooms are separated by a bridge hallway that overlooks the rooms below.

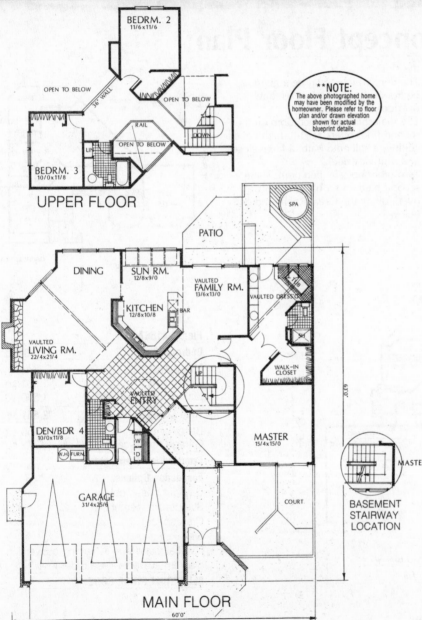

**NOTE:
The above photographed home may have been modified by the homeowner. Please refer to floor plan and/or drawn elevation shown for actual blueprint details.

Plans P-7663-3A & -3D

Bedrooms: 3+	Baths: 3
Living Area:	
Upper floor	569 sq. ft.
Main floor	2,039 sq. ft.
Total Living Area:	**2,608 sq. ft.**
Daylight basement	2,039 sq. ft.
Garage	799 sq. ft.
Exterior Wall Framing:	2x4
Foundation Options:	**Plan #**
Daylight basement	P-7663-3D
Crawlspace	P-7663-3A
(Typical foundation & framing conversion diagram available—see order form.)	
BLUEPRINT PRICE CODE:	**D**

TO ORDER THIS BLUEPRINT, CALL TOLL-FREE 1-800-547-5570 Plans P-7663-3A & -3D *PRICES AND DETAILS ON PAGES 12-15*

Photo by Carol Cox Smith

Ultimate in Luxury and Livability

- This popular design is loaded with features for families of the 90's.
- Entire second floor of 735 sq. ft. is devoted to a sumptuous master suite with luxurious bath, large closet and skylights.

- Sunken living room is large and includes a fireplace.
- Roomy family room adjoins handy computer room and large kitchen.
- Kitchen includes a large walk-in pantry and work island.

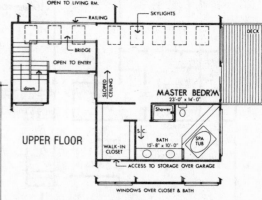

UPPER FLOOR

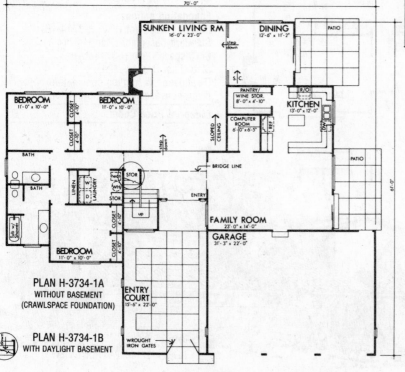

PLAN H-3734-1A
WITHOUT BASEMENT
(CRAWLSPACE FOUNDATION)

PLAN H-3734-1B
WITH DAYLIGHT BASEMENT

MAIN FLOOR

Plans H-3734-1A & -1B

Bedrooms: 4	Baths: 2½
Space:	
Upper floor:	735 sq. ft.
Main floor:	2,024 sq. ft.
Total living area:	2,759 sq. ft.
Basement:	2,024 sq. ft.
Garage:	687 sq. ft.
Exterior Wall Framing:	2x6

Foundation options:
Daylight basement, Plan H-3734-1B.
Crawlspace, Plan H-3734-1A.
(Foundation & framing conversion diagram available — see order form.)

Blueprint Price Code: D

Pure Luxury in a Choice of Styles

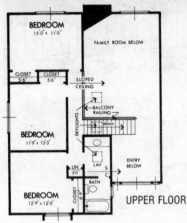

UPPER FLOOR

- Southwestern colonial or Western contemporary exteriors are available when deciding if this spacious design is for you.
- Elaborate master suite features attached screened spa room, regular and walk-in closets, and luxurious bath with skylight.

- Study, large family and living room with sloped ceilings and rear patio are other points of interest.
- Three additional bedrooms make up the second level.
- The Spanish version (M2A) offers a stucco exterior and slab foundation.

Plans H-3714-1/1A/1B/M2A

Bedrooms: 4	Baths: 3
Space:	
Upper floor:	740 sq. ft.
Main floor:	2,190 sq. ft.
Total living area:	**2,930 sq. ft.**
Basement:	1,153 sq. ft.
Garage:	576 sq. ft.
Exterior Wall Framing:	**2x6**

Foundation options:
Daylight basement (Plan H-3714-1B).
Standard basement (Plan H-3714-1).
Crawlspace (Plan H-3714-1A).
Slab (Plan H-3714-M2A).
(Foundation & framing conversion diagram available — see order form.)

Blueprint Price Code:	D

MAIN FLOOR

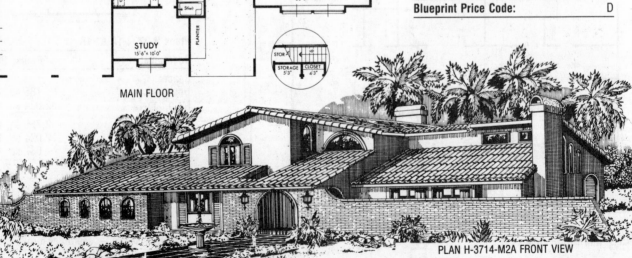

PLAN H-3714-M2A FRONT VIEW

TO ORDER THIS BLUEPRINT, CALL TOLL-FREE 1-800-547-5570 **Plans H-3714-1/1A/1B/M2A** *PRICES AND DETAILS ON PAGES 12-15*

Elegantly Different

Arched brickwork and windows lend a uniqueness and elegance that is immediately noticeable in this three-bedroom home.

A covered entry leads to a vaulted foyer opening to the formal living and dining room area. Here you'll find large windows and a vaulted ceiling that add a light airiness to the room, balanced by the coziness of a warm fireplace.

With skylights and a windowed nook opening onto the back deck, the kitchen is bright and sunny — perfect for those who enjoy cooking and entertaining. An angled island with convenient eating bar highlight the kitchen, along with a handy pantry and a centrally located desk that is ideal for household planning. A generous family room with a practical wood stove off the kitchen is certain to make this part of your home the center of family activity.

A hallway from the garage passes a utility room designed with the emphasis on "utility." The counter space lends itself to many projects, and a built-in ironing board provides convenience and saves space.

The secluded study on the lower level provides a place for work or quiet leisure activities.

Upstairs, the two children's bedrooms show their individuality — one with a window seat and the other with a bay window. The master bedroom is a treat,

with an octagonal sitting area to capture the view, a large walk-in closet, and a bath area with a step-up spa tub and double vanity.

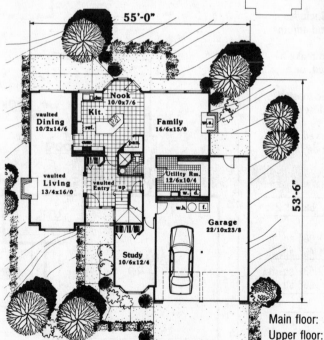

Exterior walls are 2x6 construction.
Crawlspace foundation only.

Main floor:	1,460 sq. ft.
Upper floor:	1,005 sq. ft.
Total living area: (Not counting garage)	2,465 sq. ft.

Blueprint Price Code C
Plan R-2117

Three-Sided Porch Adds Country Charm

- This inviting wrap-around porch invites visitors to come up and say "Howdy."
- The interior is just as welcoming, with its large family room with a fireplace, and the adjoining dining/living rooms.
- The open-design kitchen includes a convenient work island and adjoins a bright breakfast nook.
- A den off the foyer would make a nice home office, if needed, or a fourth bedroom as well.
- Upstairs, note the majestic master suite with a big walk-in closet and luxury bath.
- Bedrooms 2 and 3 are served by a second full bath and include large closets.

Plan I-2531-A

Bedrooms: 3-4	Baths: 2½

Space:

Upper floor:	1,064 sq. ft.
Main floor:	1,467 sq. ft.
Total living area:	**2,531 sq. ft.**
Garage:	608 sq. ft.

Exterior Wall Framing:	2x6

Foundation options:
Crawlspace.
(Foundation & framing conversion diagram available — see order form.)

Blueprint Price Code:	D

UPPER FLOOR

MAIN FLOOR

TO ORDER THIS BLUEPRINT, CALL TOLL-FREE 1-800-547-5570

Plan I-2531-A

PRICES AND DETAILS ON PAGES 12-15

Nostalgic Exterior Appeal

- Projecting bay windows, a covered front porch, large half-round windows and Victorian gable details create a nostalgic exterior appeal.
- A stunning two-story foyer awaits guests at the entry, with light flooding in from the half-round window above.
- The formal living and dining rooms lie to the right of the entry, while straight ahead, under the balcony bridge, lies the informal living area. This area includes an island kitchen with bay-windowed breakfast room overlooking the skylit family room with corner fireplace and sliders to the patio.
- There are four bedrooms upstairs, including a lavish master bedroom with sloped ceiling, walk-in closet and private bath.

Plan AX-90305

Bedrooms: 4	Baths: 2½

Space:

Upper floor:	1,278 sq. ft.
Main floor:	1,237 sq. ft.
Total living area:	**2,515 sq. ft.**
Basement:	1,237 sq. ft.
Garage:	400 sq. ft.

Exterior Wall Framing:	2x4

Foundation options:
Standard basement.
Slab.
(Foundation & framing conversion diagram available — see order form.)

Blueprint Price Code:	D

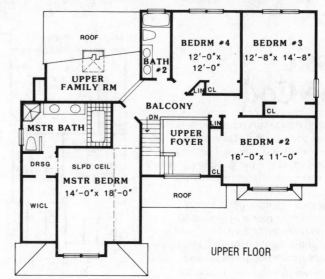

UPPER FLOOR

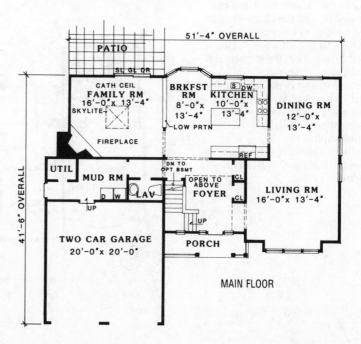

MAIN FLOOR

TO ORDER THIS BLUEPRINT,
CALL TOLL-FREE 1-800-547-5570

Plan AX-90305

PRICES AND DETAILS
ON PAGES 12-15

211

Classic
Cape Cod

- An isolated downstairs master suite with three bedrooms up is just one of the keynotes of this sophisticated design.
- Attention-getting dormer windows and a charming front porch distinguish the exterior.
- The spacious first floor offers formal living and dining rooms as well as a spacious family living area.
- The skylighted, vaulted family room has a fireplace flanked by windows and French doors. A half-bath is close by.
- The sunny breakfast room has a rear window wall, and the kitchen has an angled counter to keep the cook in touch with family activities. A laundry is accessible from both the kitchen and the garage.
- The deluxe master bedroom suite has a vaulted ceiling, two walk-in closets, a shower and a separate commode area, not to mention a skylighted spa tub and dual-sink vanity.
- The three bedrooms upstairs share another full bath and a view to the family room below.

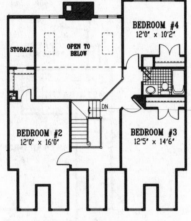

UPPER FLOOR

Plan CH-445-A	
Bedrooms: 4	**Baths:** 2½
Living Area:	
Upper floor	988 sq. ft.
Main floor	1,707 sq. ft.
Total Living Area:	**2,695 sq. ft.**
Partial basement	1,118 sq. ft.
Garage	802 sq. ft.
Exterior Wall Framing:	2x4

Foundation Options:
Partial daylight basement
Partial basement
Crawlspace
(Typical foundation & framing conversion
diagram available—see order form.)

BLUEPRINT PRICE CODE:	D

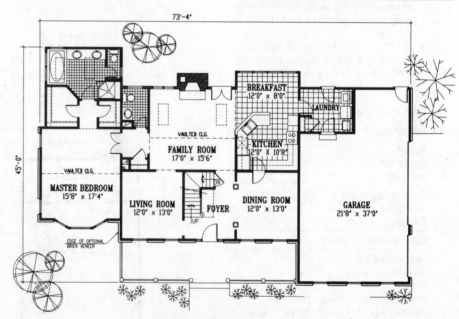

MAIN FLOOR

TO ORDER THIS BLUEPRINT,
CALL TOLL-FREE 1-800-547-5570   Plan CH-445-A   *PRICES AND DETAILS*
ON PAGES 12-15

Sunlit Elegance

- This elegant contemporary design offers just about all the amenities today's families expect in a home.
- The formal dining room is large enough for a good-sized dinner party.
- The living room is sunken and vaulted and includes a handsome fireplace.
- The spacious kitchen includes a large island and a pantry, and is open to the vaulted family room.
- Upstairs, the master bedroom is impressive, with a private master bath, large closets and easy access to a private deck. (If the greenhouse is built, stairs go from the master bath down to the hot tub.)
- The second floor also includes a roomy library and a bonus room or extra bedroom.
- The plan also offers an optional solar greenhouse, which may contain a hot tub or simply offer a great space for green plants and sunbathing.

Plan S-8217

Bedrooms: 3-4	Baths: 2
Living Area:	
Upper floor	789 sq. ft.
Main floor	1,709 sq. ft.
Bonus room	336 sq. ft.
Total Living Area:	**2,834 sq. ft.**
Partial basement	1,242 sq. ft.
Garage	441 sq. ft.
Exterior Wall Framing:	2x6

Foundation Options:

Partial basement
Crawlspace
Slab
(Typical foundation & framing conversion diagram available—see order form.)

BLUEPRINT PRICE CODE:	D

UPPER FLOOR

MAIN FLOOR

50'·6"

62'

FRONT VIEW

Dramatic Western Contemporary

REAR VIEW

- Dramatic and functional building features contribute to the comfort and desire of this family home.
- Master suite offers a spacious private bath and luxurious hydro spa.
- Open, efficient kitchen accommodates modern appliances, a large pantry, and a snack bar.
- Skylights shed light on the entryway, open staircase, and balcony.
- Upper level balcony area has private covered deck, and may be used as a guest room or den.

UPPER FLOOR

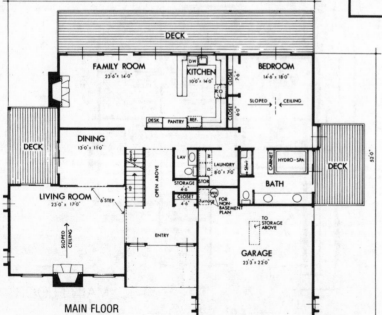

MAIN FLOOR

Plans H-3708-1 & -1A

Bedrooms: 4	Baths: 2½

Space:	
Upper floor:	893 sq. ft.
Main floor:	2,006 sq. ft.

Total living area:	2,899 sq. ft.
Basement:	approx. 2,006 sq. ft.
Garage:	512 sq. ft.

Exterior Wall Framing:	2x6

Foundation options:
Daylight basement (Plan H-3708-1).
Crawlspace (Plan H-3708-1A).
(Foundation & framing conversion diagram available — see order form.)

Blueprint Price Code:	D

TO ORDER THIS BLUEPRINT, CALL TOLL-FREE 1-800-547-5570

Plans H-3708-1 & -1A

PRICES AND DETAILS ON PAGES 12-15

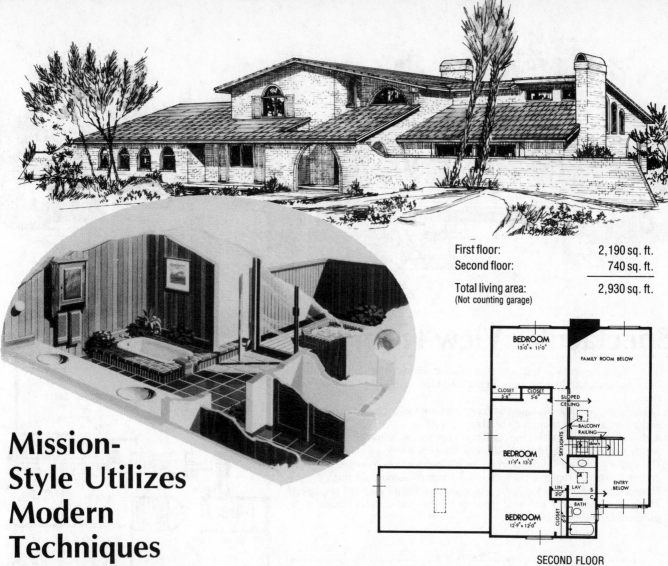

First floor: 2,190 sq. ft.
Second floor: 740 sq. ft.
Total living area: 2,930 sq. ft.
(Not counting garage)

Mission-Style Utilizes Modern Techniques

The beauty of shake-style concrete roof tile is never more apparent than on a hacienda such as this where Old World heritage and charm are married to modern building methods and concepts. Concrete block veneer in the distinctive "slump block" style simulating ancient adobe bricks is the perfect companion for this beautiful roof.

Once past the garden walls and flower festooned patios, one becomes aware of modern living concepts unimagined by the conquistadors or their successors: Living and dining areas whose vaulted ceilings are softly lighted through clerestory windows high overhead; U-shaped kitchen; a marvel of electronic equipment unimagined in the days of Pancho Villa; a master bedroom suite suitable for the grandest senor or senora with 1,600 cubic feet of wardrobe space; a Roman-style walk-up bath; enclosed shower and toilet rooms; separate lavatories; and perhaps most luxurious of all, a private hydro-spa in a private corner of a private patio.

Many more areas of interest will become evident as one studies the nearly 3,000 sq. ft. of living space enclosed in this modern hacienda.

SECOND FLOOR
740 SQUARE FEET

(Exterior walls are 4x4x16 concrete block veneer over 2x6 framing.)

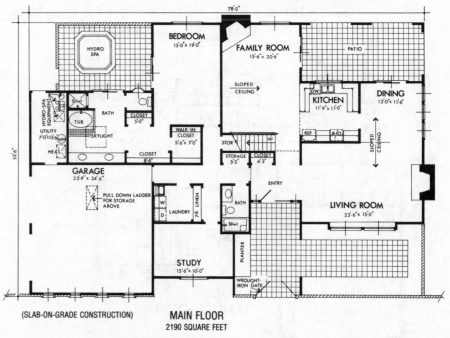

(SLAB-ON-GRADE CONSTRUCTION)

MAIN FLOOR
2190 SQUARE FEET

Spectacular View From Loft

- A soaring foyer and vaulted, step-down parlor with fireplace and decorative brick columns can be seen from an overhead loft in this distinguished two-story.
- Flanking the parlor are a vaulted library with built-in shelves along two walls and a formal dining room with brilliant 12' ceiling.
- Rich-looking brick borders the cooktop in the roomy island kitchen with a handy pantry; an adjoining bayed breakfast room offers a sunny patio.
- The exciting sunken family room off the kitchen features a unique gambrel ceiling, massive fireplace, corner windows and refreshing wet bar.
- Three steps up from the loft is the spacious master suite with private, bayed sitting area and lavish bath with separate vanities and walk-in closets, a garden tub and romantic deck.

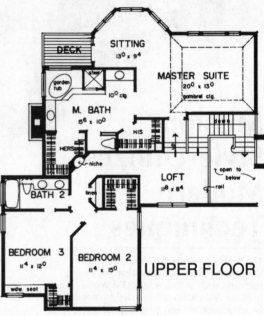

UPPER FLOOR

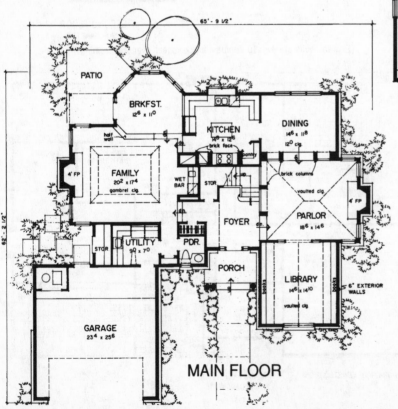

MAIN FLOOR

Plan DW-3108	
Bedrooms: 3	**Baths: 2 ½**
Space:	
Upper floor	1,324 sq. ft.
Main floor	1,784 sq. ft.
Total Living Area	**3,108 sq. ft.**
Basement	1,784 sq. ft.
Garage	595 sq. ft.
Exterior Wall Framing	2x6
Foundation options:	
Standard Basement	
Crawlspace	
Slab	
(Framing conversion diagram available—see order form.)	
Blueprint Price Code	E

**TO ORDER THIS BLUEPRINT,
CALL TOLL-FREE 1-800-547-5570**

Plan DW-3108

*PRICES AND DETAILS
ON PAGES 12-15*

UPPER FLOOR

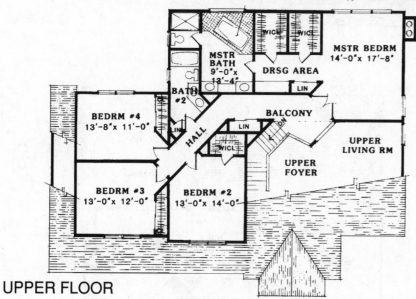

MSTR BEDRM
14'-0"x 17'-8"

WICL WICL

MSTR BATH
9'-0"x 13'-4"

DRSG AREA

LIN

BATH #2

BEDRM #4
13'-8"x 11'-0"

HALL

LIN LIN

BALCONY

DN

WICL

UPPER LIVING RM

UPPER FOYER

BEDRM #3
13'-0"x 12'-0"

BEDRM #2
13'-0"x 14'-0"

Interior Excitement

- This roomy four-bedroom home offers interior excitement with an open stairway off the vaulted foyer and adjoining sunken living and family rooms.
- The sunken family room at the rear accepts traffic from three sides; it features a corner fireplace and doors that open to an optional patio.
- The island kitchen and breakfast room combine for a spacious, yet intimate atmosphere; a butler's pantry is located off the formal dining room.
- A massive master bedroom with dressing area, dual walk-in closets and luxury bath joins three additional bedrooms on the upper level.

Plan AX-91307

Bedrooms: 4	Baths: 2 ½
Space:	
Upper floor	1,448 sq. ft.
Main floor	1,684 sq. ft.
Total Living Area	**3,132 sq. ft.**
Basement	1,503 sq. ft.
Garage	420 sq. ft.
Exterior Wall Framing	2x4

Foundation options:
Standard Basement
(Foundation & framing conversion diagram available—see order form.)

Blueprint Price Code	**E**

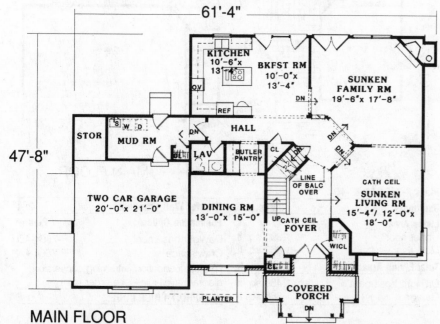

61'-4"

47'-8"

KITCHEN
10'-6"x 13'

BKFST RM
10'-0"x 13'-4"

SUNKEN FAMILY RM
19'-6"x 17'-8"

OV

REF

DN

STOR

S W D

MUD RM

DN

HALL

LAV

BUTLER PANTRY

CL

DN

DN

DN

TWO CAR GARAGE
20'-0"x 21'-0"

DINING RM
13'-0"x 15'-0"

UP CATH CEIL FOYER

LINE OF BALC OVER

CATH CEIL

SUNKEN LIVING RM
15'-4"/ 12'-0"x 18'-0"

WICL

CL

COVERED PORCH

DN

PLANTER

MAIN FLOOR

TO ORDER THIS BLUEPRINT,
CALL TOLL-FREE 1-800-547-5570

Plan AX-91307

PRICES AND DETAILS
ON PAGES 12-15

217

Creative Spaces

- Here's a home that is not only large, but extremely creative in its use of indoor space.
- A huge area is created by the combination of the vaulted living and dining rooms, which flow together visually but are separated by a railing.
- Another expansive space results from the kitchen/nook/family room arrangement, and their easy access to deck and patio.
- Upstairs, the master suite includes a lavish bath and generous closets.
- Three large secondary bedrooms share another full bath, and each has its own unique design feature.

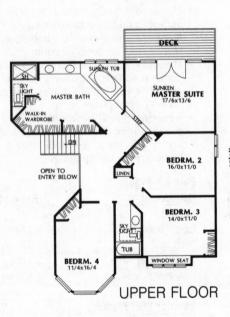

UPPER FLOOR

BASEMENT STAIRWAY LOCATION

MAIN FLOOR

Plans P-7664-4A & -4D

Bedrooms: 4+	Baths: 2½
Living Area:	
Upper floor	1,301 sq. ft.
Main floor	1,853 sq. ft.
Total Living Area:	**3,154 sq. ft.**
Daylight basement	1,486 sq. ft.
Garage	668 sq. ft.

Exterior Wall Framing:	2x4
Foundation Options:	**Plan #**
Daylight basement	P-7664-4D
Crawlspace	P-7664-4A
(Typical foundation & framing conversion diagram available—see order form.)	
BLUEPRINT PRICE CODE:	E

Lower Level Opens to Rear in Spacious Hillside Design

- A huge living room with fireplace and dining room with railing overlook the stairway to the lower level of this walk-out, hillside design.
- The spacious country kitchen offers an island cooktop and unique skywall.
- Three to four bedrooms, an optional hobby room, and a family room with second fireplace, wet bar and attached deck occupy the lower level.

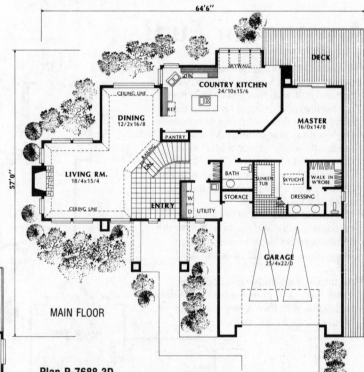

MAIN FLOOR

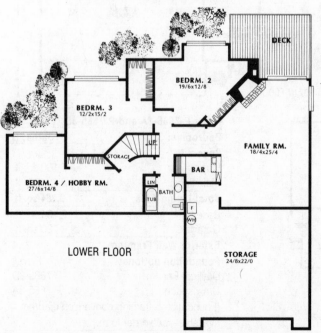

LOWER FLOOR

Plan P-7688-3D

Bedrooms: 3-4	Baths: 2½
Space:	
Main floor:	1,624 sq. ft.
Lower floor:	1,624 sq. ft.
Total living area:	3,248 sq. ft.
Garage:	557 sq. ft.
Storage:	620 sq. ft.
Exterior Wall Framing:	2x4

Foundation options:
Daylight basement.
(Foundation & framing conversion
diagram available — see order form.)

Blueprint Price Code:	E

TO ORDER THIS BLUEPRINT,
CALL TOLL-FREE 1-800-547-5570

Plan P-7688-3D

PRICES AND DETAILS
ON PAGES 12-15

219

Anyone for Fun?

- A spectacular sunken game room with a corner window, vaulted ceilings, wet bar and half-wall that separates it from the family room is ideal for the active family or for those who like to entertain.
- The exciting atmosphere continues to the family room, also at a level lower than the rest of the home; here you'll find a fireplace, a rear window wall and a railing that allows a view of the adjoining vaulted nook.
- The spacious kitchen offers an island cooktop, pantry and pass-through to the game room hallway; formal, vaulted living areas are found opposite the entry.
- An upper-level bridge overlooks the game room and joins the two secondary bedrooms with the master suite and luxury, skylit master bath.

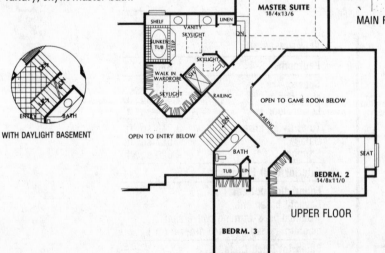

MAIN FLOOR

WITH DAYLIGHT BASEMENT

UPPER FLOOR

Plans P-7665-3A and P-7665-3D	
Bedrooms: 3-4	**Baths:** 3
Space:	
Upper floor	1,160 sq. ft.
Main floor	2,124 sq. ft.
Total Living Area	**3,284 sq. ft.**
Basement	2,104 sq. ft.
Garage	720 sq. ft.
Exterior Wall Framing	2x4
Foundation options:	Plan #
Daylight Basement	P-7665-3D
Crawlspace	P-7665-3A
(Foundation & framing conversion diagram available—see order form.)	
Blueprint Price Code	E

TO ORDER THIS BLUEPRINT,
CALL TOLL-FREE 1-800-547-5570   **Plans P-7665-3A & -3D**

PRICES AND DETAILS
ON PAGES 12-15

Attractive European Look

- Arched windows with keystones, the stucco finish with corner quoins and many other fine flourishes give this European-style home its good looks.
- The two-story foyer flaunts a handsome open stairway to the upper floor. A second stairway is offered in the family room.
- Columns act as dividers between the formal living spaces to the left of the foyer. Double doors in the dining room close off the kitchen, which features a center island, a walk-in pantry and a handy freezer room.
- A bright, bayed breakfast area is nestled between the kitchen and the family room and offers access to the deck.
- The vaulted family room also opens to the deck and has a fireplace and two built-in bookcases.
- A bonus room or fourth bedroom shares the upper floor with three other bedrooms, three full baths and a convenient laundry room.

Plan APS-3302

Bedrooms: 4+	Baths: 4
Living Area:	
Upper floor	1,276 sq. ft.
Main floor	1,716 sq. ft.
Bonus room	382 sq. ft.
Total Living Area:	**3,374 sq. ft.**
Standard basement	1,716 sq. ft.
Garage	693 sq. ft.
Exterior Wall Framing:	2x4

Foundation Options:
Standard basement
(Typical foundation & framing conversion diagram available—see order form.)

BLUEPRINT PRICE CODE:	E

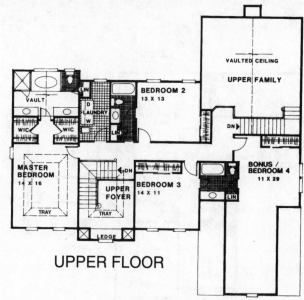

UPPER FLOOR

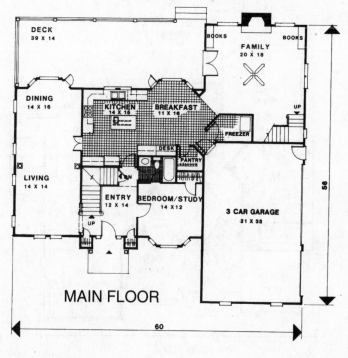

MAIN FLOOR

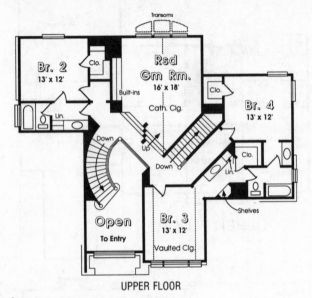

UPPER FLOOR

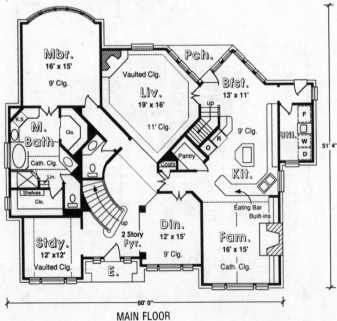

MAIN FLOOR

Dramatic Angles and Curves

- This award-winning design utilizes angular forms to create a logical and functional flow of traffic.
- Dramatic rooflines and window treatments adorn the beautiful brick exterior.
- Inside, the two-story foyer reveals the first of two stairways to the upper level; the other stairway is located in the breakfast room at the rear of the home.
- Highlights on the first floor include volume ceilings throughout and a spectacular central living room with a corner fireplace and a rear window wall overlooking the porch. A huge island kitchen boasts a sunny breakfast nook. An angled eating bar separates the kitchen from the family room, which features built-ins that flank a second fireplace.
- A spacious master bedroom on the main floor and a fantastic raised game room surrounded by three large bedrooms on the second floor complete this exciting, spacious home.

Plan KLF-921	
Bedrooms: 4-5	**Baths:** 3 ½
Space:	
Upper floor	1,150 sq. ft.
Main floor	2,383 sq. ft.
Total Living Area	**3,533 sq. ft.**
Exterior Wall Framing	2x4
Foundation options:	
Slab	
(Foundation & framing conversion diagram available—see order form.)	
Blueprint Price Code	**F**

TO ORDER THIS BLUEPRINT, CALL TOLL-FREE 1-800-547-5570

Plan KLF-921

PRICES AND DETAILS ON PAGES 12-15

Spacious Spanish Elegance

A spacious 3,944 sq. ft. of exciting living area is surrounded by archways, heavily escutcheoned wooden doors, and protective tiled roofs, which enhance the stucco exterior of this home.

Tile floors and the sunken living room please the eye from the very first glance. A sliding glass door provides access to the secluded patio from the elegant living room. From the entry, one passes through folding doors into the homey atmosphere of the family room/kitchen area. From the adjoining hobby room, a circular stairway leads to the elevated recreation room complete with outdoor deck. Note that the

recreation area provides 399 sq. ft. of usable floor space.

For that special guest, the fourth bedroom and an adjacent bath are separated from the main bedroom area. The bedroom wing boasts three large bedrooms, including a master suite with its own private bath. A second bath serves the remaining two bedrooms. A half-bath near the front entry brings the total number of bathrooms to four. The covered front porch leads to the breezeway between the three-car garage and main house, where there is a separate entrance into the sewing or hobby room.

First floor:	3,545 sq. ft.
Second floor:	399 sq. ft.
Total living area: (Not counting garage)	**3,944 sq. ft.**

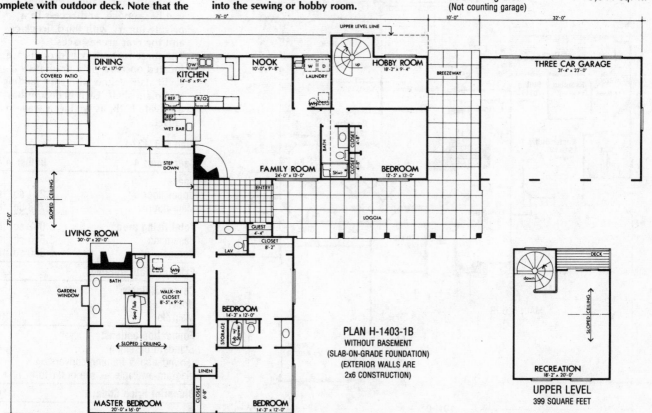

PLAN H-1403-1B
WITHOUT BASEMENT
(SLAB-ON-GRADE FOUNDATION)
(EXTERIOR WALLS ARE 2x6 CONSTRUCTION)

RECREATION
18'-2" x 20'-0"

UPPER LEVEL
399 SQUARE FEET

Blueprint Price Code F
Plan H-1403-1B

PRICES AND DETAILS ON PAGES 12-15

Brimming with Traditional Charm

- This stately luxury residence has all the right stuff for today's busy executive family.
- The exterior is brimming with the traditional charm of half-round windows, brick with special coursing, narrow lap and shake siding and multiple repeated gables.
- The interior houses 5,042 sq. ft. of well-laid-out floor space. The main floor is zoned into three main living areas; formal, informal, and master suite.
- Guests enter the formal living/entertaining area from the sunken living room with fireplace and corner glass overlooking one of many outdoor brick planters.
- The informal zone centers around the large island kitchen with built-in desk and handy access to the three car garage via the mud/laundry area. The kitchen also oversees the breakfast and sunroom eating areas, as well as the dramatic sunken family room. This inviting space features a corner focal point fireplace, vaulted ceilings, wet bar service, and access to a private library with third fireplace and the rear greenspaces.
- The three secondary bedrooms are located upstairs via a dramatic skylit stair atrium with split landing and plant shelf. Each bedroom has a private bath, as well as a walk-in closet.

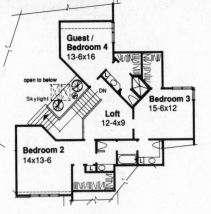

UPPER FLOOR

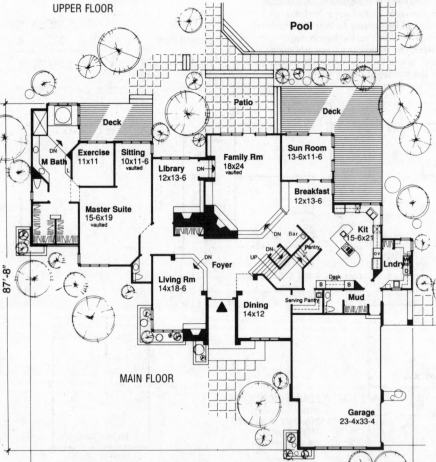

MAIN FLOOR

Plan B-87137-L

Bedrooms: 4	Baths: 4½

Space:	
Upper floor:	1,244 sq. ft.
Main floor:	3,798 sq. ft.

Total living area:	5,042 sq. ft.
Basement:	3,600 sq. ft.
Garage:	590 sq. ft.

Exterior Wall Framing:	2x4

Ceiling Heights:	
Upper floor:	8'
Main floor:	10'

Foundation options:
Standard basement.
(Foundation & framing conversion diagram available — see order form.)

Blueprint Price Code:	G

Plan B-87137-L

PRICES AND DETAILS
ON PAGES 12-15